Ministry of Agriculture, Fisheries and Food

National Food Survey 1998

Annual Report
on
Food Expenditure, Consumption and
Nutrient Intakes

LONDON : THE STATIONERY OFFICE

Published with the permission of the Ministry of Agriculture, Fisheries and Food on behalf of the Controller of Her Majesty's Stationery Office.

©Crown Copyright 1999.

All rights reserved.

Copyright in the typographical arrangement and design is vested in the Crown. Applications for reproduction should be made in writing to the Copyright Unit, Her Majesty's Stationery Office, St Clements House, 2 – 16 Colegate, Norwich NR3 1BQ.

First published 1999

ISBN 0 11 243052 X

Preface

The National Food Survey (NFS) has provided information on household food purchases and the nutritional value of the domestic diet in Great Britain since 1940. In 1994 the survey was extended to cover eating out in Great Britain. In 1996, the household food part of the survey was extended to cover Northern Ireland and this has enabled some results to be presented for the United Kingdom.

The Survey provides comparisons of household food consumption and expenditure data in 1998 with those from the previous year, and a decade ago, as well as developments in respect of eating out and nutrient intakes. This years' report contains a special section (Section 5) which provides NFS-based estimates of nutrient intakes by age and gender with comparison of nutrient intakes from home supplies and from food eaten out. Some comparisons with the results from the National Diet and Nutrition Surveys, jointly sponsored by the Ministry and the Department of Health, are also given. This analysis was conducted by Professor Andrew Chesher, a member of the NFS Committee.

The Ministry of Agriculture, Fisheries and Food is grateful to the households which participated in the Survey and to those organisations responsible for the fieldwork, notably the Office for National Statistics and the Northern Ireland Statistics and Research Agency. Thanks are also due to the National Food Survey Committee, whose advice on the conduct of the survey is invaluable. A particular mention should be made of the contributions of Dr John Slater (Chairman of the Committee), Mr Jim Burns and Dr Roger Whitehead all of whom retired from the Committee. Thanks are also due to the staff of the Ministry's NFS Branch and Nutrition Unit who manage the large and complex datasets and compile this report.

David Thompson

Chairman – National Food Survey Committee

The National Food Survey Committee

David THOMPSON [a]
   Ministry of Agriculture, Fisheries and Food, Chairman

Richard ALDRITT [a]
   National Assembly for Wales

Dr Caroline BOLTON-SMITH
   University of Dundee

Dr Judith BUTTRISS [a]
   British Nutrition Foundation

Professor Andrew CHESHER
   University College, London

Susan CHURCH
   Ministry of Agriculture, Fisheries and Food

Douglas GREIG [a]
   Scottish Executive Rural Affairs Department

Dr Spencer HENSON [a]
   University of Reading

Dr Richard HUTCHINS [a]
   Institute of Grocery Distribution

Dr Michael NELSON [a]
   Kings College, London

Stuart PLATT
   Ministry of Agriculture, Fisheries and Food

Robert PRICE
   Food and Drink Federation

Tom STAINER
   Department of Agriculture for Northern Ireland

Professor Martin WISEMAN
   Burson-Marsteller, London

Secretary

Stan SPELLER
   Ministry of Agriculture, Fisheries and Food

(a) New members from June 1999

Report of the National Food Survey Committee 1998/99

The National Food Survey (NFS) Committee provides advice to MAFF on all aspects of the Survey. The Committee met in June 1999 to assess current and future developments and to review the content of the annual report.

The main issue was the possible merger of the data collection stages of the Family Expenditure Survey and the National Food Survey from April 2001. A final decision on whether or not it goes ahead will be taken in the autumn of 2000.

One of the conclusions of the GSS review of major Government Statistical Surveys was that the overlap between the National Food Survey (NFS) commissioned by MAFF and the Family Expenditure Survey (FES) commissioned by the Office for National Statistics (ONS) should be investigated. A combination of the two surveys was considered in the early 1980's but foundered on evidence suggesting that the response rate of a combined survey would fall to unacceptable levels. However, with improved IT and survey techniques and the fact that the coverage and methodology of the two surveys have become more similar in recent years, it was felt that the idea of combining the two surveys should be re-considered. A joint ONS/MAFF project was therefore set up to examine the feasibility of merging the data collection, validation, imputation and clean file production stages of the two surveys. The analysis and reporting would remain with the two separate departments.

The design proposed for the merged survey is based on the current FES design, enhanced to provide additional information on food, mainly by asking respondents to record quantities and additional details of food bought as well as expenditure. The survey would consist of household and individual interviews, a diary of expenditure and food quantities to be completed by every person aged 16 or over and a simplified diary to be completed by every child aged 7 to 15 years.

The 1998 FES User Group Workshop organised by the Data Archive was extended to include NFS users. It was held at the Royal Statistical Society in October 1998. ONS and MAFF gave presentations on plans for the merger. An article was issued in various statistical and nutrition journals and was placed on the Ministry's Website (see the back page of this annual report). Readers were invited to write to the authors (FES or NFS) with any views or suggestions on the merger. Another joint workshop will be held by the Data Archive in December 1999 and will provide the opportunity for discussion.

A feasibility study has been undertaken, on the recommendation of the Committee, to identify the best method of collecting information on the source and amount of food that is purchased by consumers but not consumed and the reasons for the waste. This information is needed primarily for use in interpreting results from the Ministry's National Food Survey. Coding and analysis of the diaries is ongoing but initial recommendations on methodology have been made. The preferred method, in terms of accuracy and respondent burden, involved respondents weighing each individual item of waste and recording the details in a diary. It was also recommended that the diary should record details of the items of food and drink consumed at each meal occasion.

Contents

		Page
Section 1	Summary of results and Introduction	1
	Introduction	3
Section 2	Household food: expenditure and consumption	7
	National averages	9
	Regional comparisons	17
	Income group comparisons	20
	Household composition comparisons	24
	Household composition and income comparisons	28
	Age of main diary keeper comparisons	28
Section 3	Household food: Nutrient intakes	31
	National averages	31
	Regional, income group and household composition differences	33
Section 4	Eating out: expenditure, consumption and nutrient intakes	35
	Expenditure and consumption	36
	Results by household characteristics	38
	Results by personal characteristics	43
	Eating out: nutrient intakes	46
	Results by household characteristics	47
	Results by personal characteristics	52
	Household food and eating out: nutrient intakes	54
Section 5	Age and gender variation in food energy and nutrient intakes, 1974 - 1998	57
	Introduction	57
	Household average energy and nutrient intake	58
	Variations in energy and nutrients from home supply, 1974 - 1998	61
	Variations in energy and nutrients from food eaten out and from home supplies, 1974 - 1998	65
	Section 5 charts	69
	Comparison with other sources	88
	Supplementary tables	94
Appendix A	Structure of the Survey	103
	Household food and drink	103
	Food and drink eaten out	112

Appendix B　　Supplementary Tables for the Main Survey　　119

Appendix C　　Supplementary Tables for the Eating out Survey　　149

Glossary and additional information　　153
　　　　　　　　　　Symbols and conventions used　　157
　　　　　　　　　　　　　　Additional Information　　157

Section 1

Summary of results and Introduction

Expenditure

- In 1998 average expenditure in Great Britain on household food was £14.79 per person per week. This was 0.8 per cent higher than in 1997. Expenditure inclusive of soft and alcoholic drinks and confectionery (home consumption) was £16.94 per person per week, 1.4 per cent higher than in 1997.

- Expenditure on food and drink eaten out was £6.73 per person per week in 1998, up 1.8 per cent on 1997 and representing 28 per cent of the combined total of home and eating out expenditure on food and drink of £23.67.

Consumption

- Household consumption of milk and cream (including yoghurt and dairy desserts) fell by 2 per cent in 1998 and included a rare recorded fall (of 2 per cent) in the consumption of skimmed milks. Cheese consumption decreased by 5 per cent.

- Purchases of carcase beef and veal remained close to their 1997 levels with consumption of boned joints rising to compensate for the ban on beef on the bone introduced in December 1997.

- Household consumption of mutton and lamb was up by 5 per cent on 1997 whilst the consumption of primary poultry, pork and fish showed little change on the levels seen in 1997. However, consumption of fresh fatty fish such as salmon and mackerel increased for the fourth year running.

- Household purchases of eggs was 2 per cent lower than in 1997 and 35 per cent lower than in 1988.

- Consumption of oils and fats fell by 4 per cent in 1998 due to reduced fat spreads falling back to their 1995 level. Consumption of low fat spreads was virtually the same as in 1997.

- Purchases of sugar for home use fell by 7 per cent to an historical low.

- Household consumption of fresh potatoes fell by 4 per cent but, with much higher prices than in 1997, expenditure rose by a third.

- Household consumption of fresh green vegetables, other fresh vegetables and processed vegetables all fell by close to 2 per cent. Within processed vegetables, household consumption of potato products rose by 2 per cent and consumption of other processed vegetables fell by 4 per cent. Fresh vegetable prices (other than potatoes) were up 6 per cent on 1997.

- Household consumption of fresh fruit showed virtually no change on 1997 after increasing in most recent years and by 20 per cent since 1988. Prices were up 4 per cent on 1998. There was a 10 per cent rise in the consumption of fruit juices in 1998 and a 44 per cent increase in the last decade.

- The consumption of bread has fallen slightly every year since 1994 mainly due to lower consumption of brown (including wholemeal) bread. Cereal consumption, excluding bread, fell by 5 per cent reflecting reduced purchases of cakes, biscuits, rice and oatmeal products.

- Household consumption of tea and coffee was about the same as in 1997 though more than 20 per cent down on a decade ago.

- Home consumption of soft drinks fell by 5 per cent on 1997, though consumption of the low calorie ready to drink variety continued to increase.

- Home consumption of wine rose by 13 per cent in 1998 but this was offset by a recorded fall of 17 per cent in home consumption of beer. Lager consumption was unchanged.

Nutrient intakes

- Energy intake from household food fell to 1,740 kcal in 1998 accompanied by a slight decrease in the assessed intakes of several nutrients. Energy intake has fallen by 13 per cent in the last decade.

- The proportion of food energy derived from fat continued to decline, from 42.0 per cent in 1988 to 39.1 per cent in 1997 and 38.8 per cent in 1998. The proportion of food energy derived from saturated fatty acids (15.2 per cent) was similar to that in 1997 but lower than in 1988 (17.2 per cent).

Introduction

The annual report on the National Food Survey has provided national data on food expenditure, consumption and nutrient intakes since 1950. This edition presents the data for 1998, and includes comparisons with both one and ten years ago. As in other recent reports, it would have been possible to base this year's report on results for the United Kingdom, rather than Great Britain, because the Survey was extended to Northern Ireland in January 1996. However, in order to preserve continuity and to present comparisons with earlier years, most data presented are for Great Britain. Nevertheless some United Kingdom and Northern Ireland data are included. Detailed results for Northern Ireland are published by the Department of Agriculture for Northern Ireland and are obtainable from the Northern Ireland National Food Survey Section in Belfast (02890 – 524850).

The results for Great Britain are derived from the responses of a random sample of some 6,000 private households throughout the country. Each of the participating households recorded details of all items of food brought into the home for human consumption during the course of a week. Soft drinks, alcoholic drinks and confectionery brought into the home were also covered. Some information on the numbers of meals eaten outside the home, but not the content or cost of such meals, was recorded for all the households. In addition, a half of the selected households in Great Britain also recorded details of all meals, snacks and drinks consumed outside the home.

As the data presented in this report are based on a sample, they are subject to sampling error and small changes over time or differences between groups should not necessarily be regarded as statistically significant. Appendix A contains details of the structure and methodology of the Survey, including sampling errors. A glossary of terms is given at the end of the report.

The main household consumption and expenditure data for 1998 are presented in Section 2 and Appendix B of this report. They show averages per person per week for each type of food.

Results for Great Britain as a whole are followed by results classified according to various geographical and household characteristics. These provide some insight into patterns of consumption and expenditure in different types of households but need to be interpreted with some care as an observed difference cannot necessarily be attributed solely to the classification difference under consideration. For example, differences in the level of expenditure between income groups may, in part, reflect differences in the numbers and ages of household members and the number of meals eaten outside the home.

It is important to note that the NFS classifies food in the form in which it is acquired by consumers and that, in the case of household food, food purchased (together with own-produced and free food consumed) is used as a proxy for consumption. As a result of the first point, NFS data on the consumption of a particular food ingredient excludes any of that ingredient which is consumed in other forms e.g. sugar consumed as chocolate is "chocolate" in the NFS and pork consumed in pork pies is coded as "meat pies", not as pork.

A summary of nutrient intake data for household food and drink is presented in Section 3 with reference to the Tables in Appendix B. Section 4 and Appendix C present expenditure, consumption and nutrient intake data derived from the Eating Out component of the Survey. Section 5 presents NFS-based estimates of nutrient intakes by age and gender with comparison of nutrient intakes from home supplies and from food eaten out. Comparisons with the results from the National Diet and Nutrition Surveys, jointly sponsored by the Ministry and the Department of Health, are also given.

Background

An estimated £54 billion was spent on household food (excluding alcoholic drinks) in 1998. This was an increase of 1.2 per cent on 1997 and compares with an increase of 5.0 per cent for total consumers' expenditure. As a result, expenditure on food as a percentage of total consumers' expenditure continued to decline (Table 1.1).

Table 1.1 Household final consumption expenditure in the United Kingdom at current prices[1]

	1988 £ b	1988 %	1997 £ b	1997 %	1998 £ b	1998 %
Expenditure on household food	36.5	12.9	53.2	10.7	53.9	10.3
Total consumers' expenditure	283.4	100.0	498.3	100.0	525.5	100.0
Related series:						
Expenditure on alcoholic drinks	18.6	6.6	29.1	5.8	29.8	5.7
Expenditure on catering (meals and accommodation)	23.7	8.4	43.0	8.6	47.5	8.8

Source: Office for National Statistics

Retail food prices, as measured by the annual average Retail Prices Index, rose by 1.3 per cent between 1997 and 1998 (Figure 1.2). Within this, the annual index for non-seasonal food rose by 0.6 per cent. This is only the second time since 1961 that the rise in this index has been below 1.0 per cent. This low rate of increase partially reflects a 1.0 per cent fall in UK food manufacturers' output prices which in turn partially reflects a 5.0 per cent fall in the prices paid by manufacturers for their materials and fuel.

The annual all items Retail Price Index increased by 3.4 per cent in 1998 implying that food prices fell by 2.0 per cent in real terms. This was the eighth annual fall in food prices in real terms since 1988 so that prices in 1998 were 9.9 per cent lower in real terms than a decade ago. Figure 1.3 shows average food prices in 1998 up by 43 per cent from the RPI base (January 1987) compared with a rise of 67 per cent for all items except food.

---

[1] Estimates of Consumers' Expenditure now conform to the European System of Accounts 1995 (ESA95) and have therefore been re-titled 'Household final consumption expenditure'

Figure 1.2 Annual percentage changes in the Retail Price Index: All items and Food

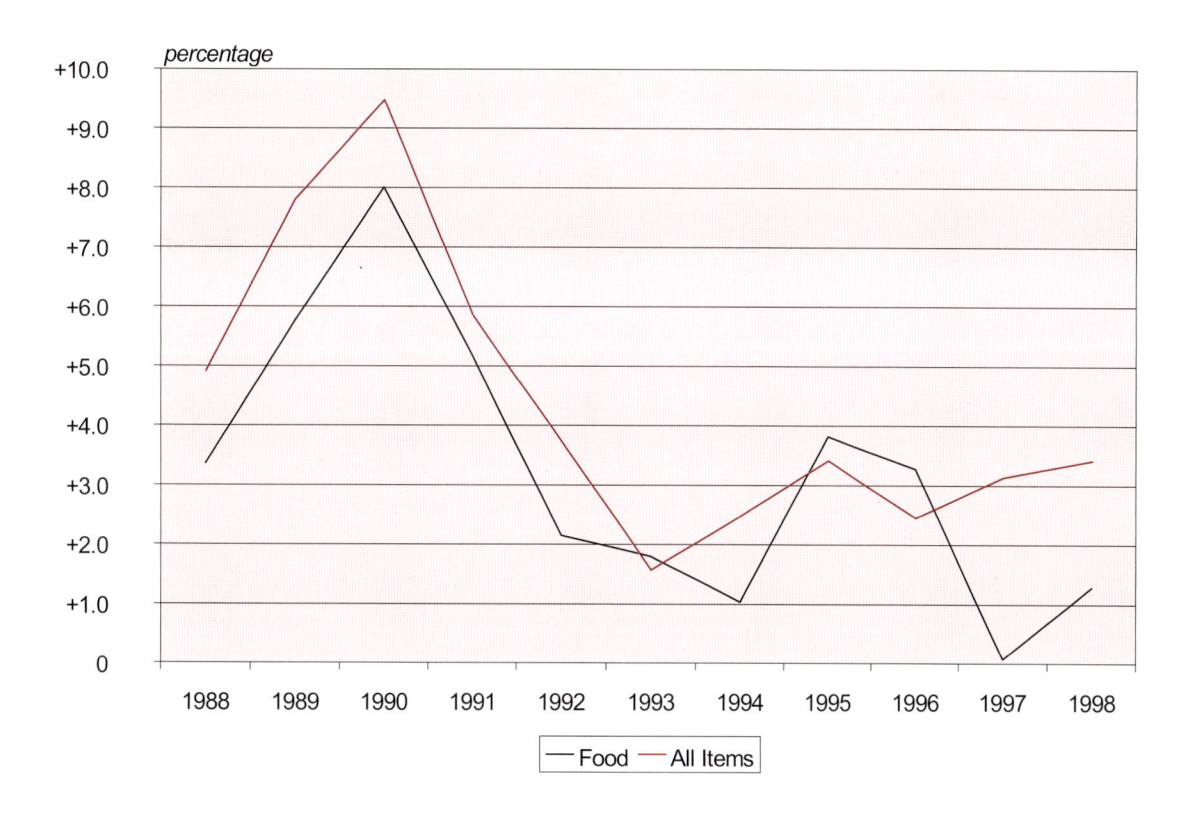

Figure 1.3 Retail Price Index: All items, food and alcoholic drinks, 1998

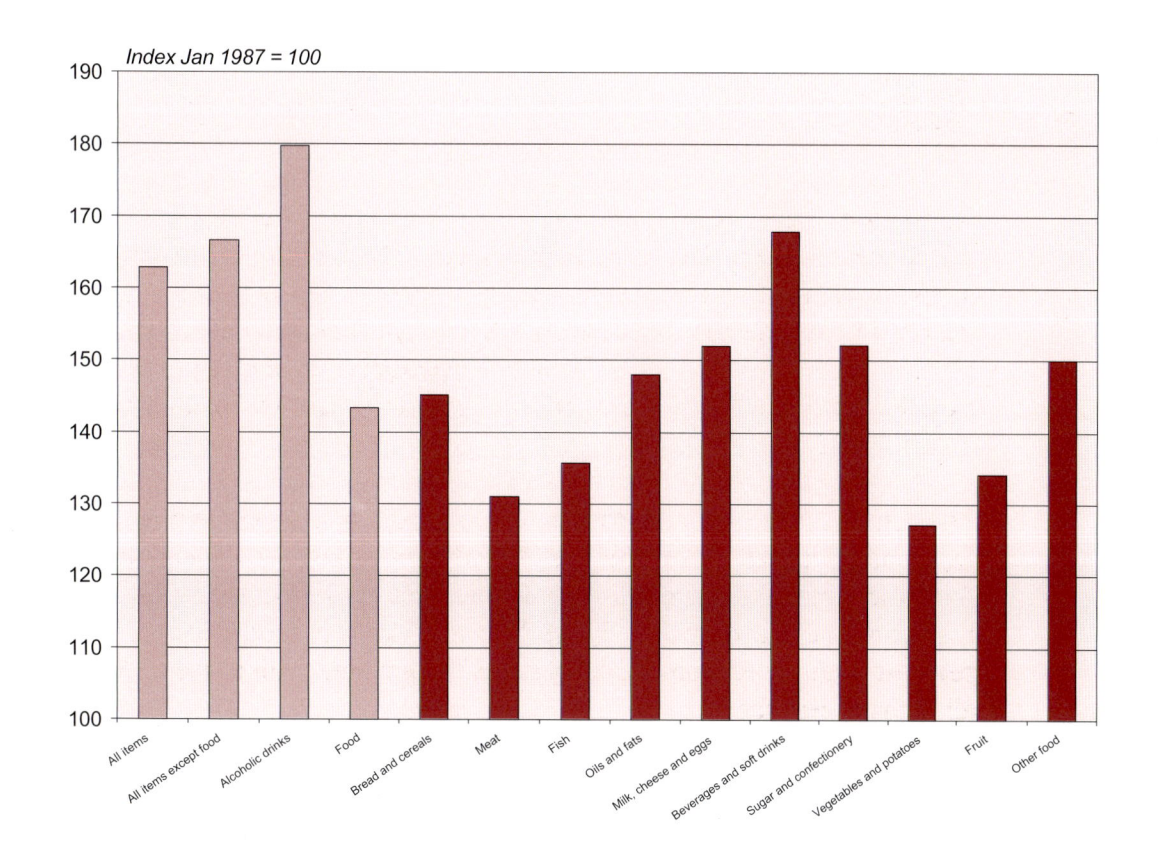

Section 2

Household food: expenditure and consumption

This Section presents results for food brought into the home i.e. household food, and a short section on the number of meals eaten outside the home. As in past years, results of the Survey are given for Great Britain. However, with the inclusion of Northern Ireland in the Survey as from January 1996, some United Kingdom results, particularly on expenditure, are included for comparison. In 1998, average expenditure on household food in Great Britain rose by 0.8 per cent to £14.79 per person per week (Table 2.1). The notional value of supplies from gardens, allotments and free sources, at 18 pence per person per week, was close to the corresponding figure for 1997. Spending on alcoholic and soft drinks and confectionery for home consumption, added a further £2.15 to the average expenditure per person per week. Details of consumption and expenditure by food code are given in Appendix Table B1 and B7 respectively.

Table 2.1 Household food expenditure and total value of food obtained for consumption

per person per week

	Expenditure			Value of garden and allotment produce, etc [a]		Value of consumption [b]		
	1997	1998	Change	1997	1998	1997	1998	Change
Food	£	£	%	£	£	£	£	%
1st Quarter	14.59	14.49	-0.7	0.11	0.12	14.70	14.61	-0.6
2nd Quarter	14.97	15.22	1.7	0.11	0.17	15.08	15.39	2.1
3rd Quarter	14.19	14.68	3.5	0.32	0.25	14.51	14.93	2.9
4th Quarter	14.96	14.76	-1.3	0.12	0.16	15.08	14.92	-1.1
Yearly average	**14.68**	**14.79**	**0.8**	**0.17**	**0.18**	**14.85**	**15.00**	**1.0**
Soft drinks	0.52	0.52	...	...	0.5	0.52	0.52	...
Alcoholic drinks	1.20	1.33	10.8	...	1.6	1.20	1.33	10.8
Confectionery	0.31	0.30	-3.2	...	0.7	0.31	0.30	-3.2
Total food and drink, (GB)	**16.71**	**16.94**	**1.4**	**0.18**	**0.19**	**16.89**	**17.13**	**1.4**
Total food and drink, (UK)	**16.67**	**16.87**	**1.2**	**0.18**	**0.18**	**16.85**	**17.06**	**1.2**

(a) valued at average prices paid for comparable purchases
(b) expenditure on food purchased for consumption in the home plus the estimated value of garden and allotment produce, etc.

The estimate of total household expenditure on food, soft drinks and confectionery (but not including alcoholic drinks) in the United Kingdom, at £15.56 per person per week, was 13 per cent lower than the estimate from the Family Expenditure Survey (FES). The change in expenditure between 1997 and 1998 was 0.5 per cent from the National Food Survey compared with 2.6 per cent from the FES.

Table 2.2 Comparison of expenditure on household food with the Family Expenditure Survey

	1996	1997	1998	% change 97-98
Family Expenditure Survey, (UK)				
Expenditure on household food [a] per household per week	42.28	42.56	43.35	1.9
Persons per household	2.46	2.43	2.41	-0.7
Estimated expenditure per person per week	17.19	17.51	17.96	2.6
National Food Survey, (UK)				
Expenditure on household food [a] per person per week	15.33	15.49	15.56	0.5
Percentage shortfall of NFS	11	12	13	

(a) Excluding alcoholic drinks
Source: Office for National Statistics - The Family Expenditure Survey

The 0.8 per cent rise in per capita expenditure on household food in Great Britain in 1998 reflected a 1.6 per cent increase in prices and a 0.8 per cent fall in the volume of food purchased. Per capita expenditure on convenience foods rose by 3.5 per cent and seasonal foods by 6.6 per cent; expenditure on other foods fell by 3.4 per cent. Further details of the average prices paid for individual food items are given in Appendix Table B2.

Figure 2.3 Percentage changes in expenditure, prices and quantity of food purchased, 1997 to 1998

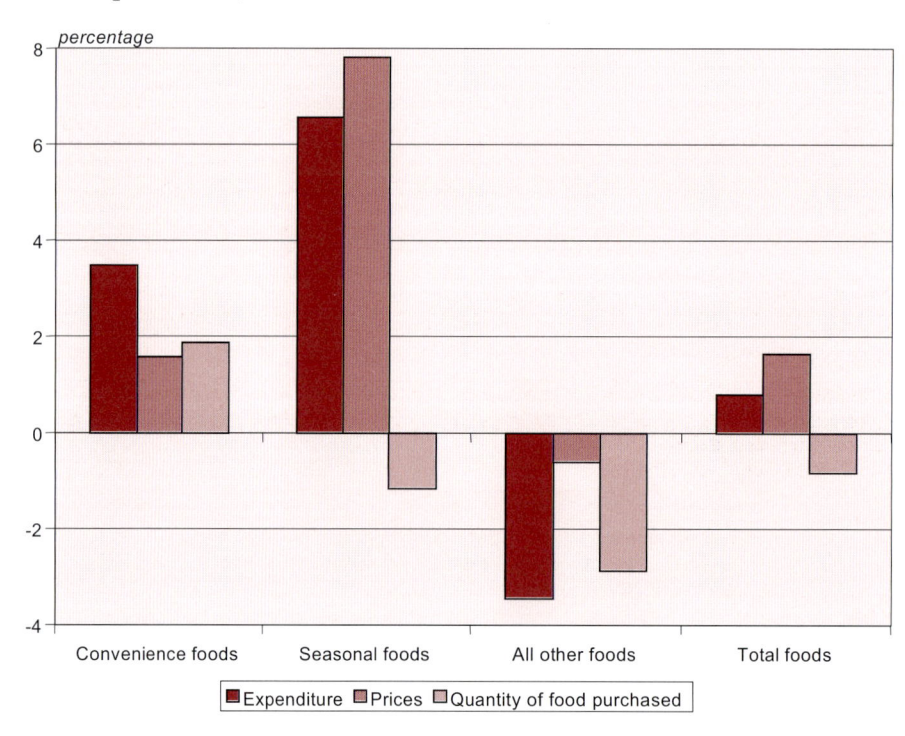

National averages

This sub-section gives 1998 consumption and expenditure results for Great Britain and compares them with those for 1988 and 1997 (Tables 2.4 to 2.13 and Table B1). Per capita expenditure on household food increased by 0.8 per cent in 1998. Expenditures on fish, fruit, vegetables, beverages and alcoholic drinks all increased. These increases were mainly due to higher prices as only in the case of fruit and fruit products did consumption also increase. Expenditures on eggs, fats and oils and sugar and preserves fell, mainly due to lower consumption.

Table 2.4 Consumption and expenditure for main food groups [a]

per person per week

		Consumption 1988	Consumption 1997	Consumption 1998	Expenditure 1988	Expenditure 1997	Expenditure 1998
		(grams)[b]			(pence)		
Milk and cream	(ml or eq ml)	2280	2095	2045	112.4	138.3	134.4
Cheese		117	109	104	38.2	55.0	51.7
Meat and meat products		1037	940	941	303.3	393.7	387.8
Fish		143	146	146	57.6	74.7	77.3
Eggs	(no)	2.67	1.78	1.74	19.3	17.7	17.0
Fats and oils		280	203	195	34.6	37.7	36.2
Sugar and preserves		249	169	156	17.7	18.2	16.8
Vegetables and vegetable products		2352	2061	2005	145.9	214.4	227.8
Fruit and fruit products		905	1068	1090	81.4	125.6	131.5
Cereal products		1535	1518	1478	180.2	268.3	267.9
Beverages		75	59	58	42.4	44.2	48.9
Miscellaneous		na	na	na	43.6	80.2	81.7
Total food, (GB)		**na**	**na**	**na**	**£10.77**	**£14.68**	**£14.79**
Soft drinks [c]	(ml)	885	1454	1384	na	51.9	52.0
Alcoholic drinks	(ml)	na	391	388	na	120.3	132.9
Confectionery		na	57	56	na	30.5	30.1
Total all food and drink, (GB)		**na**	**na**	**na**	**na**	**£16.71**	**£16.94**
Total all food, (UK)		**na**	**na**	**na**	**na**	**£14.57**	**£14.74**
Total all food and drink, (UK)		**na**	**na**	**na**	**na**	**£16.67**	**£16.87**

(a) the constituents of food groups are shown in Appendix Table B1. It should be noted in particular that 'milk and cream' includes yoghurt, fromage frais and dairy desserts and 'vegetables' includes potatoes unless otherwise stated
(b) except where otherwise stated
(c) converted to unconcentrated equivalent

Figure 2.5 Composition of expenditure on household food

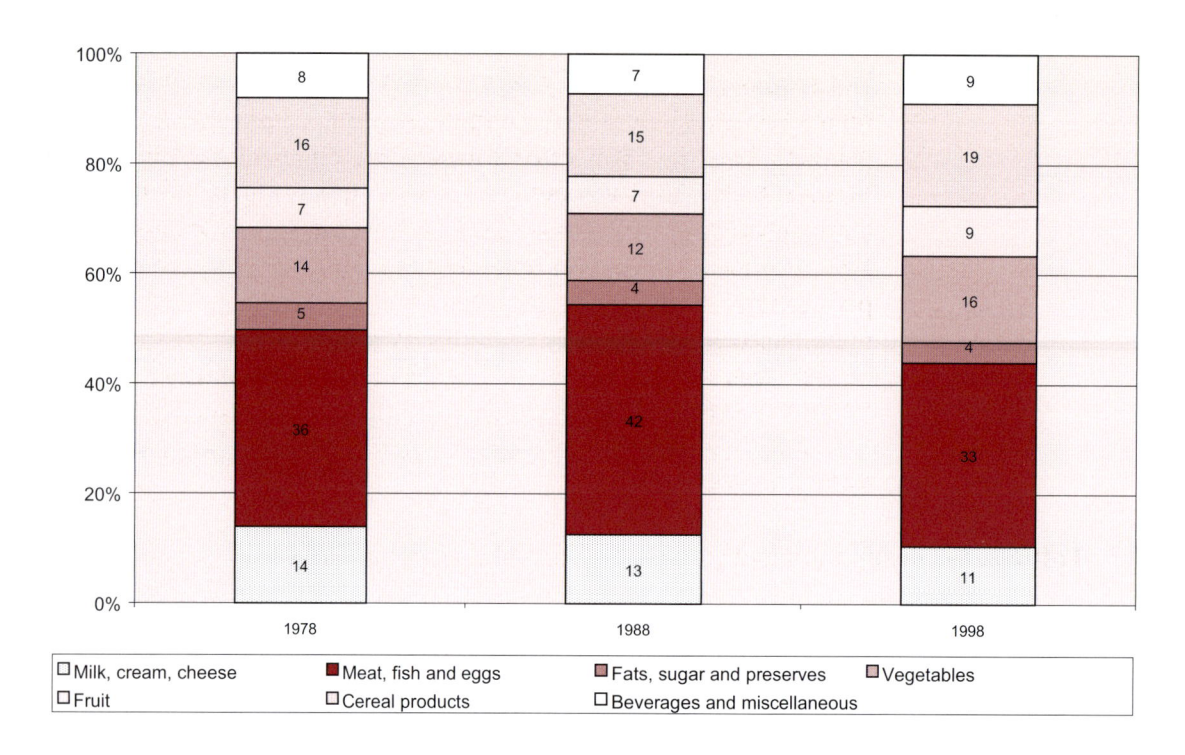

[Stacked bar chart showing composition percentages for 1978, 1988, 1998]

Category	1978	1988	1998
Milk, cream, cheese	14	13	11
Meat, fish and eggs	36	42	33
Fats, sugar and preserves	5	4	4
Cereal products	14	12	16
Fruit	7	7	9
Vegetables	16	15	19
Beverages and miscellaneous	8	7	9

Milk, cream and cheese

Consumption of liquid whole milk, skimmed milks and yoghurts and fromage frais each fell by 2 per cent in 1998 in spite of slight falls in prices. Whole milk consumption was 55 per cent down on 1988. Although consumption of semi-skimmed milks was nearly three times as high as then, consumption of fully-skimmed milk was slightly lower. Fully-skimmed milk represented 15 per cent of consumption of skimmed milks in 1998 compared with 34 per cent ten years ago. Cheese consumption fell by 5 per cent in 1998 and by 11 per cent compared with 1988 (Tables 2.6 and B1).

Table 2.6 Consumption and expenditure for milk and cheese

per person per week

		Consumption			Expenditure		
		1988	1997	1998	1988	1997	1998
		(millitres)[a]			(pence)		
MILK AND CREAM:							
Liquid whole milk, full price		1479	684	667	65.6	35.2	33.6
Welfare and school milk		34	28	26	0.1	0.4	0.4
Skimmed milks		527	1136	1110	23.3	57.4	55.5
Other milks and dairy desserts	(eq ml)	136	104	99	7.1	14.1	14.3
Yoghurt and fromage frais		89	128	126	12.5	26.8	26.1
Cream		15	16	17	3.8	4.4	4.5
Total milk and cream, (GB)		**2280**	**2095**	**2045**	**112.5**	**138.3**	**134.4**
Total milk and cream, (UK)		**na**	**2101**	**2056**	**na**	**138.7**	**134.9**
CHEESE:							
Natural	(g)	109	98	94	35.2	49.6	46.8
Processed	(g)	8	11	10	3.0	5.4	4.9
Total cheese, (GB)	(g)	**117**	**109**	**104**	**38.2**	**55.0**	**51.7**
Total cheese, (UK)	(g)	**na**	**106**	**103**	**na**	**54.7**	**51.2**

(a) except where otherwise stated

Meat, fish and eggs

Household purchases of carcase meat and uncooked poultry remained close to their 1997 levels in 1998. Within the total, consumption of lamb increased by 5 per cent but the other three meats were up or down by only about 1 per cent. Within the total for beef and veal, consumption of boned beef joints rose compensating for the ban on beef on the bone introduced in December 1997. With falls in price of nearly 10 per cent for lamb and pork, 3 per cent for poultry and 2 per cent for beef, expenditure was down for all four meats. Home consumption of meat-based ready and takeaway-ready meals continued to increase. Consumption of fish was also close to its 1997 level but expenditure was up by 3 per cent. Within the total, consumption of fresh fatty fish, such as salmon and mackerel, increased for the fourth year running to nearly 15 grams per person per week in 1998, twice as high as in 1988.

Table 2.7 Consumption and expenditure for meat, fish and eggs

per person per week

		Consumption			Expenditure		
		1988	1997	1998	1988	1997	1998
		(grams)[a]			(pence)		
MEAT:							
Beef and veal		180	110	109	70.5	54.6	52.7
Mutton and lamb		78	56	59	24.6	26.2	24.6
Pork		94	75	76	26.2	28.8	27.0
Total carcase meat		**352**	**241**	**244**	**121.4**	**109.5**	**104.2**
Bacon and ham, uncooked		99	72	76	30.5	36.2	35.9
Bacon and ham, cooked including canned		32	41	40	14.1	26.1	25.1
Poultry, uncooked		213	221	218	41.8	68.7	65.8
Poultry, cooked, not canned		16	33	33	6.9	17.1	17.4
Other meat and meat products		325	331	330	88.7	136.0	139.3
Total meat, (GB)		**1037**	**940**	**941**	**303.3**	**393.7**	**387.8**
Total meat, (UK)		**na**	**940**	**937**	**na**	**394.4**	**387.3**
FISH:							
Fresh		32	31	33	13.6	16.8	17.9
Processed and shell		15	17	14	7.8	11.9	10.6
Prepared including fish products		49	53	52	21.5	26.0	28.1
Frozen, including fish products		45	46	46	14.7	20.0	20.7
Total fish, (GB)		**143**	**146**	**146**	**57.6**	**74.7**	**77.3**
Total fish, (UK)		**na**	**145**	**144**	**na**	**74.2**	**76.5**
EGGS, (GB)	(no)	2.67	1.78	1.74	19.3	17.7	17.0
EGGS, (UK)	(no)	na	1.81	1.74	na	18.0	17.0

(a) except where otherwise stated

Fats and oils

Following its slight up-turn in 1996, consumption of fats and oils fell in both 1997 and 1998, to be back in line with its previous rate of long-term decline of around 3 per cent per annum. The fall was almost entirely due to a drop in reduced-fat spreads with other fats and oils, including low fat spreads, remaining close to their 1997 levels.

Table 2.8 Consumption and expenditure for fats and oils

per person per week

		Consumption			Expenditure		
		1988	1997	1998	1988	1997	1998
FATS:			(grams) [a]			(pence)	
Butter		57	38	39	12.6	11.8	12.2
Margarine		108	26	26	10.1	2.8	2.9
Low fat and reduced fat spreads		38	77	69	6.0	14.3	12.7
Vegetable and salad oils	(ml)	40	48	49	3.0	6.5	6.1
Other fats and oils (mainly lard)		9	14	13	1.5	2.3	2.3
Total fats, (GB)		**280**	**203**	**195**	**34.6**	**37.7**	**36.2**
Total fats, (UK)		**na**	**203**	**195**	**na**	**37.8**	**36.4**

(a) except where otherwise stated

Sugar and preserves

Purchases of sugar and preserves fell by 8 per cent in 1998 to a level 37 per cent lower than that of 1988.

Table 2.9 Consumption and expenditure for sugar and preserves

per person per week

	Consumption			Expenditure		
	1988	1997	1998	1988	1997	1998
		(grams)			(pence)	
SUGAR AND PRESERVES:						
Sugar	196	128	119	11.3	9.6	8.5
Honey, preserves, syrup and treacle	53	41	37	6.4	8.6	8.3
Total sugar and preserves, (GB)	**249**	**169**	**156**	**17.7**	**18.2**	**16.8**
Total sugar and preserves, (UK)	**na**	**168**	**156**	**na**	**18.2**	**16.7**

Vegetables and fruit

Household consumption of fresh potatoes fell by 4 per cent in 1998 and was 31 per cent lower than ten years ago. In contrast, expenditure was up by a third on 1997 as prices increased by 40 per cent following a fall in supplies caused by wet weather in 1998 and lower than usual prices in 1997. Consumption of fresh green vegetables fell by 2 per cent and was 16 per cent below that of 1988. Within the total, cauliflower was up by 5 per cent on the year and by a quarter compared with ten years ago. Other fresh vegetables also fell by 2 per cent in 1998 but were 2 per cent up on ten years ago. Consumption of potato products rose by 2 per cent in 1998 to a level 45 per cent higher than a decade ago. Other processed vegetable products, which consist largely of canned vegetables, fell by 3 per cent in 1998 and by 13 per cent in the last ten years. Although consumption of fresh fruit was up by less than 1 per cent in 1998, it was a fifth higher than in 1988 having increased in almost every year. Fruit juice consumption rose by 10 per cent in 1998 and by 44 per cent over ten years ago.

Table 2.10 Consumption and expenditure for vegetables and fruit

per person per week

		Consumption			Expenditure		
		1988	1997	1998	1988	1997	1998
		(grams)[a]			(pence)		
VEGETABLES:							
Fresh potatoes		1033	745	715	22.3	25.6	34.1
Fresh green		293	251	246	19.1	30.9	32.9
Other fresh		475	497	486	41.3	58.8	61.2
Processed potatoes, frozen		76	106	111	5.9	10.9	12.2
Other frozen vegetables		109	94	88	12.0	15.4	14.3
Processed potatoes, not frozen		62	90	89	19.8	38.8	39.1
Other vegetables, not frozen		303	278	271	25.6	34.0	34.0
Total vegetables, (GB)		**2352**	**2061**	**2005**	**145.9**	**214.4**	**227.8**
Total vegetables, (UK)		**na**	**2067**	**2007**	**na**	**213.7**	**226.5**
FRUIT:							
Fresh		595	712	716	52.5	87.0	91.3
Fruit juices	(ml)	211	277	304	15.2	21.7	24.3
Other fruit products		98	79	70	13.7	16.9	16.0
Total fruit, (GB)		**905**	**1068**	**1090**	**81.4**	**125.6**	**131.5**
Total fruit, (UK)		**na**	**1056**	**1078**	**na**	**124.5**	**130.2**

(a) except where otherwise stated

Bread, cereals and cereal products

After being fairly stable between 1991 and 1996, household consumption of bread fell in both 1997 and 1998, though neither fall was statistically significant. However, consumption of sliced white premium bread and sliced soft-grain bread was up in 1998, whilst brown bread (including wholemeal) consumption fell in 1998 after its steady downward trend of the last ten years was interrupted in 1997. There has been an increase in consumption of French bread and Vienna bread in recent years but consumption of these did not change between 1997 and 1998. Consumption of most other cereal products fell or remained steady in 1998 (see Table 2.11).

Table 2.11 Consumption and expenditure for bread, cereals and cereal products

per person per week

	Consumption			Expenditure		
	1988	1997	1998	1988	1997	1998
	(grams)			(pence)		
BREAD:						
White bread	441	431	442	27.5	28.4	28.7
Brown bread	110	80	69	8.6	6.8	6.0
Wholemeal bread	123	91	81	9.3	7.3	6.6
Rolls and sandwiches	na	74	77	na	14.8	16.3
Other bread	na	71	73	na	13.8	14.6
Total bread, (GB)	**859**	**746**	**742**	**66.3**	**71.2**	**72.2**
Total bread, (UK)	**na**	**749**	**744**	**na**	**71.6**	**72.4**
OTHER CEREALS AND CEREAL PRODUCTS:						
Flour	103	54	55	3.7	2.1	2.2
Cakes and pastries	73	93	88	20.0	30.9	30.3
Buns, scones and tea-cakes	32	43	41	5.3	9.2	9.0
Biscuits	149	138	137	28.2	37.9	37.1
Oatmeal and oat products	18	16	11	2.8	1.8	1.4
Breakfast cereals	126	135	136	22.4	35.6	36.2
Cereal convenience foods	96	144	173[a]	21.7	51.6	58.2[a]
Other cereals (including rice)	78	149	97[a]	10.4	28.0	21.4[a]
Total cereals including bread, (GB)	**1535**	**1518**	**1478**	**180.2**	**268.3**	**267.9**
Total cereals including bread, (UK)	**na**	**1519**	**1478**	**na**	**269.0**	**267.9**

(a) fresh and dried pasta was included under other cereals until 1998 when it was re-allocated to cereal convenience foods. Consumption was 42 grams and expenditure 8.3 pence per person per week for fresh and dried pasta in 1998.

Beverages and miscellaneous foods

Household consumption of tea and coffee in 1998 was little changed from its 1997 level. However, household consumption of each was more than 20 per cent down on a decade ago. Consumption of mineral water was marginally down on its peak year (1997) and consumption of ice-cream and ice-cream products was also down, possibly as a result of poorer summer weather.

Table 2.12 Consumption and expenditure for beverages and miscellaneous foods

per person per week

	Consumption			Expenditure		
	1988	1997	1998	1988	1997	1998
	(grams)[a]			(pence)		
BEVERAGES:						
Tea	47	36	35	17.4	17.9	19.2
Coffee	20	14	16	22.1	22.3	26.4
Cocoa and drinking chocolate	5	3	3	1.6	1.3	1.8
Branded food drinks	4	5	3	1.3	2.7	1.5
Total beverages, (GB)	**75**	**59**	**58**	**42.4**	**44.2**	**48.9**
Total beverages, (UK)	**na**	**59**	**58**	**na**	**43.9**	**48.5**
MISCELLANEOUS:						
Mineral water (ml)	26	125	124	1.0	5.2	5.5
Soups, canned, dehydrated and powdered	83	73	74	8.0	11.0	12.0
Pickles and sauces	63	92	96	9.1	22.1	24.1
Ice-cream and ice-cream products (ml)	90	105	95	9.2	15.6	15.1
Other foods [b]	na	45	na	35.6	26.3	25.0
Total miscellaneous, (GB)	**na**	**na**	**429**	**43.6**	**80.2**	**81.7**
Total miscellaneous, (UK)	**na**	**na**	**426**	**na**	**79.8**	**78.6**

(a) except where otherwise stated
(b) including spreads, salt and other miscellaneous food items

Soft and alcoholic drinks and confectionery brought home

As with other estimates in this Section, estimates for drinks and confectionery shown in Table 2.13 refer only to household consumption and exclude those purchases not taken home or not brought to the attention of the main diary keeper or the interviewer. Consumption of soft drinks fell by 5 per cent in 1998, although the consumption of low-calorie unconcentrated drinks continued to increase. The increase in the volume of alcoholic drinks consumed in the home in recent years levelled off in 1998 with decreases for beer being offset by increases for wine. Consumption of lager and continental beers and spirits was unchanged.

Table 2.13 Consumption and expenditure for drinks and confectionery brought home

per person per week

	Consumption 1988	Consumption 1997	Consumption 1998	Expenditure 1988	Expenditure 1997	Expenditure 1998
	(millilitres)			(pence)		
SOFT DRINKS :[a]						
Concentrated	102	101	94	7.1	9.4	8.6
Ready to drink	296	483	473	12.6	25.2	26.1
Low-calorie, concentrated	na	40	33	na	3.6	3.1
Low-calorie, ready to drink	na	266	276	na	13.7	14.2
Total soft drinks[b], (GB)	**885**	**1454**	**1384**	**22.9**	**51.9**	**52.0**
Total soft drinks[b], (UK)	**na**	**1460**	**1389**	**na**	**52.5**	**52.2**
ALCOHOLIC DRINKS:						
Lager and beer [c]	na	210	195	na	34.3	32.9
Wine	na	120	135	na	51.4	67.2
Other	na	60	58	na	34.7	32.8
Total alcoholic drinks, (GB)	**na**	**391**	**388**	**na**	**120.3**	**132.9**
Total alcoholic drinks, (UK)	**na**	**383**	**380**	**na**	**118.0**	**130.6**
	(grams)			(pence)		
CONFECTIONERY:						
Chocolate confectionery	na	41	40	na	23.1	22.7
Mints and boiled sweets	na	13	13	na	5.9	5.8
Other	na	3	3	na	1.5	1.6
Total confectionery, (GB)	**na**	**57**	**56**	**na**	**30.5**	**30.1**
Total confectionery, (UK)	**na**	**57**	**55**	**na**	**30.3**	**29.8**

(a) excluding pure fruit juices which are recorded in the Survey under fruit products
(b) converted to unconcentrated equivalent
(c) including low alcohol lager and beers

Meals eaten outside the home

Section 4 reports on food purchased and eaten outside the home in terms of expenditure, consumption and nutrient intakes. This section shows the number of mid-day and total number of meals bought and eaten outside of the home (based on three meals a day) (Table 2.14 and Appendix Table B3). It also shows the source of the food eaten at mid-day by children aged 5 to 14 years (Figure 2.15 and Table B4). As in past years, one of the highest levels of eating out (of the three main meals per day) was recorded by single-parent households. In 1998, persons in such households averaged 4.10 meals out per person (out of a possible 21) against an overall average of 3.01. This was the highest of any household composition group (as defined in Appendix Table B3). In Great Britain as a whole in 1998, 25 per cent of mid-day meals taken by children aged 5 years to 14 years were meals provided at school; the same percentage as in 1997 (all households are included in the survey over a weekend and some would have been in the sample during school holidays; these are included in these results). In each of the last three years, children in Wales have been more likely to take school dinners, and children in Scotland less likely, than those in England as a whole.

Table 2.14 Number of meals out (not from household supply)

	1993	1996	1997	1998
				per person per week
Mid-day meals out	1.77	1.73[a]	1.80	1.83
All meals out [b]	2.91	2.92	3.07	3.01

(a) based on April 1996 to March 1997
(b) based on a pattern of three meals consumed a day

Figure 2.15 Average number of mid-day meals per week per child aged 5 to 14 years by source of meal by country

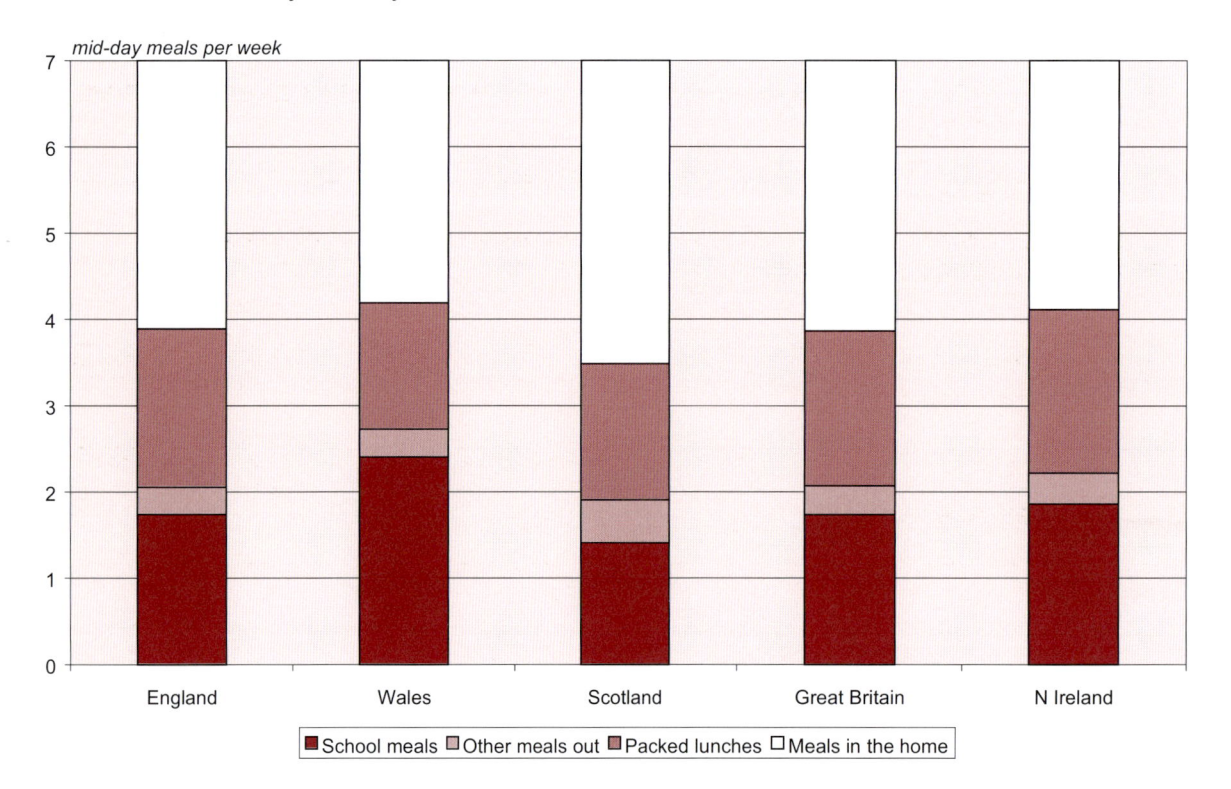

Regional comparisons

The National Food Survey is designed to be representative of the United Kingdom as a whole, but it also provides regional comparisons. Practical considerations limit the number of separate areas from each region that can be surveyed in any one year (see Appendix A, Table A2). For this reason, comparisons between regions and comparisons between years, for the same region, must be interpreted with a degree of caution. Differences in relative prices and in various other factors including household composition and income and the propensity to eat away from the home also affect the comparisons for household food.

As in 1997, per capita expenditure on household food and drink in Northern Ireland (£14.56) was below that of the other three countries while in Scotland (£18.16) it was higher. Regional figures for total weekly expenditure on household food and drink in England in 1998 ranged from £15.19 per person per week in the North West through the average for England of £16.74 to £18.21 in the South East (Table 2.17). Main deviations of household consumption from the Great Britain average are given in Table 2.16. An entry is only made in this table if the region shown recorded the minimum (or maximum) consumption relative to the GB average in both 1997 and 1998 (though the 1998 percentage alone is shown). Northern Ireland has been excluded from this table (but not from Table 2.17) because of its separate publication (see Section 1). Further analysis for fruit and vegetables are given in Figures 2.18 and 2.19.

Table 2.16 Household consumption: main deviations from the Great Britain average, 1998

percentage deviations from Great Britain average

North East	15% *higher* on eggs		
London	12% *lower* on bread		
	22% *higher* on fish	27% *higher* on other fresh vegetables	19% *higher* on fruit
South West	23% *higher* on fresh green vegetables		
Wales	7% *higher* on milk and cream	15% *higher* on other meat and products	22% *higher* on fresh potatoes
	27% *higher* on beverages		
Scotland	16% *lower* on fish	31% *lower* on green vegetables	14% *lower* on other fresh vegetables
	13% *higher* on soft drinks		

Table 2.17 Consumption and expenditure for selected foods, by Government Office Region, 1998

grams per person per week, unless otherwise stated

		North East	North West (a)	Yorkshire and the Humber	East Midlands	West Midlands	East	London	South East	South West	England	Wales	Scotland	N Ireland
Number of respondents		891	1784	1233	997	1395	1294	1474	2135	1353	12556	838	1341	2100
CONSUMPTION														
Milk and cream	(ml)	1942	2169	2006	2182	2170	1881	1986	1968	2113	2046	2183	1946	2409
Cheese		96	94	94	118	103	100	92	117	126	105	103	103	66
Carcase meat		242	264	245	265	239	256	244	211	256	245	227	242	267
Other meat and meat products		793	696	675	631	657	655	662	690	713	684	802	750	588
Fish		152	130	154	137	147	151	178	140	145	147	160	122	93
Eggs	(no)	2.00	1.72	1.89	1.71	1.56	1.64	1.72	1.71	1.76	1.73	1.68	1.84	1.62
Fats and oils		186	190	190	206	186	158	220	191	211	193	235	184	209
Sugar and preserves		147	143	143	182	172	145	146	168	158	156	175	147	139
Vegetables		2051	1844	1795	2099	2104	1949	2136	2001	2253	2019	2277	1712	2052
Of which:														
Fresh potatoes		767	702	603	766	780	678	695	703	822	720	874	566	1033
Fresh green vegetables		223	209	235	273	238	272	278	255	302	253	265	171	143
Other fresh vegetables		445	424	447	479	436	498	616	501	526	488	570	418	355
Processed potatoes		224	185	184	202	226	177	188	191	218	198	203	220	187
Other processed vegetables		392	324	326	379	424	324	359	351	385	360	365	337	334
Fruit		981	935	1024	968	981	1203	1295	1203	1229	1102	1137	957	674
Bread		793	720	786	799	776	668	656	714	796	738	789	748	807
Other cereals		774	674	744	664	752	723	780	736	771	734	726	714	687
Beverages		53	58	56	57	65	56	52	54	67	57	73	53	47
Soft drinks (b)	(ml)	1537	1204	1202	1397	1414	1564	1231	1424	1487	1374	1256	1572	1506
Alcoholic drinks	(ml)	481	271	374	409	359	346	367	422	396	375	475	458	135
Confectionery		52	48	49	65	54	57	46	59	59	54	64	62	41
													pence per person per week	
EXPENDITURE														
Milk and cream		127.6	138.6	127.7	137.4	135.1	129.8	134.4	135.9	144.6	135.1	140.8	123.9	153.3
Cheese		44.8	43.1	44.4	51.3	48.8	51.1	48.7	62.7	64.6	51.8	52.8	50.6	33.7
Carcase meat		97.0	113.0	100.5	98.9	100.9	116.0	108.1	96.5	105.3	104.3	95.0	109.4	121.6
Other meat and meat products		299.0	270.1	258.3	242.11	267.0	285.8	289.0	305.1	271.6	278.4	306.6	317.9	251.6
Fish		79.7	65.7	77.5	66.2	72.8	85.4	91.9	82.6	74.3	77.6	84.8	70.3	47.9
Eggs		17.8	16.0	16.4	16.5	14.7	17.7	18.6	17.7	16.4	16.9	15.6	18.7	15.6
Fats and oils		33.2	33.4	31.7	35.2	33.9	31.6	39.7	37.7	41.6	35.6	46.0	35.8	42.0
Sugar and preserves		14.0	14.0	15.2	17.8	16.8	16.0	17.4	19.0	18.7	16.7	20.9	14.9	16.0
Vegetables		214.5	197.1	196.1	214.0	229.3	224.9	271.9	246.1	248.8	228.7	231.9	216.6	187.6
Fruit		105.8	112.9	116.6	108.5	112.1	146.9	162.5	151.5	149.0	132.1	142.8	119.2	88.6
Bread		74.7	70.6	72.9	74.5	69.2	65.0	70.5	70.33	79.0	71.5	74.5	77.2	79.5
Other cereals		218.7	173.4	189.5	166.4	186.2	189.0	200.3	208.6	210.5	193.8	200.9	210.5	185.5
Beverages		46.6	46.6	46.9	48.7	52.3	48.2	40.7	48.7	56.6	48.3	63.2	45.9	35.0
Other foods		81.0	67.5	75.6	66.2	84.7	76.38	90.9	96.7	85.3	81.6	81.2	83.3	59.7
Total food		£14.54	£13.62	£13.69	£13.44	£14.24	£14.84	£15.84	£15.80	£15.66	£14.72	£15.57	£14.94	£13.18
Soft drinks		50.6	41.6	40.8	54.1	50.4	56.1	58.3	53.6	48.4	50.4	40.8	74.7	57.6
Alcoholic drinks		156.2	88.8	99.4	117.0	101.7	124.3	127.5	156.0	125.8	121.9	171.3	211.4	60.2
Confectionery		26.1	26.4	23.7	33.2	27.9	34.0	27.4	31.7	31.6	29.2	34.3	36.3	20.3
Total all food and drink		£16.87	£15.19	£15.33	£15.48	£16.04	£16.98	£17.97	£18.21	£17.72	£16.74	£18.03	£18.16	£14.56

(a) throughout this Report Merseyside Government Office Region is included under "North West"

(b) converted to unconcentrated equivalent by applying a factor of 5 to concentrated and low calorie concentrated soft drinks

Figure 2.18 Consumption of vegetables by Government Office Region, 1998

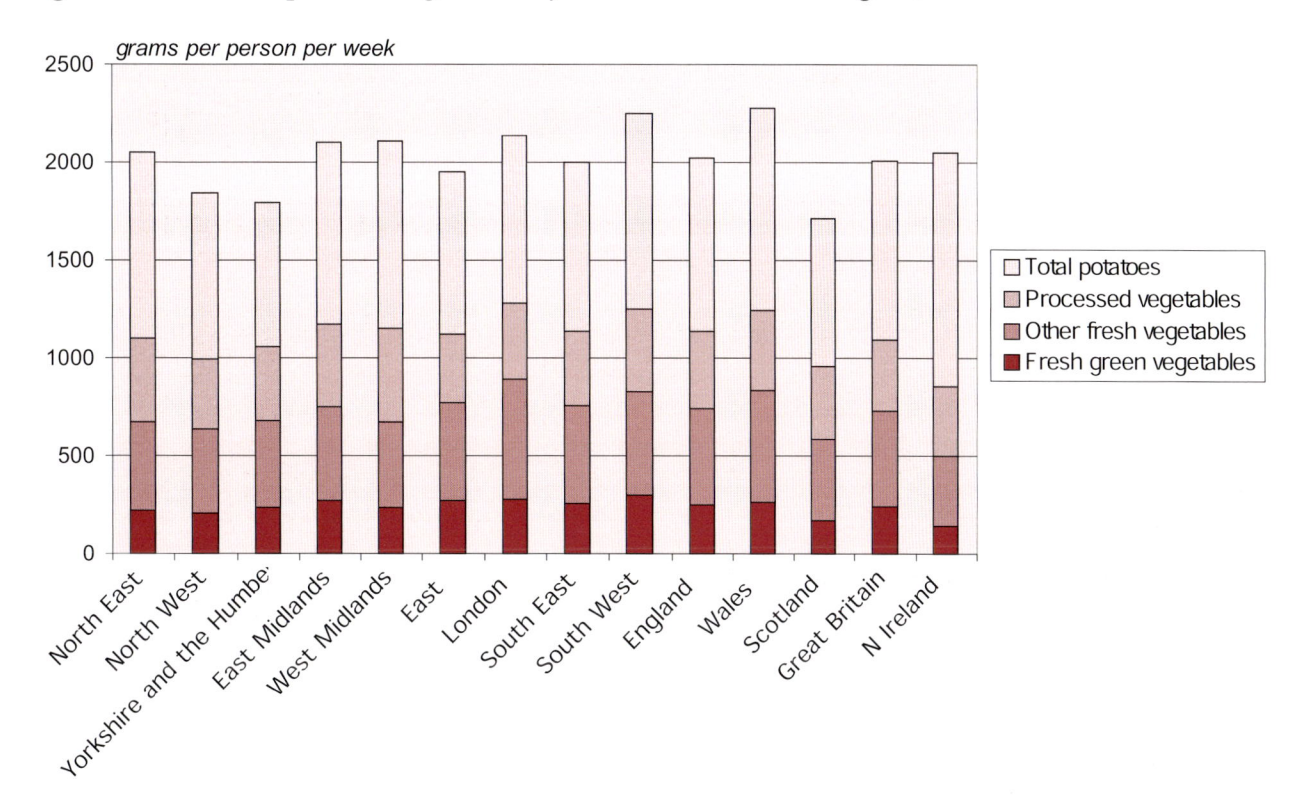

Figure 2.19 Consumption of fresh fruit by Government Office Region, 1998

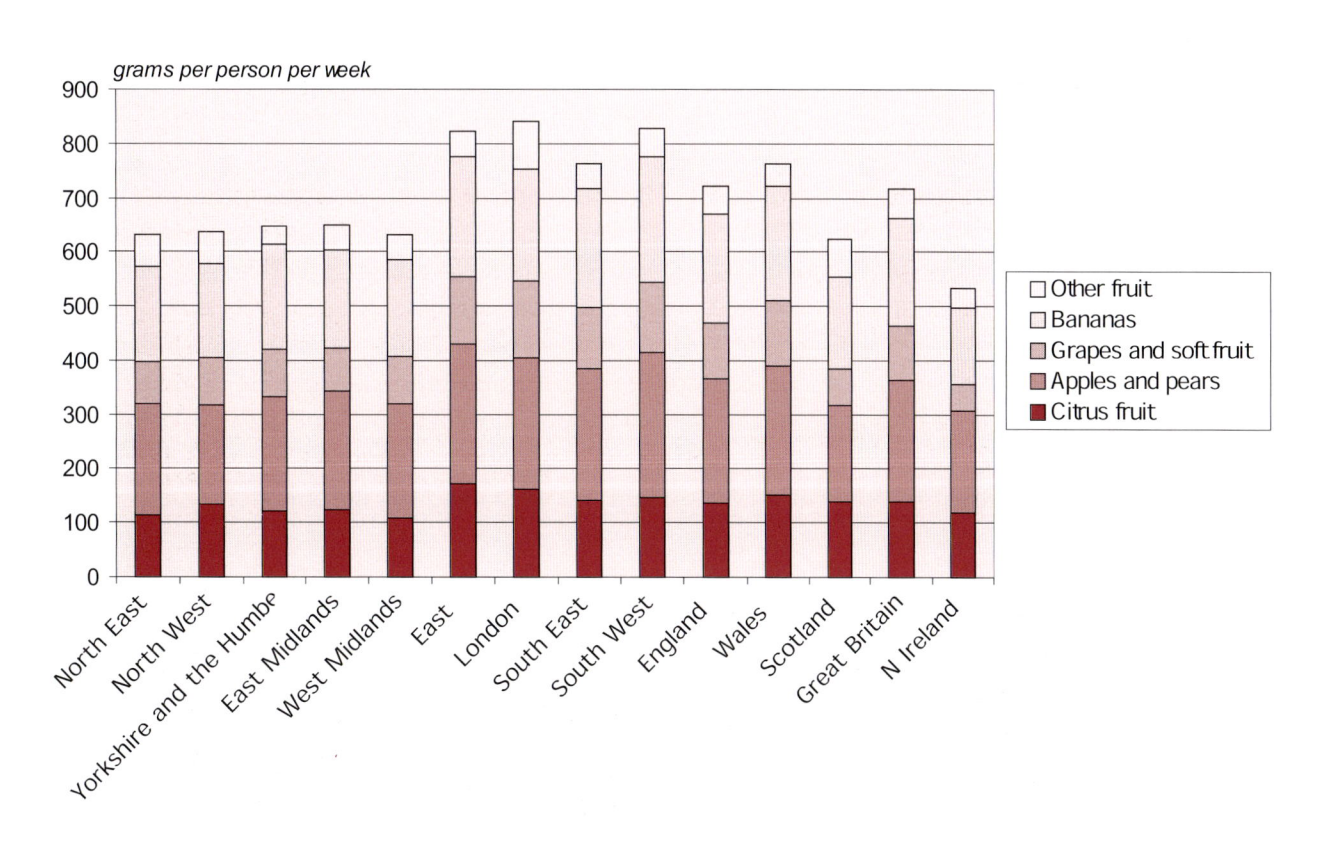

Income group comparisons

Average household consumption and expenditure for different head-of-household gross income groups in 1998 is shown in Table 2.20. The sample distribution of households by income group always differs slightly from the target distribution and from that of previous years (Appendix Table A4). This means that estimates of food consumption and expenditure will not always be entirely comparable with those of earlier years. Some consistent patterns of food purchasing between households with differing levels of head of household income are, however, revealed in the results which are given in more detail by type of food in Appendix Tables B5 and B6. The composition of the survey sample in terms of income groups is shown in Appendix Table A3.

Households in which the head of household was receiving less than £160 per week (D or E2) spent £13.13 per person per week on household food and drink in 1998. This was £3.81 per person per week (22 per cent) less than the average expenditure per capita over all households in Great Britain (£16.94). The difference reduces to £2.83 (19 per cent) if soft and alcoholic drinks and confectionery are excluded. These households consumed less than the average amounts of fruit, fresh vegetables other than potatoes (see Figures 2.21 and 2.22) and alcoholic drinks. However, taken together, they consumed more whole milk and sugar than the average for all households.

Pensioner households (OAP) in Great Britain spent £16.69 per person per week on food and drink in 1998. This was slightly below the GB average (of £16.94) but slightly above if soft and alcoholic drinks and confectionery are excluded (£15.25 compared with the GB average of £14.79). These households consumed above average amounts of most foods and were the largest consumers of liquid milk (whole-cream and skimmed together) and cream, meat and meat products, eggs, fats and oils, sugar, fresh potatoes and tea.

In Sections 5 and 6 of the National Food Survey Report for 1997 (November 1998, ISBN 0-11-243044-9), net family income per person decile groups were used as the income measure. That measure was seen as more likely to indicate the resources available for food than the traditional head-of-household income measure used above and for many years. One reason was that the latter takes no account of the number of persons in the household; another was that it is based on gross income. For the period covered in the two sections (1995-97), the two measures of income did not correlate as closely as might be assumed. About a quarter of households in the lowest decile group were not in the two lowest head-of-household income groups (D and E2). Similarly about three-fifths of households in head-of-household income Groups D and E2 were not in the lowest NFI decile.

The correlation between the two measures of income is complicated by the fact that the so-called head-of-household income groups are not specified purely in terms of income; whether the income is earned or the household is a pensioner household (OAP) is also relevant.

It is also of relevance when considering expenditure on, and consumption of, food that the proportion of adult-only households was much lower (at 24 per cent) in the lowest decile income bands than in the lowest head-of-household income groups D and E2 (at 58 per cent and 66 per cent respectively).

Head-of-household income may therefore not be the best proxy for resources available to a household for food purchases. This issue is being pursued but changes are not likely to be made until the survey for the year 2001.

This lack of correlation between the two measures is important, particularly in relation to estimates of food consumption and nutrient intakes, whose relationship to income differed in a number of respects between the two measures.

Table 2.20 Consumption and expenditure for selected foods by income group of head-of-household, 1998

grams per person per week, unless otherwise stated [a]

		INCOME GROUP [a]						
		\multicolumn{4}{c	}{Households with one or more earners}	\multicolumn{2}{c	}{Households without an earner}	
		\multicolumn{4}{c	}{Gross weekly income of head of household}			
		£640 and over	£330 and under £640	£160 and under £330	Under £160	£160 and over	Under £160	OAP
		A	B	C	D	E1	E2	
Number of respondents		1267	4476	4448	1000	1058	1524	962
CONSUMPTION								
Milk and cream	(ml or eq ml)	2020	1912	1919	2012	2440	2295	2487
Of which:								
Wholemilk	(ml)	503	579	658	791	657	1070	982
Skimmed milks	(ml)	1171	1091	1047	1018	1471	1009	1260
Cheese		122	108	105	80	131	86	85
Carcase meat		226	223	254	193	306	245	296
Of which:								
Beef and veal		96	102	119	101	122	102	113
Mutton and lamb		61	49	57	33	94	65	95
Pork		69	73	78	59	89	77	88
Other meats and meat products		692	675	709	612	760	689	775
Of which:								
Bacon and ham, uncooked		58	68	68	75	117	89	104
Bacon and ham, cooked, including canned		41	38	41	37	46	36	48
Poultry, uncooked		239	216	216	171	248	197	261
Poultry, cooked, not canned		42	30	35	31	41	24	29
Fish		154	142	122	122	227	139	208
Eggs	(no)	1.59	1.43	1.67	1.79	2.16	2.12	2.59
Fats and oils		168	167	190	181	264	207	294
Of which:								
Butter		47	33	31	38	70	28	67
Margarine		18	16	28	23	27	37	51
Low fat spreads		15	25	21	17	32	19	30
Reduced fat spreads		27	45	44	34	64	51	64
Sugar and preserves		105	114	143	187	218	217	288
Fruit and fruit products		1579	1121	909	786	1728	851	1144
Of which:								
Fresh fruit		964	704	606	505	1215	588	835
Fruit juices	(ml)	533	359	252	235	355	192	184
Vegetables		1976	1884	1933	1865	2489	2089	2420
Of which:								
Fresh potatoes		574	605	689	799	854	883	1028
Fresh green vegetables		278	229	216	181	405	216	363
Other fresh vegetables		621	497	432	355	704	405	531
Processed potatoes		164	204	228	205	165	194	147
Other processed vegetables		341	349	368	325	361	391	351
Cereals (including bread)		1446	1427	1453	1381	1726	1518	1631
Of which:								
Bread		637	699	748	766	856	775	854
Breakfast cereals		166	137	126	109	161	140	125
Beverages		47	46	55	58	96	60	99
Of which:								
Tea		24	26	33	34	50	40	76
Total food expenditure, (GB)		**£19.00**	**£15.08**	**£13.67**	**£11.56**	**£19.57**	**£12.23**	**£15.25**
Total food expenditure, (UK)		**£18.89**	**£14.99**	**£13.42**	**£11.67**	**£19.23**	**£12.37**	**£15.14**
Soft drinks [a]	(ml)	1364	1507	1485	1271	1125	1356	798
Alcoholic drinks	(ml)	683	471	354	228	426	197	199
Of which:								
Beers	(ml)	76	72	77	26	54	35	59
Lagers and continental beers	(ml)	108	181	142	93	81	64	35
Wine	(ml)	440	152	88	39	185	55	41
Confectionery		57	57	55	45	72	48	57
Total food and drink expenditure, (GB)		**£23.78**	**£17.39**	**£15.44**	**£12.73**	**£22.45**	**£13.40**	**£16.69**
Total food and drink expenditure, (UK)		**£23.63**	**£17.20**	**£15.10**	**£12.80**	**£22.22**	**£13.51**	**£16.50**

(a) converted to unconcentrated equivalent by applying a factor of 5 to concentrated and low calorie concentrated soft drinks

Figure 2.21 Consumption of vegetables by income group of head-of-household, 1998

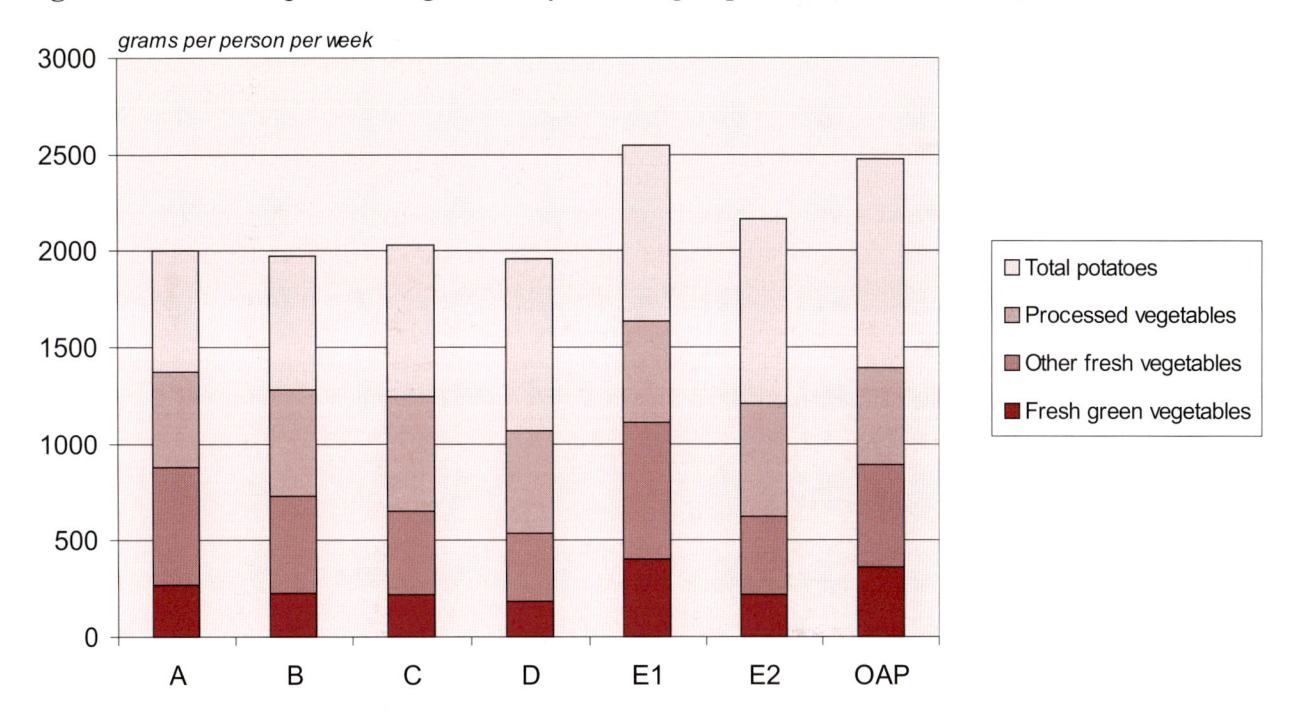

Figure 2.22 Consumption of fresh fruit by income group of head-of-household, 1998

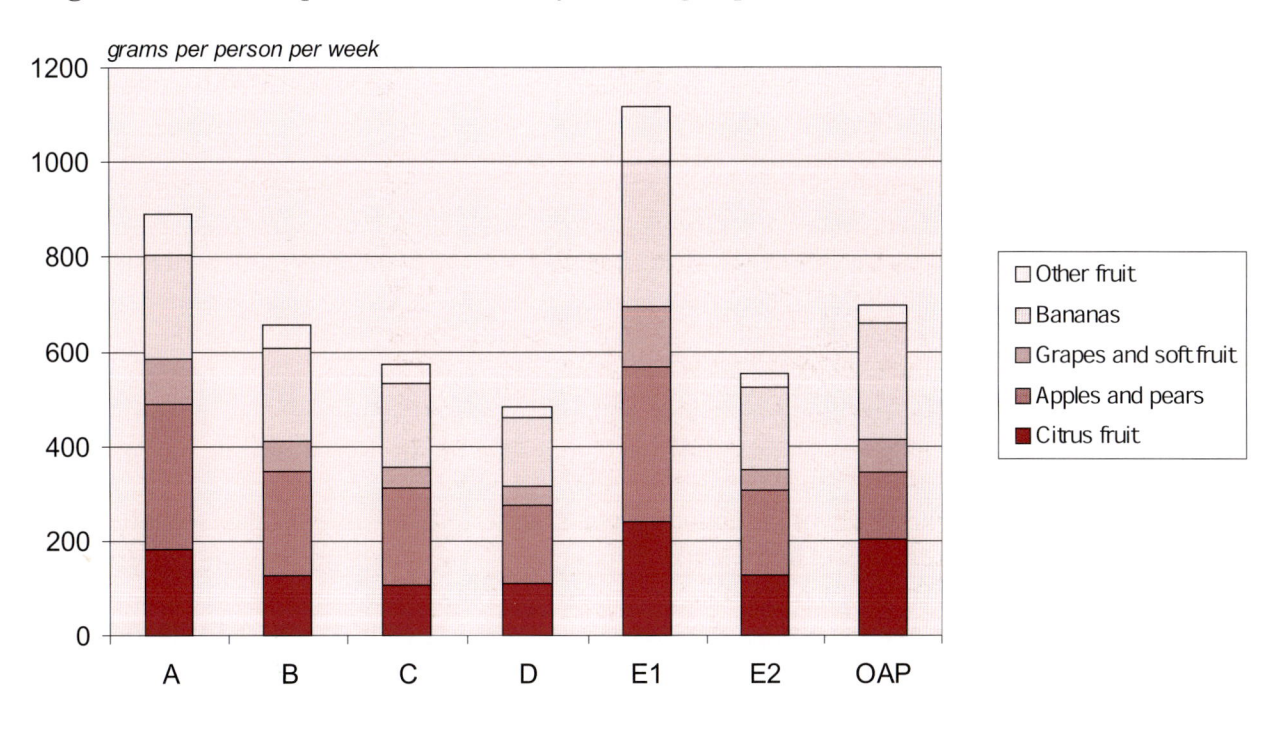

Household composition comparisons

The size and composition of a household has a significant effect on household food consumption and expenditure. Table 2.23 shows total expenditure per person per week and consumption for groups of foods classified by the numbers of adults and children in the household. Appendix Table B7 shows expenditure by household composition and detailed food type. As seen in previous years, per capita expenditure on food was highest in households with one or two adults and no children, any further increase in household size resulting in lower average spending on food per capita.

Taken as a whole, households with children spent 18 per cent less per capita on food and drink than the average household. They consumed over 20 per cent less of fish, eggs, fats, sugar, fresh vegetables, fresh fruit (see Figures 2.24 and 2.25), tea and coffee. They spent more than the average household on only potato products, soft drinks and, marginally, breakfast cereals.

As in previous years, for adult-only households, per capita expenditure on food was highest where there were two adults (Figure 2.26). However for liquid whole-milk, sugar and bread per capita expenditure was highest in one-adult households before declining with each additional adult (Table B7).

Figure 2.27 (which is based on Table B7) illustrates comparisons of expenditure between households with two adults and differing numbers of children. The greatest reduction in expenditure per person occurs between adult-only households and the households with one child. An exception to this, as in earlier years, was the higher (home) consumption of soft drinks by two-adult households with children than such households without children. Per capita expenditure on most foods declined gradually with addition of extra children to the household.

The reduced per capita expenditure observed in households with children may be attributed to various factors, including the lower food requirements of younger children, potential economies of scale, and reduced wastage in larger households. There may also be some effect due to less income being available for spending on each person, especially if the presence of children is associated with a decrease in the number of income-earning adults. As the relationship between household size and per capita expenditure may be influenced by a number of factors, the data do not lend themselves to simple interpretation.

The following section gives a descriptive view of the separate effects of income and household composition on food expenditure and consumption. The results of a modelling approach to separating out the various factors was given in Section 6 of the 1997 report (November 1998, ISBN 0-11-243044-9).

Table 2.23 Consumption of selected foods by household composition, 1998

grams per person per week [a]

						Households with						
Number of adults		1				2				3	3 or more	4 or more
Number of children		0	1 or more	0	1	2	3	4 or more	0	1 or 2	3 or more	0
Number of respondents		1510	966	3920	1452	2488	1045	499	1179	1009	127	540
CONSUMPTION												
Milk and cream (ml or eq ml)		2371	1915	2117	2050	1939	1924	1868	2019	2026	1912	1847
Of which:												
Wholemilk (ml)		768	921	529	757	721	817	996	560	788	1109	486
Skimmed milks (ml)		1316	836	1319	984	989	839	690	1263	1061	729	1154
Cheese		114	84	123	109	89	80	75	114	90	39	135
Carcase meat		235	159	316	257	183	155	155	335	219	126	262
Of which:												
Beef and veal		98	83	140	114	84	69	61	149	99	15	139
Mutton and lamb		71	30	78	60	40	30	63	76	48	97	54
Pork		67	46	99	83	58	57	32	110	72	13	69
Other meat and meat products		752	594	790	733	595	541	496	796	644	392	852
Of which:												
Bacon and ham, uncooked		83	42	114	68	44	43	31	92	64	17	103
Bacon and ham cooked, inc canned		45	32	48	41	36	30	27	41	32	24	45
Poultry, uncooked		198	179	254	239	190	168	159	253	214	186	257
Poultry, cooked, not canned		43	26	35	28	27	22	25	45	27	17	46
Fish		191	90	197	128	110	96	77	180	100	76	143
Eggs (no)		2.26	1.29	2.12	1.60	1.33	1.16	1.43	2.03	1.40	1.50	2.06
Fats and oils		223	139	248	176	141	125	110	237	200	96	254
Of which:												
Butter		58	14	55	32	26	20	14	50	24	20	48
Margarine		30	23	27	25	16	21	26	36	27	28	35
Low fat spreads		23	16	31	19	18	14	9	34	20	0	26
Reduced fat spreads		57	38	59	37	41	31	26	49	33	8	49
Sugar and preserves		223	117	204	132	104	111	80	173	151	75	155
Fresh potatoes		735	678	884	677	530	515	599	809	646	553	911
Fresh green vegetables		322	127	367	206	164	127	90	305	182	105	263
Other fresh vegetables		567	298	666	433	374	334	278	564	360	403	514
Processed potatoes		182	226	174	211	216	226	247	193	204	157	231
Other processed vegetables		394	340	407	407	285	306	303	399	309	164	416
Fresh fruit and fruit products		1392	660	1376	940	1002	814	531	1096	934	1027	1103
Of which:												
Fresh fruit		946	410	654	581	586	481	369	766	612	684	727
Fruit juices (ml)		348	226	303	304	372	291	139	261	276	320	338
Cereals		1680	1298	1608	1444	1370	1324	1248	1505	1449	1242	1438
Of which:												
Bread		891	629	821	719	662	625	647	778	675	477	809
Cakes and pastries		108	58	108	72	74	80	52	100	80	61	81
Buns, scones and teacakes		55	33	50	36	37	38	24	39	35	4	38
Biscuits		157	139	145	130	133	144	118	118	131	67	132
Cereal convenience foods		140	200	162	206	189	180	144	156	182	111	160
Breakfast cereals		147	123	135	138	140	151	147	126	130	92	108
Beverages		90	31	81	45	37	37	24	67	45	19	62
Of which:												
Tea		60	18	48	25	21	23	12	39	32	16	39
Total food expenditure, (GB)		**£17.43**	**£10.53**	**£18.11**	**£14.68**	**£12.77**	**£10.79**	**£8.57**	**£16.73**	**£12.45**	**£8.62**	**£15.61**
Total food expenditure, (UK)		**£17.35**	**£10.54**	**£17.91**	**£14.61**	**£12.62**	**£10.85**	**£9.00**	**£16.52**	**£12.82**	**£10.55**	**£14.81**
Soft drinks [b] (ml)		1018	1561	1089	1548	1584	1838	1649	1371	1592	864	1520
Alcoholic drinks (ml)		443	130	562	403	358	249	214	409	213	47	323
Confectionery		60	39	60	50	59	55	49	55	49	39	61
Total food and drink expenditure, (GB)		**£19.82**	**£11.67**	**£20.96**	**£16.60**	**£14.99**	**£12.29**	**£9.63**	**£18.95**	**£14.02**	**£9.46**	**£17.65**
Total food and drink expenditure, (UK)		**£19.68**	**£11.63**	**£20.66**	**£16.57**	**£14.72**	**£12.32**	**£10.01**	**£18.71**	**£14.35**	**£11.42**	**£16.64**

(a) except where otherwise stated
(b) converted to unconcentrated equivalent by applying a factor of 5 to concentrated and low calorie concentrated soft drinks

Figure 2.24 Consumption of vegetables by household composition, 1998

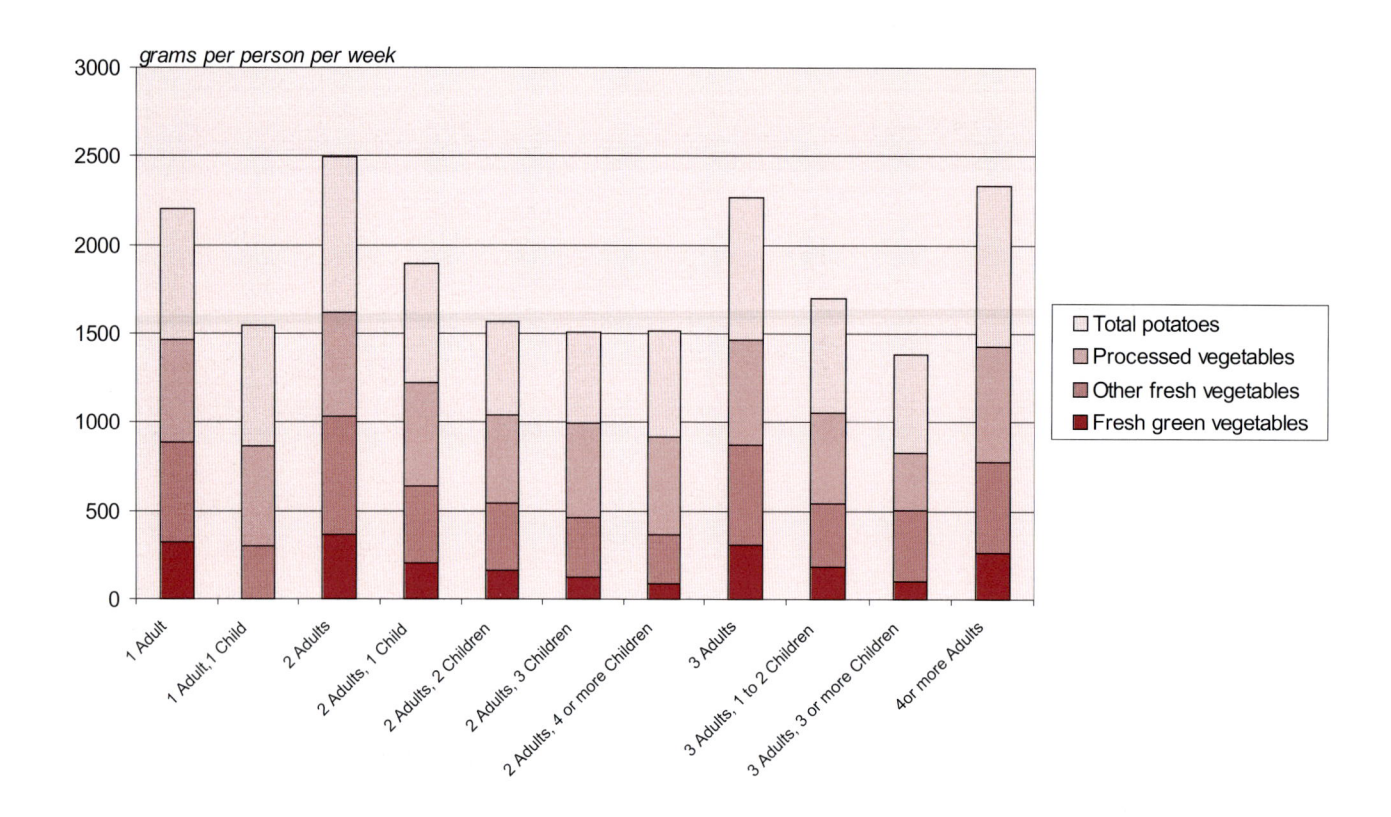

Figure 2.25 Consumption of fruit by household composition, 1998

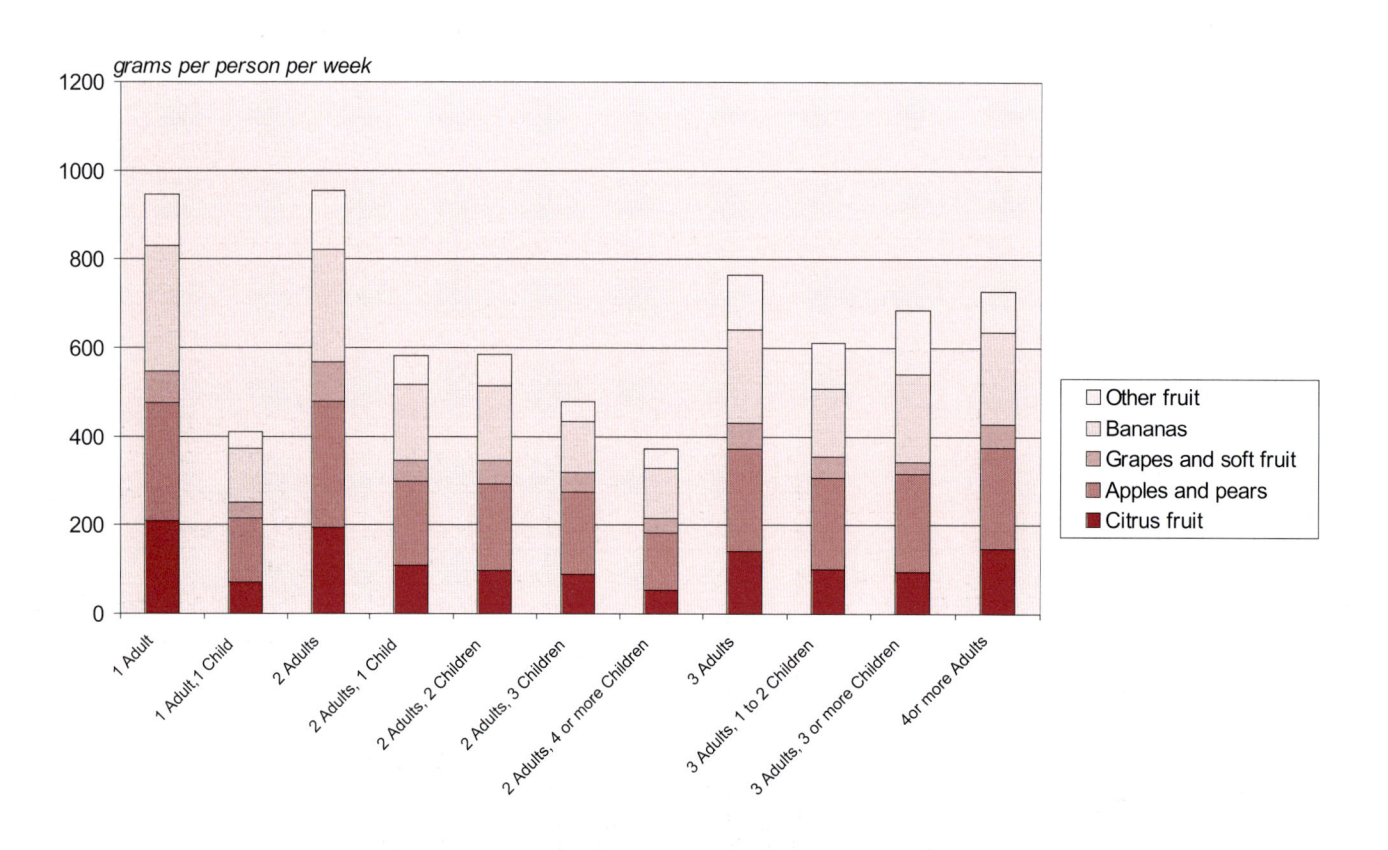

Figure 2.26 Expenditure on main food groups by number of adults in adult-only households, 1998

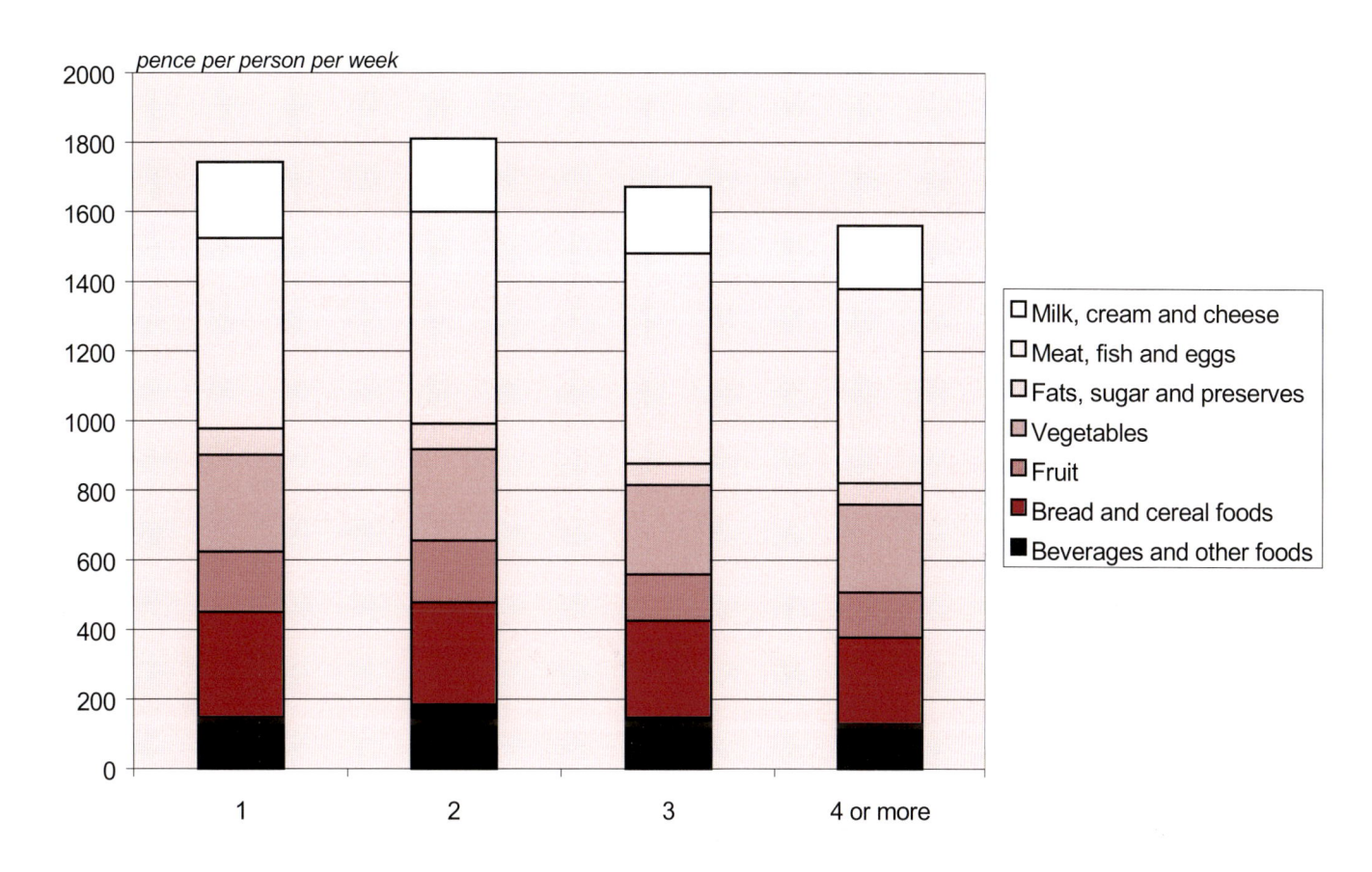

Figure 2.27 Expenditure on main food groups by number of children in two-adult households, 1998

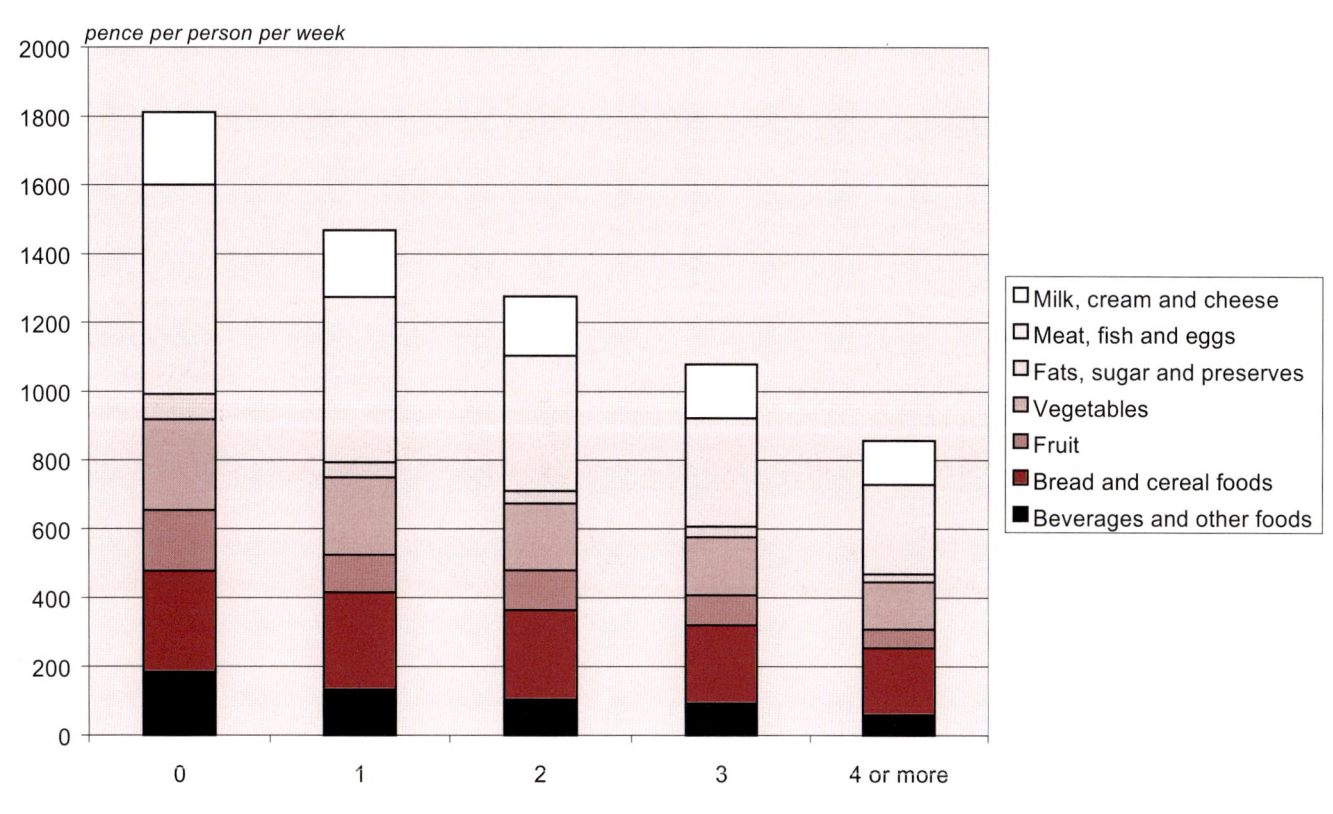

Household composition and income comparisons

Average expenditure on household food showed greater variation per person between households of different composition, particularly those with and without children, than between those in the (head of household) income groups illustrated in Figure 2.28 (see also Appendix Table B8). The decrease in per capita expenditure with declining income generally held for each household type. For adult-only households, average weekly per capita expenditure on food and drink was £29.12 for those in the highest head-of-household income group (A) and £16.60 for those in the lower income groups (D and E2). For households with two adults and two children, the range was £22.44 for the highest income group and £11.31 for the two lowest income groups combined.

Figure 2.28 Household food expenditure for selected household composition groups within head-of-household income groups, 1998.

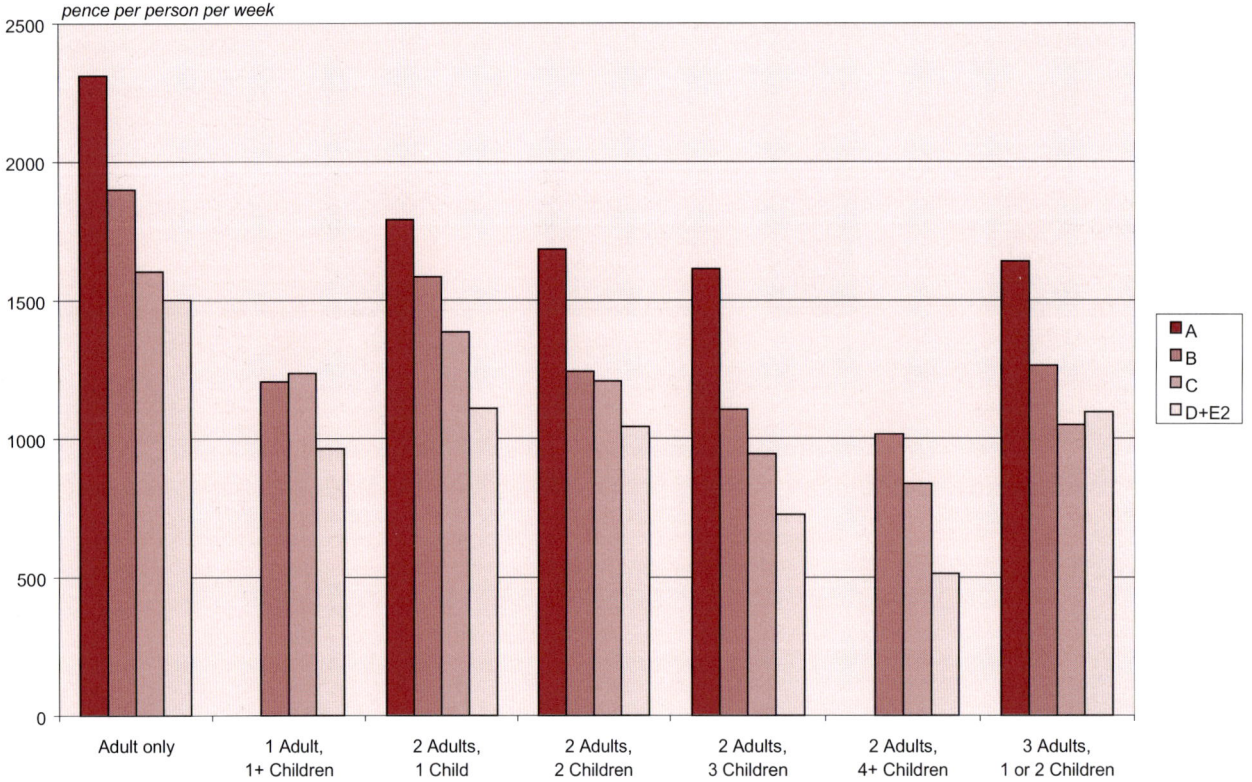

Age of main diary keeper comparisons

The main diary keeper is that person within the household who is mainly responsible for the purchase of food and for the provision of meals. The age of this person is often related to the composition of the household and, to a lesser extent, its income group and level of eating out. The survey results by age of the main diary keeper therefore have to be interpreted with caution.

Table 2.29 Consumption and expenditure for selected foods by age of main diary keeper, 1998

per person per week

		\multicolumn{7}{c}{Age of main diary-keeper}
		Under 25	25-34	35-44	45-54	55-64	65-74	75 plus
Number of respondents		658	3327	4056	2897	1746	1278	764
CONSUMPTION		\multicolumn{7}{c}{(grams)[a]}
Milk and cream	(ml or eq ml)	1701	1863	1906	2038	2349	2490	2463
Of which:								
Wholemilk	(ml)	723	745	684	577	618	754	1000
Skimmed milks	(ml)	728	865	1014	1243	1450	1441	1178
Cheese		85	84	101	126	119	118	92
Carcase meat		151	151	209	309	363	319	266
Of which:								
Beef and veal		69	73	103	135	146	135	101
Mutton and lamb		39	26	43	75	101	95	87
Pork		42	51	63	98	116	89	78
Other meats and meat products		535	577	646	823	804	822	665
Of which:								
Bacon and ham, uncooked		50	43	49	95	119	127	109
Bacon and ham, cooked inc canned		23	29	38	44	50	57	43
Poultry, uncooked		145	155	208	279	268	263	185
Poultry, cooked, not canned		35	26	31	37	41	38	26
Fish		98	97	116	159	213	234	202
Eggs	(no)	1.23	1.29	1.42	1.89	2.41	2.63	2.26
Fats		148	125	151	233	270	286	288
Of which:								
Butter		13	20	26	47	53	81	71
Margarine		16	17	20	32	32	39	40
Low fat spreads		20	16	18	26	33	29	32
Reduced fat spreads		28	34	39	50	60	67	63
Sugar and preserves		97	84	118	176	232	270	289
Fresh potatoes		526	492	586	856	950	1053	897
Fresh green vegetables		126	126	182	299	403	421	368
Other fresh vegetables		301	355	413	582	660	677	512
Processed potatoes		276	218	218	190	178	158	121
Other processed vegetables		362	327	335	391	407	389	310
Fruit and fruit products		728	775	987	1212	1480	1505	1284
Of which:								
Fresh fruit		401	462	588	833	1049	1074	972
Fruit juices	(ml)	305	274	352	316	299	289	180
Cereals		1270	1274	1401	1586	1702	1745	1580
Of which:								
Bread		636	624	690	812	879	908	770
Cakes and pastries		39	60	74	100	112	131	144
Buns, scones and teacakes		22	29	39	41	61	62	45
Biscuits		106	113	133	143	151	176	161
Cereal convenience foods		206	204	183	182	105	117	85
Breakfast cereals		102	124	137	143	140	154	135
Beverages		33	33	41	64	90	105	101
Of which:								
Tea		25	19	24	36	55	68	69
Soft drinks [b]	(ml)	1627	1503	1484	1551	1182	927	756
Alcoholic drinks	(ml)	364	339	384	489	455	287	225
Of which:								
Beers	(ml)	53	40	49	95	111	69	48
Lagers and continental beers	(ml)	158	156	141	161	73	49	31
Wine	(ml)	69	99	149	158	189	104	62
Confectionery		40	44	54	60	71	62	63

(a) except where otherwise stated
(b) converted to unconcentrated equivalent by applying a factor of 5 to concentrated and low calorie concentrated soft drinks

Table 2.29 *continued*

per person per week

	\multicolumn{7}{c}{Age of main diary-keeper}
	Under 25	25-34	35-44	45-54	55-64	65-74	75 plus
EXPENDITURE				(pence)			
Milk and cream	95.7	120.5	121.8	136.2	163.4	166.3	167.2
Of which:							
Wholemilk	29.7	33.8	31.9	28.9	32.3	42.1	57.5
Low fat milk	33.4	40.5	48.7	63.8	76.3	75.0	64.1
Cheese	38.4	40.6	48.8	62.9	61.5	60.7	47.6
Carcase meat	56.6	61.0	88.7	132.5	152.8	148.4	124.4
Other meat and meat products	207.3	249.3	261.6	336.0	315.6	322.5	270.9
Fish	44.9	47.7	59.7	90.5	113.2	124.1	115.2
Eggs	11.9	12.2	13.1	18.8	24.9	25.9	23.9
Fats	20.1	23.1	26.5	42.0	52.5	60.6	56.5
Of which:							
Butter	3.5	6.2	8.1	14.6	16.8	26.0	24.1
Margarine	1.8	2.2	2.3	3.3	3.5	4.7	4.6
Reduced and low fat spreads	8.9	9.3	10.0	14.1	17.7	18.4	17.9
Sugar and preserves	8.4	9.3	11.2	18.9	24.4	31.1	36.1
Fresh potatoes	20.9	24.0	27.6	40.5	47.9	48.7	43.6
Fresh green vegetables	15.7	21.0	26.0	38.9	49.8	53.6	40.4
Other fresh vegetables	40.4	51.4	52.9	72.1	77.8	78.4	55.7
Processed potatoes	63.6	56.0	57.7	53.0	44.1	34.0	25.9
Other processed vegetables	44.4	43.3	45.5	55.0	55.9	51.2	40.9
Fruit and fruit products	73.8	95.4	112.4	146.6	185.1	189.4	163.5
Cereals	222.4	248.2	255.7	295.3	292.4	292.1	258.0
Beverages	24.3	28.2	36.7	57.1	76.7	84.4	70.8
Miscellaneous (expenditure only)	72.5	77.1	77.5	89.9	91.4	88.9	66.1
Total food, (GB)	**£10.61**	**£12.09**	**£13.23**	**£16.86**	**£18.29**	**£18.60**	**£16.07**
Total food, (UK)	**£10.07**	**£11.74**	**£12.83**	**£15.90**	**£17.41**	**£18.41**	**£16.23**
Soft drinks	61.0	52.1	53.2	64.8	46.4	36.9	26.9
Alcoholic drinks	89.1	100.5	137.0	149.6	177.8	120.0	112.4
Confectionery	22.1	23.7	29.1	32.0	38.8	33.9	36.9
Total food and drink, (GB)	**£12.33**	**£13.85**	**£15.43**	**£19.32**	**£20.92**	**£20.51**	**£17.83**
Total food and drink, (UK)	**£12.06**	**£13.49**	**£14.65**	**£18.39**	**£19.74**	**£20.44**	**£17.94**

Expenditure on household food and drink varied from £12.33 per person per week in households where the main diary keeper was under 25 years to £20.92 where he or she was aged 55 to 64 years. Consumption of most food items, but especially milk and cream, fish, eggs, fresh potatoes, fresh vegetables, fruit and fruit products and cereals, all rose steadily with the age of the main diary keeper, and usually to a peak in the 65 to 74 age group. The main exceptions were in the consumption of whole milk, which was lowest for the 45 to 54 age group and potato products and other processed vegetables which were both highest in the under 25 age group. Alcoholic drinks consumption at home was highest in the 45 to 54 age group. However the highest consumption of both wine and beer at home was seen at 55 to 64 years with the 45 to 54 age group consuming the greatest volume of lagers and continental beers at home.

Section 3

Household food: nutrient intakes

National averages

This section of the report summarises the information on the nutritional value of the food brought into homes throughout Great Britain in 1998, and compares results with selected earlier years. In addition, following the inclusion of Northern Ireland in the National Food Survey from 1996, information is presented on nutrient intakes for the UK as a whole. Appendix A describes how energy and nutrient intakes are calculated from the data on purchases recorded in the Survey. More details of nutrient intakes in 1998 are given in Appendix Tables B9 to B12; Table B9 shows average intakes of a wide range of nutrients, while Tables B10 to B12 show similar information for households in different regions and income groups and with different household compositions. For each category of household, intakes are given not only in absolute amounts but, where possible, they are also compared with the Reference Nutrient Intakes (RNIs) published by the Department of Health in 1991 (see Appendix A for further details)[1]. In addition, each table shows the amounts of selected nutrients provided by soft and alcoholic drinks and confectionery. The contributions made by selected foods to average intakes of a number of nutrients are shown in Appendix Table B13. Information on food and drink consumed out of the home and their contribution to the average intake of energy and nutrients is provided in Section 4. A special statistical analysis giving National Food Survey-based estimates of age and gender variation in energy and nutrient intakes is included in Section 5. Contributions to nutrient intakes from pharmaceutical sources in the form of dietary supplements are not recorded in the survey.

Energy

The energy content of the average British household diet, excluding soft and alcoholic drinks, and confectionery, was 1,740 kcal per person per day, compared with 1,790 kcal in 1997 in line with the well established downward trend in energy intake (Appendix Table B9, which also gives values in MegaJoules). The energy contribution of soft and alcoholic drinks and confectionery brought home in 1998 raised the average energy intake to 1,840 kcal per person per day compared with 1,900 kcal in 1997. Energy intakes for the United Kingdom as a whole (i.e. including Northern Ireland) were the same as those for Great Britain. Compared with 1997, the largest decreases in energy intakes were seen for cereals (-18 kcal), sugars and preserves (-7 kcal) and milk and milk products, meat and meat products, and fats (all -6 kcal) (Table 3.1).

---

[1] Department of Health, *Dietary Reference Values for Food Energy and Nutrients for the United Kingdom*, HMSO, 1991

Table 3.1 Contributions made by groups of foods to GB household energy intake in selected years

	1988 kcal[a]	1988 %[b]	1997 kcal[a]	1997 %[b]	1998 kcal[a]	1998 %[b]
Milk and cream [c]	208	10	185	10	179	10
Cheese	63	3	56	3	54	3
Meat and meat products	314	16	260	15	254	15
Fish	32	2	27	2	27	2
Eggs	27	1	19	1	19	1
Fats	291	7	198	11	192	11
Sugar and preserves	131	15	88	5	81	5
Vegetables	189	9	190	11	187	11
Fruit	75	4	80	4	79	5
Cereal products	617	31	628	35	610	35
Other foods	51	2	57	3	54	3
Total food	**1998**	**100**	**1788**	**100**	**1736**	**100**
		%[e]		%[e]		%[e]
Soft drinks [d]	na	na	45	2	43	2
Alcoholic drinks [d]	na	na	30	2	30	2
Confectionery [d]	na	na	36	2	35	2
Total food and drink	**na**	**na**	**1900**		**1844**	

(a) kcal per person per day
(b) percentage contribution to total food energy
(c) see footnote (a) under Table 2.4
(d) information on soft and alcoholic drinks and confectionery has only been collected since 1992. Previous estimates were based on supply figures and are not comparable.
(e) percentage contribution to total food and drink energy

Energy content of the household food supply has decreased considerably over the last 10 years with the largest changes in the energy intake from fats (-99 kcal in 1998 compared with 1988), meat and meat products (-60 kcal), sugars and preserves (-50 kcal) and milk and milk products (-29 kcal). However, when expressed as a percentage of total food energy, the contribution from sugar and preserves has decreased markedly and that from fat has actually increased.

Fats, carbohydrate and fibre

The total fat content of the food brought into the home in GB decreased from 78 g per person per day in 1997 to 75 g per person per day in 1998. Intake of saturated fatty acids also decreased, from 30.3 g per person per day in 1997 to 29.3 g per person per day in 1998. Intakes for the UK as a whole were very similar.

Since there was also a decrease in energy intake between 1997 and 1998, the average proportion of food energy obtained from total fat and saturated fatty acids fell, less sharply, to 38.8 per cent and 15.2 per cent respectively (Table 3.2). This shows further progress towards the population average targets recommended in the report on Dietary Reference Values[1], which were for the proportion of food energy from total fat to be no more than 35 per cent and that from saturated fatty acids to be 11 per cent. When the contributions from soft and alcoholic drinks and confectionery were included, the average proportion of food energy obtained from total fat and saturated fatty acids were 37.3 per cent and 14.7 per cent respectively. The comparable targets for total energy are 33 per cent and 10 per cent respectively.

---

[1] Department of Health, *Dietary Reference Values for Food Energy and Nutrients for the United Kingdom*, HMSO, 1991

Table 3.2 Trends in percentage energy from fat and saturated fatty acids

	Fat		Saturated fatty acids	
	g per person per day[a]	percentage of food energy [a]	g per person per day[a]	percentage of food energy [a]
1988	93	42.0	38.3	17.2
1989	90	41.9	36.9	17.1
1990	86	41.6	34.6	16.6
1991	85	41.4	33.7	16.4
1992	86	41.7	33.6	16.3
1993	84	41.3	32.7	16.1
1994	80	40.5	31.1	15.7
1995	78	39.8	30.8	15.6
1996	82	39.7	31.6	15.4
1997	78	39.1	30.3	15.3
1998	75	38.8	29.3	15.2

(a) excluding soft and alcoholic drinks and confectionery

The average carbohydrate content of the household food supply (excluding soft and alcoholic drinks and confectionery) in 1998 was 214g per person per day (in both GB and the UK), compared with 221g per person per day in 1997. Soft and alcoholic drinks contributed a further 18g bringing the average daily intake to 232g. Intake of fibre, expressed as non-starch polysaccharide, in the average household diet was 12.1g per person per day, a decrease compared with 1997.

Minerals and vitamins

The average intake from household food in 1998 of a range of vitamins and minerals, both with and without the additional contributions made by soft and alcoholic drinks and confectionery, is set out in Appendix Table B9. These are compared with intakes in 1996 and 1997, in Great Britain, and the weighted Reference Nutrient Intakes (RNIs) (see Appendix A). The intakes of many minerals and vitamins in 1998 decreased compared with those in 1997, as might be expected with the decrease in energy intake. Exceptions were slight increases in absolute intakes of niacin equivalent and vitamin C and no change for vitamin B6 intake. For vitamin C only, the increase was still apparent when expressed as a percentage of the RNI.

The average daily intake remained well above the RNI for calcium. Average intakes of iron and zinc were close to the RNI (95 per cent) while those of magnesium and potassium were somewhat below the RNI. The average daily intake of sodium from household food, excluding the contribution from table salt, was 171 per cent of the RNI. Average intakes of vitamins in 1998 were well above the RNIs, where these have been set, for all age groups.

Regional, income group and household composition differences

Nutrient intakes in 1998 in households in different regions and income groups, and with different household compositions, are shown in Appendix Tables B10 to B12. The main sections of these tables do not include the contributions from soft or alcoholic drinks or from confectionery, but their contributions to energy, fat, total carbohydrate and alcohol intake are shown in section (iv) of each table. As in previous years, the variations in nutrient intakes were generally smaller than the variations in dietary patterns (shown in Appendix Tables B5 to B8) because foods of broadly similar nutritional value tend to be substituted for one another.

Table B10 shows nutrient intake by Government Office Regions (GORs). Energy intake was highest in Wales and lowest in Northern Ireland while the proportion of food energy derived from fat was highest in Scotland and lowest in England. For many other nutrients, intakes were highest in Wales and lowest either in Northern Ireland or Scotland, especially when compared with RNIs. Within England, energy intake was highest in the South West and lowest in the East. The proportion of food energy obtained from fat was highest in the North West and also lowest in the East. For many other nutrients, intakes were highest in the South West and lowest either in the North West or the East. However, notable exceptions included polyunsaturated fatty acids and vitamin C, where intakes were highest in London, and proportion of food energy derived from saturated fatty acids, which was lowest in London.

Differences in nutrient intakes between households of different income groups, as defined by income of the head of household, are shown in Table B11. In marked contrast to 1997 and previous years, intakes of energy and most nutrients, with some exceptions, were generally least for the lowest head-of-household income group (D) due to a sharp fall in the recorded intakes for this group in 1998. This fall occurred in most months of 1998 and in most food groups and regions. Indications from data for the first half of 1999 suggest only a partial recovery in intakes for group D but reductions for the highest income group (A). As in past years, energy intakes for households without an earner were least in the lowest income group (E2). Intakes were below the RNI for energy, potassium and magnesium across all income groups. However, for iron and zinc, pensioner households (OAP) and the higher income group amongst households without an earner (E1) and had intakes above the RNI whereas the lower non-earning income group (E2) was below the RNI. Additionally, for zinc the highest income group amongst earners had intakes above the RNI.

As in previous years, differences in nutrient intakes varied more with the composition of the household (Table B12) than between regions or income groups. As expected, households that contained only adults generally had the highest average daily intake of energy per person, reflecting the lower energy requirements of children. However, in many cases, the average intakes expressed as a percentage of the Estimated Average Requirement (EAR)[1] (which takes account of the different requirements of the survey sample) were also lower in households with children than in adult-only households. Adult-only households also tended to have higher intakes of minerals and vitamins, both in absolute terms and, in most cases but less markedly, when expressed as a percentage of the RNI.

---

[1] Department of Health, *Dietary Reference Values for Food Energy and Nutrients for the United Kingdom,* HMSO, 1991

Section 4

Eating out: expenditure, consumption and nutrient intakes

Introduction

The Eating Out (EO) part of the National Food Survey (NFS) complements the household part by recording information about household members' food and drink consumption and expenditure which is additional to that brought home and recorded in the Main Survey. Eating out is defined as consumption of food and drink outside the home that is not obtained from the household's stocks. It therefore covers a range of situations from, for example, food purchased from fast food outlets at lunchtime through to a formal evening meal in a restaurant. However, food consumed outside the home but taken from household supplies, such as picnics and packed lunches, is covered within the main part of the Survey rather than the EO part. The recording of expenditure on food and drink is restricted to personal expenditure; expenditure for business purposes is excluded. Similarly expenditure on food and drink purchased with other goods or services, e.g. with accommodation, entertainment or school fees, is not included unless it is separately identifiable.

The EO Survey is carried out on a sub-sample of the Main Survey households in Great Britain; Northern Ireland is not included. Half of the addresses selected in each of the postcode sectors covered by the Main Survey are also included in the EO survey. A description of the structure of the EO survey is given in Appendix A. This shows that the 1998 EO Survey was based on 2,663 households (Tables A6 and A9), compared with 5,973 households in the Main Survey in Great Britain (Tables A1 and A3).

This difference in sample size is reflected in higher percentage standard errors for the EO Survey (3.1 per cent) for expenditure on food and drink than for the Main Survey (1.0 per cent) (Tables A5 and A10). Non-sampling errors are also larger on the EO survey than the Main Survey. Firstly there is some evidence of under-recording and this may vary over time. This is particularly the case for alcoholic drink consumption, for which it is notoriously difficult to obtain reliable information. Secondly there are likely to be some differences in the choice of food code from the 1,600 available in the EO Survey. In 1996, new survey contractors took over the fieldwork for the Survey and the inevitable changes in coding practice which occurred mean that some comparisons of detailed food codes before and after 1996 are subject to additional, un-quantifiable errors.

Appendix A also describes how each food code is allocated a portion size for estimating consumption and a set of conversion factors for estimating intakes of energy and the various nutrients.

Expenditure and consumption

National averages

Expenditure

Table 4.1 shows the main expenditure results for both the Eating Out Survey and the Main Survey for the five published years of the Eating Out Survey to date. Appendix Table A10 shows sampling errors for 1998 EO expenditure estimates. The national average expenditure on food and drink consumed outside the home in 1998 was £6.73 per person per week, a slight, but not statistically significant, increase on the previous year. Expenditure on household food and drink also increased slightly (Section 2). The increases in expenditure on both household food and in eating out in 1998 were both just above food price inflation as measured by the Retail Price Index for food (1.3 per cent). As in 1996 and 1997, expenditure on food and drink eaten out in 1998 represented 28 per cent of total food and drink expenditure. Excluding alcoholic drinks, expenditure on eating out has increased by 23 per cent since 1994 compared with an increase of 12 per cent for household food and non-alcoholic drinks. In contrast, recorded expenditure on alcoholic drinks consumed outside the home has barely increased since 1994 while expenditure on alcoholic drinks consumed at home has increased by 45 per cent in the same period.

Table 4.1 Expenditure on eating out and household food and drink

£ per person per week

Source:	1994	1995	1996	1997	1998	% change 97/98
Food and drink eaten out	5.74	5.83	6.53	6.61	6.73	1.8
Household food and drink	14.83	15.63	16.46	16.71	16.94	1.4
Total	**20.57**	**21.46**	**22.99**	**23.32**	**23.67**	**1.5**
of which alcoholic drinks:						
Consumed out	1.49	1.52	1.70	1.58	1.52	-4
Consumed at home	0.92	1.08	1.14	1.20	1.33	11
Total	**2.41**	**2.6**	**2.84**	**2.78**	**2.85**	**3**

Comparison with FES expenditure results

Information on household expenditure, including eating out, is also available from the Family Expenditure Survey (FES). However, there are some methodological differences between the FES and the NFS Eating Out Survey which mean that some adjustments have to be made to normally published NFS data in order to make more meaningful comparisons. In particular, the NFS estimates have to be restricted to average expenditure by those aged over 16 years.

Table 4.2 shows that National Food Survey estimates for expenditure on eating out have been consistently lower than those of the FES, notably for alcoholic drinks in which the EO survey produces an annual estimate less than half of the FES. There are several possible factors for the differences in the estimates. Perhaps of greatest importance, the FES requires more active co-operation of all members of a household aged 16 or over in record-keeping and offers a monetary reward to each diary-keeper, which is only paid if all members agree to co-operate. The FES may also include slightly more money spent by adults on children, which the NFS Eating Out Survey would record against the children if they actually made the purchase. The two-week recording period of the FES may also affect the averages per week.

Table 4.2 Comparison of expenditure on eating out with the Family Expenditure Survey

£ per person (aged 16 yrs or more) per week

		1994	1995	1996	1997	1998
Food, soft drinks and confectionery	NFS	4.84	4.93	5.68	6.01	6.07
	FES	5.74	6.30	6.66	7.20	7.44
Percentage shortfall of NFS		16	22	15	17	18
Alcoholic drinks	NFS	1.92	1.94	2.20	2.03	1.93
	FES	3.93	3.65	3.83	4.34	4.39
Percentage shortfall of NFS		51	47	43	53	56
Total food and drink	NFS	6.76	6.86	7.88	8.05	8.01
	FES	9.67	10.00	10.49	11.32	11.62
Percentage shortfall of NFS		30	31	25	29	31

Source: Office for National Statistics – The Family Expenditure Survey

Consumption

Table 4.3 shows average per capita consumption on food and drink eaten outside the home for the five published years of the Eating Out Survey to date. Comparisons before and after 1996 should be treated with care because a switch to a new data collection contractor in 1996 would have had some impact on the choice of food codes from amongst the 1600 available. Standard errors for the 1998 estimates are given in Appendix A, Table A10. These are particularly important when interpreting the detailed consumption estimates given in Table C1 but are also relevant to the other statistics in this Section, including those in Table 4.3.

Consumption of meat and meat products outside of the home increased for the second year running after dropping by 8 per cent in 1996 when the main BSE crisis occurred. Within the group total, consumption for all but one of the meat products identified in Table C1 remained at the same level or slightly higher than in 1997. The exception was meat-based dishes (such as casserole, lasagne and chilli con carne) for which recorded consumption in 1998 was slightly lower than in 1997.

Per capita consumption of potatoes increased again, this time due to an increase of 7 per cent in consumption of chips. Consumption of other vegetables was virtually the same as in 1997. Following an increase in 1997, consumption of fruit decreased by almost the same amount in 1998.

Consumption of ethnic foods (outside the home) continued to increase, due to an increase in the consumption of curry in 1998. Consumption of sandwiches and rolls fell in 1998, after large increases in 1997. Per capita consumption of beverages outside the home fell for the first time since 1994 and was back to its 1996 level. This was mainly due to a fall of 6 per cent in the volume of coffee consumed outside the home. The consumption of soft drinks also fell for the first time since 1994 to below its level in 1995. This was due to a fall in consumption of all soft drinks, except for milk-based drinks, such as milkshakes, which has remained the same since 1996 (Table C1).

Table 4.3 Average consumption of food and drink eaten out, 1994-1998

		\multicolumn{5}{c}{*grams per person per week, unless otherwise stated*}
		1994	1995	1996	1997	1998
Number of respondents		8620	8751	8425	6430	6165
Ethnic foods		28	26	32	38	41
Meat and meat products		109	108	99	107	110
Fish and fish products		(a)	(a)	23	23	25
Cheese and egg dishes and pizza		27	26	28	27	27
Potatoes		(a)	(a)	114	119	123
Vegetables (excluding Potatoes)		(a)	(a)	65	73	74
Salads		(a)	(a)	17	22	21
Rice, pasta and noodles		20	18	24	27	27
Soup	(ml)	18	16	17	16	16
Breakfast cereals		1	1	1	1	1
Fruit (fresh and processed)		17	17	18	22	19
Yoghurt		6	4	5	6	6
Bread		13	14	14	14	15
Sandwiches		36	37	35	50	45
Rolls		25	26	24	31	28
Sandwiches/rolls extras		9	10	7	8	8
Beverages	(ml)	383	389	392	406	392
Ice creams, desserts and cakes		57	49	51	56	51
Biscuits		6	5	12	11	11
Crisps, nuts and snacks		10	9	12	11	10
Other foods		34	31	32	31	29
Soft drinks, including milk	(ml)	310	330	336	348	318
Alcoholic drinks	(ml)	539	535	483	490	435
Confectionery		21	19	23	19	17

(a) comparative data not available

Results by household characteristics

Regional comparisons

Table 4.4 shows consumption and expenditure on food and drink eaten out in 1998 by Government Office Region. Eating out results are obtained from a subset of those households chosen for the Main Survey sample. This subset, like the main sample, is designed to be representative of Great Britain as a whole. However, since a limited number of areas are covered within each region during a year, comparisons between regions and between years should be interpreted with caution.

For the third time in five years, total per capita expenditure on food and drink eaten out in 1998 was highest in England (£6.78). In 1998 this was followed by Scotland (£6.64) and then Wales (£6.10) but there is considerable variation (including sampling variation) across years in the estimates for these two countries. This also applies to regional estimates, though as in 1997, within England, highest expenditures were in London, the South East and the North East (even so the high expenditure on alcohol in the North East looks like a statistical fluctuation possibly caused, for example, by a single household in the sample staging a party away from the home). The South West region has shown below average expenditure each year from 1994.

As in 1997, persons in England consumed more sandwiches and ice creams, desserts and cakes outside the home than persons in Scotland or Wales and slightly more fish, fruit and salads. The highest recording regions within England of these foods were fish (Yorkshire and the Humber), fruit (London), sandwiches (South East and North West England), ice creams (South West England), desserts (London and Yorkshire and the Humber) and cakes (South East and East England). As in 1997, the amount of soup, rolls, crisps, nuts and savoury snacks and soft drinks consumed in Scotland was greater than in any other region. In Wales, per capita consumption of meat and meat products, potatoes, and alcoholic drink was higher than in either England or Scotland.

Table 4.4 Average consumption and expenditure on food and drink eaten out by Government Office Region, 1998

	North East	North West	Yorkshire and the Humber	East Midlands	West Midlands	East	London	South East	South West	England	Wales	Scotland
Number of respondents	382	827	408	406	524	497	572	945	637	5198	384	583
Consumption										*grams per person per week, except where otherwise stated*		
Ethnic meals	24	40	34	44	38	44	73	39	27	41	34	47
Meat/meat products	122	113	97	121	101	88	111	121	102	109	118	112
Fish/fish products	23	28	34	26	22	19	31	24	20	25	21	24
Cheese and egg dishes and pizza	31	27	21	30	26	25	39	25	28	28	28	22
Potatoes	156	130	125	119	124	105	141	115	109	124	128	112
Vegetables (excl. pots)	84	68	79	80	70	63	78	85	73	75	79	58
Salads	20	27	26	15	26	18	22	22	16	21	19	15
Rice, pasta and noodles	32	19	22	23	20	26	49	25	26	27	28	29
Soup (ml)	13	16	20	13	12	11	11	15	11	14	10	43
Fruit, fresh and processed	12	18	15	15	14	13	37	26	20	20	9	19
Yoghurt	4	6	4	3	6	5	12	5	5	6	5	6
Bread	7	16	12	12	16	13	22	15	16	15	16	15
Sandwiches	48	53	50	39	49	38	50	54	37	47	28	39
Rolls	28	22	11	40	20	30	38	25	20	26	33	39
Beverages (ml)	312	359	349	340	319	391	450	488	508	404	413	274
Ice creams, desserts and cakes	52	53	57	43	36	52	61	54	61	53	41	41
Biscuits	12	11	12	16	12	8	13	13	13	12	5	9
Crisps, nuts and snacks	9	10	9	11	9	9	10	11	8	10	7	12
Other foods	48	37	49	33	30	23	44	41	33	37	48	39
Soft drinks (incl. milk) (ml)	320	307	248	355	296	253	381	324	278	308	297	418
Alcoholic drinks (ml)	700	403	463	479	484	273	426	381	459	437	488	387
Confectionery	21	16	15	18	17	15	14	18	16	17	17	18
Expenditure										*£ per person per week*		
All food and drink	8.78	6.89	5.33	6.42	5.99	5.67	8.92	6.98	5.92	6.78	6.10	6.64
Of which:												
Alcoholic drinks	2.56	1.50	1.39	1.47	1.52	0.94	1.73	1.39	1.35	1.50	1.47	1.67

Income group comparisons

Table 4.5 shows consumption and expenditure on food and drink eaten out in 1998 by the income group of the head-of-household. Households with the head of household in the highest two earning groups (A1 and A2 combined) spent £10.23 per person per week on food and drink (excluding alcoholic drinks) eaten out, almost twice the average (£5.21). Those in the lowest two income groups (D and E2) spent £2.41 per person per week, 54 per cent less than average. As in past years, pensioner households (OAP), which are households without an earner and whose income is mainly derived from the state pension or a state benefit paid instead of a state pension, spent the least on eating outside the home.

Table 4.5 Average consumption and expenditure on food and drink eaten out by income group of head-of-household, 1998

		Households with one or more earners					Households without an earner			
		£910 and over	£640 and under £910	£330 and under £640	£160 and under £330	Under £160	£160 and over	Under £160		
		A1	A2	B	C	D	E1	E2	OAP	All households
Number of respondents		164	381	1787	1863	424	475	628	443	6165
Consumption		*grams per person per week, except where otherwise stated*								
Ethnic meals		105	116	53	36	20	14	13	12	41
Meat/meat products		173	127	133	121	87	72	84	33	110
Fish/fish products		77	32	30	21	16	23	18	13	25
Cheese and egg dishes and pizza		52	32	35	28	23	21	18	6	27
Potatoes		195	121	145	127	107	98	108	52	123
Vegetables (excl. pots)		164	98	91	63	54	70	59	42	74
Salads		48	37	27	16	11	23	7	16	21
Rice, pasta and noodles		81	60	38	20	17	7	19	5	27
Soup	(ml)	32	30	19	14	11	20	8	8	16
Fruit, fresh and processed		56	29	27	16	8	12	9	9	19
Yoghurt		9	7	8	6	4	1	5	2	6
Bread		24	16	19	17	12	10	9	3	15
Sandwiches		79	67	65	48	30	15	21	6	45
Rolls		53	47	36	32	19	8	9	3	28
Beverages	(ml)	513	634	563	433	260	151	88	94	392
Ice creams, desserts and cakes		72	69	61	47	35	44	44	36	51
Biscuits		10	23	17	11	6	6	6	3	11
Crisps, nuts and snacks		9	14	13	11	8	3	6	1	10
Other foods		80	51	44	40	28	30	24	20	38
Soft drinks (incl. milk)	(ml)	495	427	392	373	305	128	195	21	318
Alcoholic drinks	(ml)	803	437	590	429	306	321	262	190	435
Confectionery		24	21	20	21	19	6	9	...	17
Expenditure									*£ per person per week*	
All food and drink		17.75	9.78	8.50	6.67	4.12	5.90	2.81	2.01	6.73
Of which:										
Alcoholic drinks		2.72	1.61	1.99	1.57	1.07	1.23	0.83	0.53	1.52

For half of the food groups, consumption increased from the lowest head-of-household income group (D) to the highest (A1). As in 1997, for biscuits and crisps, nuts and snacks and beverages, there was a fall off for the very highest group (A1). As in the previous year, income group B spent more on, and consumed, more alcohol outside the home than those in group A2, though much less than those in the highest group (A1).

Those in the lowest earning group for households without an earner (group E2, which is mainly households whose income comes mostly from state benefits) spent only two thirds of the amount on food out as those in the lowest earning group (D), compared with three quarters in 1997. However, as in 1997, they consumed more fish; more rice, pasta and noodles and more ice creams, desserts and cakes out of the home than those in group (D).

Household composition comparisons

Table 4.6 shows average consumption and expenditure on food and drink eaten out for respondents in households with different compositions. This table shows many of the same characteristics as seen in previous years. Total expenditure on food and drink eaten out (including or excluding alcoholic drinks) was again highest in adult-only households, with expenditure declining in households with children as the number of children increased. Average per capita expenditure on alcoholic drinks in 1998 was much higher in adult-only households.

As in 1997, eating out consumption of ethnic food, salads, beverages and alcoholic drinks was higher in adult-only households. Households with children consumed more meat and meat products (especially burgers and sausages), and rice, pasta and noodles as well as chips, pizzas, confectionery and ice creams, desserts and cakes.

Table 4.6 Average consumption and expenditure on food and drink eaten out by household composition, 1998

					Households with						
Number of adults		1		2				3	3 or more		4
Number of children	0	1 or more	0	1	2	3	4 or more	0	1 or 2	3 or more	0
Number of respondents	709	449	1788	607	1011	373	162	448	401	41	176
Consumption							*grams per person per week, unless otherwise stated*				
Ethnic meals	45	24	47	32	32	50	19	62	37	9	48
Meat/meat products	105	129	93	130	107	117	140	115	120	129	116
Fish/fish products	27	20	23	25	27	24	14	37	22	16	18
Cheese and egg dishes and pizza	22	40	24	30	28	30	18	25	27	79	31
Potatoes	110	184	99	123	131	141	145	123	94	141	189
Vegetables (excl. pots)	85	80	78	63	64	75	68	81	46	77	93
Salads	20	13	26	16	20	19	17	27	15	-	25
Rice, pasta and noodles	25	39	21	24	30	38	45	26	27	9	20
Soup (ml)	15	10	19	14	12	6	-	16	38	-	30
Fruit, fresh and processed	20	20	19	17	17	19	22	26	19	-	21
Yoghurt	6	8	5	5	6	7	7	2	10	-	7
Bread	16	12	17	15	13	10	11	15	15	4	24
Sandwiches	43	35	50	53	30	32	22	73	53	42	56
Rolls	23	16	30	30	27	25	14	35	32	7	37
Beverages (ml)	468	145	497	343	246	251	154	636	403	28	623
Ice creams, desserts and cakes	47	71	44	49	50	68	89	43	52	50	40
Biscuits	9	16	10	11	12	17	9	8	19	4	10
Crisps, nuts and snacks	7	12	7	13	9	12	11	11	13	10	16
Other foods	45	39	40	34	30	38	31	39	43	49	43
Soft drinks (incl. milk) (ml)	217	433	234	356	373	388	285	345	442	406	351
Alcoholic drinks (ml)	757	51	536	370	210	155	83	839	306	195	849
Confectionery	8	28	10	16	22	27	30	15	28	29	13
Expenditure									*£ per person per week*		
All food and drink	8.21	3.03	7.96	6.08	5.54	4.80	2.73	9.99	5.99	3.40	8.71
Of which:											
Alcoholic drinks	2.72	0.14	1.97	1.21	0.60	0.52	0.30	2.87	1.18	0.60	2.58

Results by personal characteristics

Gender

Table 4.7 shows consumption and expenditure on food and drink eaten out in 1998 by the gender of the respondent. In 1998, males spent £6.15 on food and drink (excluding alcoholic drinks) consumed out of the home, 40 per cent more than females and £2.53 on alcoholic drinks, four times as much as females. The 1.8 per cent increase in expenditure on food and drink eaten out in 1998 reflected a 5 per cent increase for females to just over £5 per person per week. Expenditure by males, at £8.68, was virtually unchanged.

As in previous years, males consumed more of each type of food (as categorised in Table 4.7) except salads and yoghurts. In particular, they continued to consume a much greater quantity of meat and meat products, potatoes and vegetables. They also consumed a greater volume of beverages, soft drinks and alcohol, as in 1997. Consumption of ice creams, deserts and cakes taken as a whole was the same for both males and females. Further details by gender are given in Table C2.

Table 4.7 Average consumption and expenditure on food and drink eaten out by gender, 1997-1998

		1997			1998		
		Male	Female	All persons	Male	Female	All persons
Number of respondents		3034	3396	6430	2887	3278	6165
Consumption		*grams per person per week, except where otherwise stated*					
Ethnic meals		45	32	38	43	39	41
Meat/meat products		131	86	107	137	86	110
Fish/fish products		25	22	23	26	24	25
Cheese and egg dishes and pizza		31	22	27	32	23	27
Potatoes		133	106	119	137	110	123
Vegetables (excl. pots)		81	66	73	79	70	74
Salads		19	24	22	19	23	21
Rice, pasta and noodles		31	23	27	29	25	27
Soup	(ml)	17	14	16	18	14	16
Fruit, fresh and processed		21	22	22	20	19	19
Yoghurt		5	6	6	5	7	6
Bread		15	12	14	17	13	15
Sandwiches		58	44	50	50	41	45
Rolls		36	26	31	34	22	28
Beverages	(ml)	478	342	406	461	332	392
Ice creams, desserts and cakes		57	55	56	51	51	51
Biscuits		11	11	11	11	12	11
Crisps, nuts and snacks		11	10	11	10	9	10
Other foods		41	39	40	39	37	38
Soft drinks (incl. milk)	(ml)	358	338	348	338	301	318
Alcoholic drinks	(ml)	843	173	490	746	161	435
Confectionery		21	18	19	19	15	17
Expenditure					*£ per person per week*		
All food and drink		8.65	4.78	6.61	8.68	5.01	6.73
Of which:							
Alcoholic drinks		2.65	0.62	1.58	2.53	0.62	1.52

Age group

Table 4.8 shows average consumption and expenditure by the age group of the respondent. In 1998 expenditure on food and drink (excluding alcoholic drinks) consumed outside the home rose with age to peak in the 25 to 34 years old group and then diminished with increasing age group. This group also spent the most on the consumption of alcohol outside the home. This was different from 1997 when the 35 to 44 years group spent virtually as much on food and drink (excluding alcoholic drinks) as the 25 to 34 group and the 15 to 24 group spent the most (per capita) on alcohol.

As in 1997, consumption of meat and meat products was highest for respondents aged 15 to 24 years. This reflected their consumption of burgers and kebabs. This age group was the second highest consumer of potato chips, behind the 5 to 14 age group. Apart from dipping for the 15 to 24 age group, consumption of fruit outside the home increases to age 45 to 54 years before declining. Not surprisingly, consumption of sandwiches and rolls was high for those ages covering most of the working population, i.e. 15 to 54 years, tailing off for those older than 54 years. Consumption of ice creams, desserts and cakes was over twice as high as in any other age group amongst 5 to 14 year olds, but respondents between 15 years and 24 years consumed the most confectionery out of the home. Consumption of soft and alcoholic drinks out of the home peaked amongst 15 to 24 year olds, whereas that of beverages was highest amongst 35 to 44 year olds. Further details of consumption by age and gender are given in Table C2.

Table 4.8 Consumption and expenditure on food and drink eaten out by age, 1998

		Age group							All households
		Under 5	5 - 14	15 - 24	25 - 34	35 - 44	45 - 54	55 - 64	65 - 74	75 and over	
Number of respondents		387	865	628	881	892	827	693	584	405	6165
Consumption								*grams per person per week, except where otherwise stated*			
Ethnic meals		3	22	70	78	58	44	28	12	12	41
Meat/meat products		48	161	168	152	106	111	78	43	36	110
Fish/fish products		8	28	22	27	30	34	23	17	15	25
Cheese and egg dishes and pizza		4	49	42	37	25	28	16	11	6	27
Potatoes		63	241	167	133	101	113	85	59	62	123
Vegetables (excl. pots)		32	100	60	87	79	88	76	49	44	74
Salads		7	12	20	21	29	30	22	25	8	21
Rice, pasta and noodles		14	49	36	37	31	25	14	5	2	27
Soup		2	7	16	18	23	30	10	17	11	16
Fruit, fresh and processed		19	20	15	22	24	26	18	10	9	19
Yoghurt	(ml)	7	10	5	9	4	6	4	1	-	6
Bread		4	9	17	26	20	19	12	7	4	15
Sandwiches		12	22	65	79	69	62	35	12	6	45
Rolls		3	11	44	53	43	37	15	7	1	28
Beverages	(ml)	-	10	303	696	656	725	432	143	97	392
Ice creams, desserts and cakes		36	113	33	41	42	55	42	32	37	51
Biscuits		16	18	10	14	15	11	7	4	4	11
Crisps, nuts and snacks		3	14	24	16	10	7	3	1	1	10
Other foods		13	43	37	57	44	45	32	21	22	38
Soft drinks (incl. milk)	(ml)	230	522	755	453	289	196	121	60	20	318
Alcoholic drinks	(ml)	-	...	567	771	563	606	525	358	131	435
Confectionery		6	39	43	19	13	9	5	1	...	17
Expenditure										*£ per person per week*	
All food and drink		0.29	2.69	8.82	11.41	8.59	8.92	7.02	4.75	1.88	6.73
Of which:											
Alcoholic drinks		-	...	2.19	2.70	1.83	2.23	1.94	1.04	0.40	1.52

Eating out: nutrient intakes

National averages

Table 4.9 shows the energy and nutrient intakes from food eaten out, including and excluding soft and alcoholic drinks and confectionery, for 1994 to 1998. Intakes have generally remained quite constant although the proportion of energy derived from fat and saturated fatty acids, which fell between 1994 and 1997, increased very slightly in 1998.

Table 4.9 Nutritional value of food and drink eaten out 1994 to 1998

		Nutritional value of food and drink eaten out including soft and alcoholic drinks and confectionery				
		1994	1995	1996	1997	1998
		(i) intake per person per day				
Energy	kcal	250	240	255	265	260
	MJ	1.0	1.0	1.1	1.1	1.1
Protein	g	6.9	6.9	7.1	7.7	7.7
Fat	g	12	11	11	12	12
Fatty acids:						
saturated	g	4.6	4.4	4.5	4.5	4.5
monounsaturated	g	4.4	4.2	4.3	4.4	4.3
polyunsaturated	g	1.9	1.9	1.9	2.1	2.0
Cholesterol	mg	33	33	33	34	34
Carbohydrate	g	25	24	28	29	28
of which:						
total sugars	g	12	12	14	14	13
non-milk extrinsic sugars	g	9	9	11	11	11
starch	g	13	13	14	15	15
Fibre [a]	g	1.2	1.2	1.2	1.3	1.3
Alcohol	g	2.9	2.9	2.8	2.9	2.6
Calcium	mg	73	71	73	77	75
Iron	mg	1.1	1.1	1.1	1.2	1.2
Zinc	mg	0.9	0.9	0.9	0.9	0.9
Magnesium	mg	31	30	30	32	31
Sodium	g	0.29	0.28	0.29	0.31	0.31
Potassium	g	0.33	0.32	0.32	0.34	0.34
Thiamin	mg	0.14	0.13	0.14	0.15	0.15
Riboflavin	mg	0.15	0.14	0.14	0.15	0.14
Niacin equivalent	mg	3.5	3.5	3.5	3.8	3.8
Vitamin B6	mg	0.3	0.3	0.3	0.3	0.3
Vitamin B12	µg	0.5	0.5	0.5	0.5	0.5
Folate	µg	30	30	28	30	29
Vitamin C	mg	8	8	8	9	9
Vitamin A:						
retinol	µg	85	80	61	66	64
β-carotene	µg	195	188	185	208	206
total (retinol equivalent)	µg	117	112	92	100	99
Vitamin D	µg	0.21	0.24	0.23	0.30	0.27
Vitamin E	mg	1.25	1.21	1.26	1.33	1.22
	(ii) as a percentage of energy - including soft and alcoholic drinks and confectionery					
Fat		42.3	41.8	40.3	39.7	40.1
of which:						
saturated fatty acids		16.6	16.4	15.7	15.3	15.7
Carbohydrate		38.4	38.2	41.0	41.0	41.0
Alcohol		8.1	8.4	7.6	7.7	6.9
	(iii) as a percentage of energy - excluding soft and alcoholic drinks and confectionery					
Fat		50.3	50.3	47.8	46.9	46.8
of which:						
saturated fatty acids		19.2	19.2	18.1	17.6	18.0
Carbohydrate		36.0	35.7	38.8	39.2	39.1
Alcohol		-	-	-	-	-

(a) as non-starch polysaccharides

Eighty two per cent of the energy from food and drink eaten out came from food (including beverages) while 9 per cent came from alcoholic drinks, 4 per cent from confectionery and 5 per cent from soft drinks. Food groups contributing most to energy intake were potatoes and vegetables; meats; sandwiches and rolls; alcoholic drinks; and puddings and cakes. The same groups, with the exception of alcoholic drinks, were the main contributors to fat intake.

Results by household characteristics

Region

The average intake of energy and nutrients from food and drink consumed outside the home varied little between England, Wales and Scotland (Table 4.10[1]). Within the regions of England, however, energy intake varied from 220 kcal per person per day in the East region to 295 kcal per person per day in London. The proportions of energy derived from fat and saturated fatty acids were highest in the East region (41.1 per cent) and the South West (16.2 per cent) respectively, and lowest in the North East (38.3 per cent and 14.7 per cent respectively), all of which show a slight increase on 1997 figures. However, the North East was the area with the highest intake of energy from alcohol (10.1 per cent), with the East region having the lowest intake of energy from alcohol (5.3 per cent).

Income group

Table 4.11[1] shows how energy and nutrient intake from food and drink consumed out of the home varies with the income group of the head of household. In households with an earner, energy and nutrient intakes were generally higher in the higher income groups. However, in households without an earner, energy and nutrient intakes were higher in the lower income group. Members of pensioner households (OAP) had the lowest average intake of energy and nutrients from food and drink consumed outside the home, and obtained the lowest proportion of energy from fat (39.0 per cent), but obtained the highest proportion of energy from alcohol (8.6 per cent). Those in groups C and E2 obtained the greatest proportion of energy from fat (40.5 per cent), with group C having the highest amount of energy from saturated fatty acids and group E2 having the lowest (16.0 per cent and 14.8 per cent respectively). Group D had the lowest proportion of energy from alcohol (6.2 per cent).

Household composition

The average daily intake of energy and nutrients from food and drink consumed outside the home by those in households of different compositions are shown in Table 4.12[1]. Energy intake was highest in households with three adults and no children (310 kcal per person per day), a lower figure than the 425 kcal per person per day in households of 4 or more adults recorded in 1997, but comparable with the figures from previous years. Energy intake was lowest in households with two

---

[1] Which includes contributions from soft and alcoholic drinks and confectionery

adults and four or more children (230 kcal per person per day). Households with one adult and one or more children obtained the greatest proportion of energy from fat (41.8 per cent) while households with one adult and no children obtained the lowest proportion of energy from fat (38.0 per cent). Alcohol intake and the percentage of energy derived from alcohol were markedly higher in adult-only households than in households containing children.

Table 4.10 Nutritional value of food and drink eaten out by Government Office Region, 1998

		North East	North West	Yorkshire and the Humber	East Midlands	West Midlands	East	London	South East	South West	England	Wales	Scotland
		\multicolumn{12}{c}{*(i) intake per person per day*}
Energy	kcal	280	260	245	265	245	220	295	265	250	260	250	260
	MJ	1.2	1.1	1.0	1.1	1.0	0.9	1.2	1.1	1.0	1.1	1.0	1.1
Protein	g	7.7	7.8	7.1	8.0	7.4	6.6	9.4	8.3	7.0	7.8	7.5	7.7
Fat	g	12	12	11	12	11	10	13	12	11	12	11	12
Fatty acids:													
saturated	g	4.6	4.6	4.1	4.6	4.2	4.0	5.1	4.7	4.5	4.5	4.3	4.6
monounsaturated	g	4.5	4.4	4.0	4.4	4.0	3.8	4.9	4.4	4.1	4.3	4.2	4.3
polyunsaturated	g	2.0	2.0	1.8	2.0	1.8	1.7	2.3	2.0	1.8	2.0	1.9	1.9
Cholesterol	mg	32	34	30	36	32	30	43	39	33	35	32	33
Carbohydrate	g	30	29	27	29	27	25	33	29	27	28	26	28
total sugar	g	14	13	12	13	12	11	14	14	14	13	12	13
non-milk extrinsic sugar	g	11	10	10	11	10	9	11	11	11	11	10	10
starch	g	16	16	15	15	14	13	18	15	14	15	14	15
Fibre [a]	g	1.5	1.3	1.3	1.3	1.3	1.2	1.6	1.4	1.2	1.3	1.2	1.3
Alcohol	g	4.0	2.3	2.5	2.7	2.9	1.7	2.6	2.3	2.6	2.5	2.8	2.5
Calcium	mg	79	73	71	79	71	67	87	78	74	75	70	78
Iron	mg	1.2	1.2	1.0	1.2	1.1	1.0	1.4	1.2	1.1	1.2	1.1	1.1
Zinc	mg	0.9	0.9	0.8	0.9	0.9	0.8	1.1	1.0	0.8	0.9	0.9	0.9
Magnesium	mg	34	30	29	31	30	26	36	32	30	31	30	29
Sodium	g	0.31	0.32	0.29	0.32	0.30	0.27	0.36	0.32	0.28	0.31	0.29	0.33
Potassium	g	0.36	0.34	0.33	0.33	0.32	0.29	0.39	0.35	0.32	0.34	0.33	0.32
Thiamin	mg	0.16	0.16	0.14	0.15	0.14	0.13	0.18	0.16	0.14	0.15	0.14	0.15
Riboflavin	mg	0.15	0.14	0.13	0.14	0.14	0.12	0.17	0.15	0.14	0.14	0.14	0.14
Niacin equivalent	mg	3.8	3.7	3.5	3.9	3.6	3.1	4.5	4.0	3.5	3.8	3.7	3.6
Vitamin B6	mg	0.3	0.3	0.3	0.3	0.3	0.2	0.3	0.3	0.2	0.3	0.3	0.3
Vitamin B12	µg	0.5	0.5	0.5	0.5	0.5	0.5	0.7	0.6	0.5	0.6	0.6	0.5
Folate	µg	34	28	28	30	29	25	35	30	27	29	29	27
Vitamin C	mg	10	9	8	9	8	7	11	9	8	9	9	8
Vitamin A:													
retinol	µg	51	58	37	57	66	75	81	80	59	65	69	57
β-carotene	µg	243	197	213	203	187	178	218	236	182	207	210	199
total (retinol equivalent)	µg	91	91	73	91	97	105	117	120	90	99	104	90
Vitamin D	µg	0.26	0.28	0.24	0.25	0.26	0.22	0.35	0.30	0.25	0.27	0.26	0.25
Vitamin E	mg	1.30	1.27	1.17	1.22	1.13	1.09	1.44	1.23	1.13	1.22	1.20	1.22
		\multicolumn{12}{c}{*(ii) as a percentage of total energy*}
Fat		38.3	40.8	39.2	39.9	39.1	41.1	40.0	40.4	40.3	40.0	40.4	40.4
Of which:													
saturated fatty acids		14.7	15.8	15.2	15.6	15.3	16.1	15.6	16.0	16.2	15.7	15.5	16.1
Carbohydrate		40.6	41.1	41.8	40.6	40.6	41.7	41.2	41.0	41.1	41.1	39.6	40.9
Alcohol		10.1	6.2	7.3	7.2	8.3	5.3	6.1	6.1	7.3	6.9	7.9	6.8

(a) as non-starch polysaccharides

Table 4.11 Nutritional value of food and drink eaten out by income group of head of household, 1998

		INCOME GROUP						
		Gross weekly income of head of household						
		Households with one or more earners				Households without an earner		
		£640 and over	£330 and under £640	£160 and under £330	Less than £160	£160 or more	Less than £160	OAP
		A	B	C	D	E1	E2	
		(i) Intake per person per day						
Energy	kcal	375	330	270	200	150	165	75
	MJ	1.6	1.4	1.1	0.8	0.6	0.7	0.3
Protein	g	12.4	9.8	7.9	5.6	4.8	4.7	2.5
Fat	g	17	15	12	9	7	7	3
Fatty acids:								
saturated	g	6.5	5.8	4.8	3.3	2.5	2.7	1.3
monounsaturated	g	6.1	5.4	4.5	3.3	2.5	2.9	1.2
polyunsaturated	g	2.8	2.5	2.0	1.6	1.2	1.3	0.6
Cholesterol	mg	55	43	36	23	23	19	13
Carbohydrate	g	40	36	30	23	16	18	8
Of which:								
total sugars	g	18	17	14	11	7	8	4
non-milk extrinsic sugars	g	14	13	12	9	6	6	3
starch	g	22	19	16	12	9	10	4
Fibre [a]	g	2.0	1.7	1.3	1.0	0.9	0.9	0.5
Alcohol	g	3.6	3.5	2.5	1.8	1.8	1.5	0.9
Calcium	mg	109	98	77	59	44	48	23
Iron	mg	1.8	1.5	1.2	0.8	0.7	0.7	0.4
Zinc	mg	1.4	1.1	0.9	0.7	0.6	0.6	0.3
Magnesium	mg	46	40	31	23	18	19	9
Sodium	g	0.46	0.40	0.32	0.24	0.18	0.20	0.09
Potassium	g	0.49	0.43	0.34	0.25	0.21	0.22	0.11
Thiamin	mg	0.22	0.20	0.16	0.12	0.10	0.10	0.05
Riboflavin	mg	0.21	0.18	0.14	0.10	0.09	0.08	0.06
Niacin equivalent	mg	6.0	4.9	3.9	2.6	2.3	2.1	1.2
Vitamin B6	mg	0.4	0.3	0.3	0.2	0.2	0.2	0.1
Vitamin B12	µg	0.9	0.7	0.5	0.3	0.4	0.3	0.3
Folate	µg	42	37	29	21	19	19	11
Vitamin C	mg	13	11	9	6	6	6	3
Vitamin A:								
retinol	µg	95	85	59	29	52	22	72
β-carotene	µg	359	241	187	128	202	139	133
total (retinol equivalent)	µg	154	126	90	51	85	46	94
Vitamin D	µg	0.47	0.33	0.27	0.18	0.17	0.16	0.09
Vitamin E	mg	1.80	1.55	1.25	0.94	0.77	0.83	0.38
		(ii) as a percentage of total energy						
Fat		40.0	40.0	40.5	39.3	39.6	40.5	39.0
Of which:								
saturated fatty acids		15.8	15.9	16.0	14.9	14.9	14.8	15.0
Carbohydrate		40.1	40.8	41.4	43.4	39.2	41.3	39.5
Alcohol		6.7	7.3	6.4	6.2	8.4	6.6	8.6

(a) as non-starch polysaccharides

Table 4.12 Nutritional value of food and drink eaten out by household composition, 1998

		Households with										
No of adults		1	1	2	2	2	2	2	3	3 or more	3 or more	4 or more
No of children		0	1 or more	0	1	2	3	4 or more	0	1 or 2	3 or more	0
		(i) intake per person per day										
Energy	kcal	250	270	245	260	240	265	230	310	290	240	305
	MJ	1.1	1.1	1.0	1.1	1.0	1.1	1.0	1.3	1.2	1.0	1.3
Protein	g	7	8	8	8	7	8	7	9	8	7	8
Fat	g	11	13	11	12	11	12	11	13	13	11	13
Fatty acids												
saturated	g	4.2	4.7	4.4	4.7	4.1	4.6	4.0	5.3	5.2	4.0	5.2
monounsaturated	g	3.9	4.9	4.0	4.5	4.2	4.6	4.2	4.8	4.8	4.2	4.7
polyunsaturated	g	1.9	2.2	1.8	2.0	1.9	2.1	1.8	2.3	2.1	1.9	2.2
Cholesterol	mg	35	30	37	35	30	33	27	43	34	25	37
Carbohydrate	g	26	33	25	29	28	31	28	32	34	29	32
Of which:												
total sugars	g	12	15	11	13	13	15	13	16	17	12	16
non-milk extrinsic sugars	g	9	12	9	10	10	12	10	13	14	10	13
starch	g	14	18	13	16	15	17	15	16	17	17	16
Fibre [a]	g	1.3	1.6	1.2	1.3	1.3	1.4	1.3	1.4	1.5	1.6	1.3
Alcohol	g	4.5	0.3	3.2	2.1	1.2	0.9	0.4	4.9	1.9	1.2	4.7
Calcium	mg	71	84	70	79	70	80	69	87	86	73	86
Iron	mg	1.1	1.2	1.1	1.2	1.0	1.2	1.1	1.3	1.2	1.1	1.3
Zinc	mg	0.8	1.0	0.9	0.9	0.8	0.9	0.9	1.1	1.0	0.8	1.0
Magnesium	mg	32	29	30	31	27	30	26	39	33	26	37
Sodium	g	0.29	0.33	0.29	0.33	0.30	0.32	0.28	0.36	0.35	0.30	0.36
Potassium	g	0.34	0.35	0.32	0.34	0.31	0.34	0.31	0.41	0.36	0.32	0.38
Thiamin	mg	0.14	0.18	0.14	0.16	0.15	0.16	0.14	0.17	0.18	0.16	0.15
Riboflavin	mg	0.15	0.12	0.15	0.14	0.12	0.13	0.11	0.18	0.15	0.12	0.17
Niacin equivalent	mg	3.9	3.3	3.8	3.8	3.3	3.6	3.0	4.9	3.9	2.9	4.6
Vitamin B6	mg	0.3	0.3	0.3	0.3	0.2	0.3	0.2	0.3	0.3	0.3	0.3
Vitamin B12	μg	0.6	0.4	0.6	0.5	0.4	0.5	0.4	0.7	0.5	0.4	0.6
Folate	μg	32	28	29	28	25	26	21	37	30	31	34
Vitamin C	mg	8	11	8	9	9	10	8	9	10	11	7
Vitamin A:												
retinol	μg	79	38	91	57	38	41	30	75	46	29	87
β-carotene	μg	246	208	218	182	166	202	164	228	230	254	158
total (retinol equivalent)	μg	120	73	127	87	66	75	57	113	84	71	114
Vitamin D	μg	0.28	0.24	0.28	0.27	0.23	0.27	0.26	0.34	0.27	0.24	0.28
Vitamin E	mg	1.18	1.39	1.13	1.20	1.21	1.30	1.18	1.38	1.31	1.22	1.31
		(ii) as a percentage of total energy										
Fat		38.0	41.8	40.2	41.1	40.9	40.9	41.2	38.4	39.9	40.4	38.1
Of which:												
saturated fatty acids		14.9	15.6	16.3	16.2	15.4	15.6	15.5	15.4	16.1	14.8	15.3
Carbohydrate		38.1	45.8	38.1	41.2	43.5	44.5	45.5	38.4	44.2	44.6	39.8
Alcohol		12.4	0.8	9.2	5.5	3.6	2.5	1.3	11.1	4.5	3.4	10.8

(a) as non-starch polysaccharides

Results by personal characteristics

Age and gender

The differences seen in the amounts of food and drink consumed outside the home by those in different age groups and by males and females are reflected in the average intakes of energy and nutrients shown in Table 4.13. The age and gender groupings are generally those identified as having distinct nutritional requirements in the report on Dietary Reference Values[2].

The intake of energy increased in children up to 10 years. In females, energy intake peaked in the 11 to 14 year age group (360 kcal per person per day) and then declined with increasing age. In males, energy intakes continued to rise, peaking in the 19 to 50 year age group (410 kcal per person per day), both showing decreases on 1997 figures.

Girls and boys aged 11 to 14 years had similar energy intakes. In older age groups, in general, males had a much higher intake of energy and nutrients from food and drink eaten out than females. The intake of alcohol, in particular, was higher amongst men than women with the result that in most cases men obtained more of their energy from alcohol and less from fat. The intake of non-milk extrinsic sugars was highest in the 11 to 18 year age groups for both males and females, reflecting a higher intake from soft drinks and confectionery than that found for other age groups.

---

[2] Department of Health, *Dietary Reference Values for Food Energy and Nutrients for the United Kingdom*, HMSO, 1991

Table 4.13 Nutritional value of food and drink eaten out by age and gender, 1998

		Infants	Children				Males				Females				All
		under 1	1 to 3	4 to 6	7 to 10	11 to 14	15 to 18	19 to 50	51+	11 to 14	15 to 18	19 to 50 not pregnant	19 to 50 pregnant	51+	Persons
		(i) intake per person per day													
Energy	kcal	20	110	240	275	385	370	410	190	360	355	270	290	125	260
Protein	MJ	0.1	0.5	1.0	1.2	1.6	1.6	1.7	0.8	1.5	1.5	1.1	1.2	0.5	1.1
	g	0.8	3.2	7.6	8.4	10.2	10.5	12.1	5.4	9.1	9.8	8.4	9.2	4.2	7.7
Fat	g	1	5	11	12	17	16	18	8	17	15	12	15	6	12
Fatty acids															
saturated	g	0.3	1.8	3.7	4.4	6.0	6.0	7.2	3.0	6.1	5.9	5.1	6.0	2.4	4.5
monounsaturated	g	0.3	1.9	4.2	5.0	6.9	6.5	6.6	2.9	6.4	5.8	4.4	5.3	2.2	4.3
polyunsaturated	g	0.1	0.8	1.9	2.3	3.3	2.9	2.9	1.3	3.1	2.8	2.1	2.2	1.1	2.0
Cholesterol	mg	3	10	27	30	34	35	58	29	33	33	38	39	21	34
Carbohydrate	g	3	14	30	35	50	44	42	18	46	44	29	32	14	28
Of which:															
total sugars	g	2	7	13	15	25	22	19	9	23	22	13	15	6	13
non-milk extrinsic sugars	g	1	5	10	12	21	19	16	7	20	19	10	12	5	11
starch	g	1	7	17	20	25	22	22	9	23	22	16	18	7	15
Fibre [a]	g	0.1	0.6	1.6	1.8	2.1	1.7	1.8	0.9	1.8	1.8	1.4	1.5	0.7	1.3
Alcohol	g	-					2.0	6.6	4.3		1.4	2.1	0.3	0.7	2.6
Calcium	mg	20	40	81	86	109	99	115	51	102	104	81	95	37	75
Iron	mg	0.1	0.4	1.1	1.3	1.5	1.5	1.8	0.8	1.4	1.4	1.3	1.3	0.6	1.2
Zinc	mg	0.1	0.3	0.9	1.0	1.2	1.4	1.4	0.7	1.0	1.1	1.0	1.1	0.5	0.9
Magnesium	mg	3	12	27	30	39	40	52	25	35	37	32	31	15	31
Sodium	g	0.03	0.13	0.30	0.34	0.43	0.43	0.51	0.21	0.40	0.41	0.33	0.37	0.15	0.31
Potassium	g	0.04	0.14	0.35	0.39	0.48	0.44	0.52	0.26	0.42	0.41	0.35	0.37	0.18	0.34
Thiamin	mg	0.02	0.07	0.17	0.19	0.25	0.21	0.22	0.10	0.23	0.22	0.16	0.18	0.08	0.15
Riboflavin	mg	0.02	0.06	0.12	0.13	0.15	0.16	0.24	0.13	0.14	0.15	0.14	0.14	0.07	0.14
Niacin equivalent	mg	0.3	1.3	3.0	3.4	4.0	4.6	6.5	3.0	3.7	4.2	4.1	4.0	2.0	3.8
Vitamin B6	mg		0.1	0.3	0.3	0.4	0.4	0.5	0.3	0.3	0.3	0.2	0.3	0.1	0.3
Vitamin B12	μg		0.2	0.4	0.5	0.5	0.6	0.9	0.6	0.4	0.5	0.6	0.5	0.3	0.5
Folate	μg	3	10	25	30	39	36	49	26	32	36	28	30	14	29
Vitamin C	mg	2	7	12	13	17	12	10	6	15	13	9	14	5	9
Vitamin A:															
retinol	μg	3	13	30	34	39	34	95	83	42	44	73	70	52	64
β-carotene	μg	21	72	224	287	203	162	245	187	187	191	226	190	179	206
total (retinol equivalent)	μg	7	25	67	82	73	61	136	114	73	76	111	101	82	99
Vitamin D	μg	0.02	0.09	0.23	0.27	0.27	0.27	0.43	0.22	0.27	0.24	0.30	0.25	0.17	0.27
Vitamin E	mg	0.09	0.48	1.23	1.45	2.08	1.77	1.76	0.83	1.94	1.75	1.29	1.39	0.68	1.22
		(ii) as a percentage of total energy													
Fat		34.4	39.3	39.8	40.5	40.7	39.9	39.1	37.0	41.6	39.2	41.4	44.8	42.9	40.1
Of which:															
saturated fatty acids		13.7	15.1	14.1	14.3	14.2	14.7	15.8	14.4	15.3	14.9	17.0	18.6	16.9	15.7
Carbohydrate		50.2	49.0	47.6	47.3	48.6	44.9	37.9	35.7	48.2	47.0	40.7	41.7	40.1	41.0
Alcohol		-					3.8	11.2	15.8		2.7	5.4	0.8	3.7	6.9

(a) as non-starch polysaccharides

Household food and eating out: nutrient intakes

National averages

Table 4.14 shows the nutrient intakes from food and drink from all sources, expressed as a percentage of the weighted Reference Nutrient Intakes (RNI), for 1994 to 1998. For this calculation, wastage of 10 per cent of all nutrients has been deducted from the intakes based on household purchases of food (except alcoholic and soft drinks and confectionery), but no allowance for wastage has been deducted from the recorded eating out intakes.

The average daily intakes of nutrients as a proportion of RNIs were broadly similar in 1998 compared with 1997. Intakes of all vitamins, but only two minerals (calcium and sodium), were above the RNI when the contribution from food and drink consumed outside the home was taken into account. Iron and zinc fell to levels below the RNI for the first time since 1995.

Table 4.15 shows the contribution made by food and drink from all sources to intake of energy and a range of nutrients. It thus covers food, alcoholic and soft drinks and confectionery from both household supplies[3] and eating out. The energy intake from all sources was 2,110 kcal per person per day. About 12 per cent of energy was obtained from food and drink consumed outside the home. It should be noted that additional energy (and other nutrients) would have been derived from food and drink consumed but under-recorded in the survey, in particular alcoholic drinks.

The contribution of food and drink eaten out of the home to total fat intake was about 14 per cent while the contribution to total intakes of protein and carbohydrate were about 11 per cent. The contribution of eating out to the total intake of minerals ranged from 8 per cent for calcium to 12 per cent for magnesium. Eating out contributed between 7 per cent (vitamin B12) and 13 per cent (vitamin B6) of the total intake of vitamins.

The proportion of energy derived from fat and saturated fatty acids was higher in food eaten out (40.1 per cent and 15.7 per cent respectively) than in household food (37.0 per cent and 14.7 per cent respectively). The overall proportion of energy from fat and saturated fatty acids contributed by food and drink from all sources decreased from 39.3 per cent and 15.3 per cent respectively in 1994 to 37.4 per cent and 14.8 per cent respectively, in 1998.

---

[3] The energy and nutrients from household food and drink are the averages of the households participating in the Eating Out Survey and differ slightly from those for all households shown in Section 3 (and Appendix Table B9)

Table 4.14 Nutritional value of food and drink from all sources as a percentage of weighted RNIs [a, b], 1994 to 1998

	1994	1995	1996	1997	1998
Energy [c]	94	92	98	96	93
Protein	142	142	149	149	147
Calcium	121	118	122	122	119
Iron	98	95	102	101	99
Zinc	101	98	101	101	98
Magnesium	92	90	96	95	93
Sodium	176	174	179	177	176
Potassium	84	83	88	88	87
Thiamin	156	161	175	169	166
Riboflavin	142	138	144	154	149
Niacin equivalent	191	193	205	204	203
Vitamin B6	161	169	176	175	173
Vitamin B12	350	333	331	518	491
Folate	134	131	138	137	134
Vitamin C	165	156	163	176	173
Vitamin A (retinol equivalent)	170	164	143	137	130

(a) Reference Nutrient Intakes from Department of Health, *Dietary Reference Values for Food Energy and Nutrients for the United Kingdom*, HMSO, 1991
(b) based on the intakes and requirements of the sample in the Eating Out Survey
(c) as a percentage of Estimated Average Requirements

Table 4.15 Nutritional value of food and drink from all sources for Eating Out households, 1998

		Household food and drink [a]	Eating Out	Food and drink from all sources	Percentage obtained from eating out
		(i) intake per person per day			
Energy	kcal	1850	260	2110	12
	MJ	7.8	1.1	8.9	12
Protein	g	65.1	7.7	72.8	11
Fat	g	76	12	88	14
Fatty acids:					
saturated	g	30.3	4.5	34.8	13
monounsaturated	g	27.0	4.3	31.3	14
polyunsaturated	g	13.5	2.0	15.4	13
Cholesterol	mg	226	34	260	13
Carbohydrate					
Of which:	g	234	28	262	11
total sugars	g	104	13	117	11
non-milk extrinsic sugars	g	65	11	76	14
starch	g	129	15	145	10
Fibre [b]	g	12.3	1.3	13.6	10
Alcohol	g	3.8	2.6	6.4	41
Calcium	mg	818	75	894	8
Iron	mg	10.1	1.2	11.2	10
Zinc	mg	7.6	0.9	8.5	11
Magnesium	mg	235	31	265	12
Sodium	g	2.56	0.31	2.87	11
Potassium	g	2.66	0.34	3.00	11
Thiamin	mg	1.37	0.15	1.52	10
Riboflavin	mg	1.71	0.14	1.86	8
Niacin equivalent	mg	26.9	3.8	30.6	12
Vitamin B6	mg	2.0	0.3	2.3	13
Vitamin B12	µg	6.9	0.5	7.4	7
Folate	µg	245	29	274	11
Vitamin C	mg	64	9	72	12
Vitamin A:					
retinol	µg	491	64	555	12
β-carotene	µg	1734	206	1940	11
total (retinol equivalent)	µg	780	99	879	11
Vitamin D	µg	3.19	0.27	3.46	8
Vitamin E	mg	9.85	1.22	11.07	11
		(ii) as a percentage of total energy			
Fat		37.0	40.1	37.4	
Of which:					
saturated fatty acids		14.7	15.7	14.8	
Carbohydrate		47.3	41.0	46.6	
Alcohol		1.5	6.9	2.1	

(a) including soft and alcoholic drinks and confectionery but based only on information from households participating in the Eating Out Survey
(b) as non-starch polysaccharide

Section 5
Age and gender variation in food energy and nutrient intakes, 1974 - 1998

Andrew Chesher

Introduction

The National Food Survey (NFS) is unique in providing a long continuous record of British household food acquisitions for home supplies and it is frequently used to give an overview of changes in British diet, see [1] for a recent example. In contrast the National Diet and Nutrition Survey (NDNS) programme provides detailed cross-sectional information on the diets of groups of the population at widely spaced intervals of time.

Unlike the NDNS, which record consumption of foods by individuals, the main NFS records household purchases and other acquisitions of foods and its results are usually presented in the form of household averages[1], as in Section 3 of this report.

Many dietary recommendations are specific to, and different for, men and women of different ages[2]. It is interesting to know how diet varies across people of different ages and what changes are occurring. However the National Diet and Nutrition Survey does not provide information with which to continually monitor the diet of particular groups of the British population. To date, four age groups have been studied in the NDNS and its predecessor, the Adults survey. The NDNS of adults aged 19 to 64 years will be undertaken in 2000, 14 years after the original survey.

The NFS does provide a continuous record of UK population average diet but, without special analysis, it does not give information about the diet of men and women of different ages. In this Section results of such a special analysis are presented.

The method used is essentially a "statistical disaggregation" of household energy and nutrient acquisitions to produce estimates of average energy and nutrient intakes for men and women of different ages. In the sub-sections *Household average energy and nutrient intakes* and *Variations in energy and nutrients from home supplies, 1974 – 1998*, the results are presented as 25-year time series of

---

[1] The Eating Out extension of the NFS, started in 1993, but first published in 1994, does record food consumption by individuals. Its data are studied in the sub-section *Variations in energy and nutrients from eaten out and from home supplies, 1974-1998* of this section

[2] See for example [2]

estimated average energy and nutrient intakes from home food supplies by age and gender.

These results are clearly influenced by changes during the period in the proportion of food obtained by people outside the home. Since 1993 the NFS has obtained records of food eaten out from all members of around half of the households responding to the main NFS.

In the sub-section *Variation in energy and nutrients from food eaten out and from home supplies* an average for the period 1994 to 1998 is studied. Estimates of average energy and nutrient intakes for males and females of different ages are presented separately for food at home (household food) and food eaten out. In the final sub-section, the results reported here based on NFS data are compared with those obtained from the Adults survey and the three NDNS studies for which results are available.

Before considering what the NFS can tell us about age-specific energy and nutrient intakes, the changes in household average nutrient intakes (per capita per day) from the NFS during the last 25 years are examined.

Household average energy and nutrient intakes (Figures 1 to 3)

Figures 1 and 2 show the progression over the 25-year period from 1974 to 1998 of household per capita average daily amounts of energy and of six nutrients in household food supplies - total fat, saturated fatty acids, calcium, iron, vitamin D and folate[3]. Also shown are time series of average quantities of fruit and vegetables and of fruit juices in household food supplies.

These figures reveal important trends. The average energy content of household food, and the average amounts of fats, calcium and iron in home food supplies have steadily declined, falling by about 25 per cent over the 25-year period. In contrast, amounts of fruit and vegetables[4], taken together, and of fruit juice have increased substantially.

The data on which these figures are based are acquisitions (purchases and amounts obtained free) of foods brought into the home for human consumption as recorded in one-week diaries completed in each year by

---

[3] The averages plotted here are ratios of yearly total amounts in home supplies to yearly total numbers of members in surveyed households. The series for folate starts in 1979 because nutrient conversion factors are not available prior to this date

[4] Potatoes, potato products, pulses and fruit juices are excluded from the fruit and vegetables considered here

between 5,000 and 7,000 households in Great Britain[5]. Soft and alcoholic drinks and confectionery are excluded.

These food records are converted into amounts of nutrients using conversion factors which are updated through time to reflect changes in the nutrient composition of foods. The conversion factors embody an allowance for inedible elements of foods but there is no allowance for wastage of edible food.

Some of the food recorded in the NFS diaries is intended for consumption by visitors. Since visitors eating in other's homes will tend to eat less in their own home the effect of purchase for consumption by visitors tends to cancel out across the Survey. So no adjustment is made here for visitors.

Some households buy more food than they consume during the week in which they keep records and others buy less because of purchases for and consumption from household food stores. This effect also tends to cancel out across the Survey.

These two arguments suggest that the average per capita daily nutrient acquisitions shown in Figures 1 and 2 can be interpreted as approximating average daily per capita nutrient intakes from home supplies before allowance for waste of edible food. From now on this is the interpretation that will be adopted here.

There are a number of possible causes of the dramatic decline in average energy intakes from home food supplies shown by Figure 1.

One of these is a reduction over the period in average energy needs. Work has tended to become less physically arduous during this period with the decline in manufacturing and the rise in service industries, and with effort saving changes in technology in the manufacturing and raw materials production sectors. This, together with the introduction of many labour saving devices in the home, increased amounts of space heating, and increased use of cars has led to reductions in energy needs. But there are other influences at work.

Increase in labour force participation, particularly among women, and increases in real incomes, may have led to changes in the balance between amounts of food consumed inside and outside the home.

The composition of households has changed over this period too. The figures reported in this sub-section are simple per capita averages with no allowance for the age and gender of household members. Changes in the age and gender composition of households lead to changes in the

---

[5] Data recently available for Northern Ireland are excluded in order to make these long series comparable through time

nutrient intakes of households which affect the comparison through time of simple per capita averages of the sort presented in Figures 1 and 2.

The general reduction in energy intakes over the period affects the time series of nutrient intakes shown in Figure 2. In Figure 3 this effect is largely removed by the expression of average per capita daily nutrient intakes per 1,000 kcal of food energy except for total fats and saturated fatty acids which are shown as percentage of food energy derived from fats. These graphs tell us about changes in the *composition* of British home diet. They indicate dramatic changes too.

There has been a steady reduction in the proportion of energy derived from fats, particularly from saturated fatty acids, where the decline has been of the order of 25 per cent over the 25-year period. Calcium and folate per 1,000 kcal have increased steadily since the mid 1980s, the former mainly because of increased consumption of low fat milk, the latter mainly because of increased fortification of foods. Vitamin D intake per 1,000 kcal has declined during the 1990s despite an increase in assessed intake from 1995, following the quantification of levels of Vitamin D and its metabolites in meat for the first time. Intakes per 1,000 kcal of fruit and vegetables, taken together, and of fruit juice have shown steady increases throughout the entire period.

These series suggest marked changes in the nutrient composition of British home diets between 1974 and 1998. These are of considerable interest because of their health implications. It is interesting to know whether men and women, young and old, have experienced the same decline in dietary fat content, the same increase in intakes of calcium, folate, fruit and vegetables and fruit juice.

With the aim of providing insight into questions of this sort, the next sub-section presents estimates of age and gender-specific average nutrient intakes and their variation from 1974 to 1998. This requires a relatively sophisticated approach because the NFS does not record consumption by individuals from home supplies. If such records were available, then they could be directly associated with people of different genders and ages. The main NFS records only total household food acquisitions. Statistical methods are therefore used to disaggregate household totals into age and gender specific amounts.

The results allow us to see whether there have been differential changes in dietary composition across age and gender. Such changes are of considerable public health interest. For example, adequate intakes of folate and calcium are believed to be particularly important for women, especially during child-bearing years. It is important to know whether women have experienced increases of the sort shown by the household averages in Figure 3 and whether any changes for women are restricted to particular age groups. Estimates of age and gender specific nutrient intakes reported in the next sub-section provide this information.

Some of the changes in the nutrient composition of home food supplies may reflect the increased amount of eating out that has occurred over the period 1974 to 1998. The nutrient composition of food eaten out may differ from that of food eaten at home. In the sub-section *Variations in energy and nutrients from food eaten out and from home supplies* this is studied using pooled data from 1994 to 1998 obtained from the main National Food Survey and from the Eating Out extension to the Survey which was started in 1993[6].

The final sub-section *Comparison with other sources* compares the results obtained using National Food Survey data with those reported by the National Diet and Nutrition Surveys which are based on recorded intakes of individuals, each in a specific age group.

Variations in energy and nutrients from home supplies, 1974 - 1998

This sub-section presents estimates of average daily per person nutrient intakes from home supplies by gender and age for the period 1974 to 1998. The method used is briefly described now. A detailed description and a discussion of the method can be found in [3] and [4].

Method

Average household intakes are exactly the sum of average intakes of household members because nutrients cannot be shared. As argued earlier, recorded household nutrient acquisitions are on average equal to average household intakes. Therefore the household acquisitions of nutrients recorded in the NFS can be written as equal to the sum of average intakes of male and female members of different ages plus an error term capturing (a) deviations from average intakes and (b) measurement error in recorded household acquisitions.

If we specify the relationship between the average intake of a household member and the member's age and gender, then recorded household nutrient acquisitions for a household can be written as the sum of these relationships evaluated at the ages of and for the genders of the household members, plus an error term which is the sum of member's deviations from their average intakes and measurement error. Then standard regression function estimation methods allow estimation of the age and gender specific nutrient intake functions.

---

[6] The 1993 data is not used here because during this time the Eating Out extension was in its initial phase and the data produced may be less reliable than for later years

For example if the average intake of a nutrient by males and females aged A years were respectively $\alpha_M + \beta_M A$ and $\alpha_F + \beta_F A$, independent of household composition, then the average nutrient intake of a household with N_M males and N_F females would be $\alpha_M N_M + \alpha_F N_F + \beta_M T_M + \beta_F T_F$ where T_M and T_F are the sums of the ages of respectively males and females in the household. The coefficients here could then be estimated by conventional regression estimation methods with total household nutrient acquisitions as the dependent variable and, as independent variables, the numbers of males and females in each household and the sums of their ages.

In reality the relationship between average nutrient intake and age is far more complicated than the simple linear form used in this example. The method used here and described in detail in [3] allows considerable flexibility in the form of the gender-specific nutrient intake - age relationships[7]. The method allows the data to "speak for itself" so far as the complex shape of the nutrient intake - age relationship is concerned (see the results in *Variations in energy and nutrients from food eaten out and from home supplies*) while forcing some smoothness on the relationship, a smoothness that we expect to be present in the underlying true relationship that we are trying to estimate.

The results obtained using this method have to be interpreted with care. They are affected by a number of factors, discussed in [3], so that they may give a less than perfect view of the age and gender variation in average nutrient intakes[8]. That said, only the continuous National Food Survey records, coupled with this sort of approach, can give us any long term view of trends in average nutrient intakes for men and women of different ages. So it is worth considering what, together, they produce.

Results: energy (Figure 4)

The procedure described above is applied separately to each year of the survey from 1974 to 1998. Figure 4 shows estimated average energy intakes (kcal per person per day) from home supplies for males and

---

[7] The flexibility comes through approximating the unknown age relationships by step functions with changes at each year of age and imposing a smoothness restriction which penalises large fluctuations in the age relationship over short age ranges

[8] An important assumption underlying the method used here is that average nutrient intakes for people of a given age are unrelated to the ages of other household members. Of course this is unlikely to hold exactly but evidence from weighed intake surveys suggests the effects are generally small. One effect of this sort is taken account of here. Women with small children are less likely to be in full or even part time work and so are likely to consume more in the home and less out of the home. Failing to control for labour force participation could lead to overestimation of nutrient intakes of young children. To accommodate this, indicators of labour force status were included in the estimated models. The reported results are obtained after combining estimates for non-working, part-time working and full-time working people using weights reflecting the changing representation of labour force status in the NFS data

females averaged over five year periods, 1974 to 1978, through to 1994 to 1998[9].

The fall in average energy intakes is clear at every age though it is smaller for the very young and the very old. For males the age profiles of average energy intakes from home supplies rise steeply till the late teen-age years, and then less slowly, falling past age 60 or so. For females the flattening of the age profile is less obvious and the decline starts at an earlier age[10].

A number of factors are probably responsible for these distinctive age profiles. One is, of course, changes through the life cycle in energy needs. Energy needs of the very young and very old are lower than those of others and that is partly responsible for what we see here.

It is very important to understand that, at any age considered, the age profiles in Figure 4 give average energy intakes from home supplies for people of that age, averaged across people of many different types. In particular they are averages across labour force participants and non-participants.

Many people who work outside the home make fewer demands on household supplies because they eat at the workplace or while travelling to or from it. For people in strenuous occupations this effect may be partly offset by higher energy needs. Estimating separate age profiles (not reported here) for labour force participants and non-participants suggests that the first of these effects dominates.

It is likely then that part of the age variation in average energy intakes from home food supplies shown in Figure 4 is due to age-related differences in the proportion of people in the labour force.

Another point to bear in mind is that the age profiles in Figure 4 relate to energy from *home* food supplies. The amount of eating out done varies with age as shown in the next sub-section, and part of the reason for the general increase with age in energy intakes from home supplies evident in Figure 4 is a general decrease with age among older people in the proportion of energy obtained from non-home food supplies.

In the remainder of this sub-section changes over the period 1974 to 1998 in intakes of nutrients are considered. Because of dramatic changes in energy intakes over this period the results are presented as

---

[9] Most of the results in this sub-section are presented in graphical form. Tables at the end of this Section report standard errors which give an idea of the precision of the estimates portrayed in these graphs

[10] Standard errors associated with the points plotted on these graphs are of the order of 40 kcal per person per day suggesting a 95 per cent confidence interval at any chosen age lying about 80 kcal per person per day on either side of the plotted age profiles. The changes through time are highly statistically significant at most ages. Because estimated intakes at adjacent ages are highly positively correlated, the shape of the age profile would not vary from sample to sample as much as these age-specific confidence intervals suggest, see [3]

amounts of nutrients per unit of energy intake, for total fats and saturated fatty acids as percentage of energy, and for the other nutrients as amounts per 1,000 kcal.

Results: nutrients (Figures 5 to 11)

Figures 5 to 11 show the evidence provided by the NFS on changes in the composition of diet in British households over the period 1974 to 1998. In each Figure the left and right-hand pairs of graphs show estimated intakes for respectively males and females. Results by age group for younger and older persons are shown in respectively the upper and lower pairs of graphs[11].

Figures 5 and 6 show the progression of fat intakes over the period. The youngest two age groups (1 to 10 and 11 to 20) have shown almost no change. The fat content of the diet of young people was considerably lower than that of older people until quite recently, a convergence achieved through a substantial decline since the early 1980s in the proportion of energy from fats among older people and a slight increase among the young. It seems as if women have experienced a greater decline than men, but from a higher starting point.

Figure 7 shows a higher level of calcium intake among the youngest age group and more variation with age among women than among men. Older women have substantially higher amounts of calcium per 1,000 kcal of energy intake than similarly aged men. Age variation is more easily seen in the graphs of the next sub-section. There are signs of a recent increase in the calcium content of diet, apparently somewhat larger for younger than for older people.

Figure 8 shows a general increase for people of all ages in the amount of iron per 1,000 kcal of energy in home food supplies. The marked decrease in Vitamin D per 1,000 kcal evident in the household average series shown in Figure 3 is disaggregated by age group and gender in Figure 9 which suggests the decline has been more pronounced among women than among men. Figure 10 suggests that the sharp increase in folate per 1,000 kcal has occurred in a similar fashion for men and women of most ages. Finally, Figure 11 shows common trends for men and women in fruit and vegetables as a contributor to energy in home food supplies. There are clearly very different levels of consumption of fruit and vegetables by males and females, a phenomenon more easily seen in the results presented in the next sub-section.

---

[11] The plotted values are obtained by smoothing estimated age and year specific intakes after averaging across ages within years

Remarks

The sharp decline in household average energy intakes from home food supplies during the last 25 years has been experienced by men and women, but less among the very old and very young than among others.

This decline has been accompanied by significant changes in the nutrient composition of the British home diet. Percentage of energy from fat, particularly from saturated fat, has fallen steadily, somewhat more for women than for men but for women from a higher starting value. Most of the other changes in nutrient composition have been experienced in a similar fashion by men and women of all ages.

It is clear from the results presented so far that there are substantial differences in the nutrient composition of male and female home diets and in the home diets of the young and old. These differences are the focus of the next sub-section which deals with the period 1994 to 1998. This period is especially interesting because information on food eaten outside the home is available. This allows estimates of average nutrient intakes from all food sources to be estimated and consideration of age and gender variation in these intakes.

Variations in energy and nutrients from food eaten out and from home supplies

The long time series in the previous sub-section relate to nutrient intakes from *home* food supplies. Since 1993 the National Food Survey has collected records of food eaten out[12] from around half of the households taking part in the main survey. This sub-section reports results of analysis of these eating out data and of the main household survey data for the period 1994 to 1998. This leads to estimates of age and gender specific average intakes of nutrients from all food sources[13].

The methods employed are similar to those used in the previous sub-sections[14]. The five years 1994 to 1998 are treated as a single period for analysis and estimates of average nutrient intakes by age and gender are calculated separately[15] for nutrients from home food supplies and nutrients from food eaten outside the home.

---

[12] Strictly of food eaten from non-home supplies. Packed lunches and other food taken from home food supplies do fall within the coverage of the main NFS
[13] Excluding confectionery and soft and alcoholic drinks
[14] A minor difference in the analysis of household total home nutrient intakes is that in this sub-section allowance *is* made for the presence of occasional visitors. The effect of this is to reduce energy and nutrient intakes shown in the previous sub-section by about 5 per cent
[15] There are potential estimation efficiency gains from a joint simultaneous analysis of these two data sources. The benefits of such an approach are currently under investigation

The Eating Out Survey data give person-specific records of food consumption so the aggregation problem that arises with home food supply data is not present[16]. The same flexible modelling approach is adopted with these data.

Results: energy (Figure 12)

Figure 12 shows estimated average daily energy intakes for males and females aged 0 to 90 years. The upper pane shows energy intakes from food outside the home and the central pane shows energy intakes from home supplies. The lower pane shows the result of summing these last two, namely estimates of energy intakes from all food sources considered here. Note that the scale on the eating out graph runs from 0 to 1,000 kcal per person per day in contrast to the scales on the other two graphs which run from 0 to 3,000 kcal per person per day.

There are striking features in these graphs. Note how estimated average energy intakes from food eaten-out rise steadily at younger ages and then fall, peaking later and higher for men than for women. The decline thereafter speeds up a little from age 50 onwards. Both these phenomena perhaps reflect age-related differences in labour force participation. The age variation in the home food supply profile complements to some extent the age variation in the profile for eating out.

There is a noticeable increase in estimated energy intakes for females between the ages of 35 and 45, very prominent in the results given in [3] and somewhat lessened here where food from home and non-home supplies has been included. There is the possibility of some age related under reporting of food eaten out.

Results: nutrients (Figures 13 to 17)

The remaining Figures (13 to 17) in this sub-section show estimated nutrient intakes from home and non-home food supplies and estimated total nutrient intakes, all expressed per unit of energy for the food from home supplies, food eaten out and food from both sources.

Figure 13 shows estimated proportions of energy from total fats (left hand column) and saturated fatty acids (right hand column). There is a much higher fat composition of food eaten out, close to 50 per cent of energy at its peak; the strong age dependence, with lower fat content in the non-home diet of the very young and old, and the similarity of the fat content of the non-home diets of males and females. Saturated fatty

---

[16] In the Eating Out Survey consumption is calculated using "standard portion sizes". This results in some inaccuracy in the calculation of nutrient intakes

acids, in terms of the proportion of energy derived from them, make a greater contribution to the diet of the very young.

Figure 14 shows age profiles for calcium and iron expressed per 1,000 kcal of energy for each food source. Calcium content is estimated to be much lower in food eaten out, than in food from home supplies. The very young have much higher calcium intake per 1,000 kcal than others, and women have a slightly more calcium-rich diet than men. In contrast, the estimated age profiles for iron per 1,000 kcal are very similar for men and women.

The age profiles for vitamin D shown in Figure 15 are very similar for males and females. Children have much higher intakes of Vitamin D per 1,000 kcal than others. The results for folate present a different picture with higher energy-adjusted intakes at older ages and higher intakes per 1,000 kcal for women than for men. There are striking age variations in energy-adjusted copper and zinc intakes (Figure 16) with a fall among primary school age children, but very similar profiles for males and females.

Figure 17 shows amounts (grams) of fruit and vegetables per person per day (left column) and per 1,000 kcal of energy. There are higher intakes for females than for the males and a strong age dependence.

Remarks

The statistical disaggregation of the NFS household records of food acquisitions into age-specific average energy and nutrient intakes produces plausible estimates of the age and gender variation in intakes for the period 1994 to 1998.

The results obtained for home food for 1974 – 1993, where they can be calculated, are broadly similar but, as discussed earlier, suggest differential changes in elements of the composition of diet across males and females of different ages.

Energy and most other nutrient intakes from food outside the home rise into early adult-hood and then flatten out and fall particularly after the age of about fifty years. There are off-setting changes in intakes from home food supplies. The fat content of food eaten out is far higher than that of food from home supplies with sharp variations by age, the very young and old having relatively low fat intakes from food eaten out.

Energy and other intakes from all food sources increase with age to around age 50 to 60 and then fall, and vary by gender, in a complex but plausible fashion. For some nutrients, for example calcium and vitamin D, there are sharp declines in intakes per unit of energy in early childhood. The percentages of energy from fat and from saturated fatty acids are relatively constant with age, though there is a fall in the intake of saturated fatty acids from 0 to 15 years and in fat intake after the age of 75 years. The role in diet of fruit and vegetables increases sharply with age with generally a higher representation in the diets of women than of men.

In view of the complex manipulations of the NFS data required to produce these results, it is interesting to compare them with the results of conventional dietary surveys. In the next sub-section the results are compared with estimates produced by the NDNS. There is good agreement for young people, less so for adults. Possible explanations of this are discussed below after page 87.

Section 5 Charts

		Page
Figure 1.1	Average energy in home supplies	71
Figure 2.1	Average amount of fat in home food supplies, 1974 - 1998	72
Figure 2.2	Average amount of saturated fatty acids in home food supplies, 1974 - 1998	72
Figure 2.3	Average amount of calcium in home food supplies, 1974 - 1998	72
Figure 2.4	Average amount of iron in home food supplies, 1974 - 1998	72
Figure 2.5	Average amount of vitamin D in home food supplies, 1974 - 1998	72
Figure 2.6	Average amount of folate in home food supplies, 1974 - 1998	72
Figure 2.7	Average amount of fruit and vegetables in home food supplies, 1974 - 1998	72
Figure 2.8	Average amount of fruit juice in home food supplies, 1974 - 1998	72
Figure 3.1	Percentage of energy from fat in home food supplies, 1974 - 1998	73
Figure 3.2	Percentage of energy from saturated fatty acids in home food supplies, 1974 - 1998	73
Figure 3.3	Calcium (mg) per 1,000 kcal of food energy in home food supplies, 1974 - 1998	73
Figure 3.4	Iron (mg) per 1,000 kcal of food energy in home food supplies, 1974-1998	73
Figure 3.5	Vitamin D (µg) per 1,000 kcal of food energy in home food supplies, 1974-1998	73
Figure 3.6	Folate (µg) per 1,000 kcal of food energy in home food supplies, 1979-1998	73
Figure 3.7	Fruit and vegetables (g) per 1,000 kcal of food energy in home food supplies, 1974-1998	73
Figure 3.8	Fruit juices (g) per 1000 kcal of food energy in home food supplies, 1974-1998	73
Figure 4.1	Energy from home food supplies, males, 1974-1998	74
Figure 4.2	Energy from home food supplies, females, 1974-1998	74
Figure 5.1	Percentage of energy from fat by age, home food supplies, 1974-1998, younger males	75
Figure 5.2	Percentage of energy from fat by age, home food supplies, 1974-1998, younger females	75
Figure 5.3	Percentage of energy from fat by age, home food supplies, 1974-1998, older males	75
Figure 5.4	Percentage of energy from fat by age, home food supplies, 1974-1998, older females	75
Figure 6.1	Percentage of energy from saturated fatty acids by age, home food supplies, 1974-1998, younger males	76
Figure 6.2	Percentage of energy from saturated fatty acids by age, home food supplies, 1974-1998, younger females	76
Figure 6.3	Percentage of energy from saturated fatty acids by age, home food supplies, 1974-1998, older males	76
Figure 6.4	Percentage of energy from saturated fatty acids by age, home food supplies, 1974-1998, older females	76
Figure 7.1	Calcium by age, home food supplies, 1974-1998, younger males	77
Figure 7.2	Calcium by age, home food supplies, 1974-1998, younger females	77
Figure 7.3	Calcium by age, home food supplies, 1974-1998, older males	77
Figure 7.4	Calcium by age, home food supplies, 1974-1998, older females	77
Figure 8.1	Iron by age, home food supplies, 1974-1998, younger males	78
Figure 8.2	Iron by age, home food supplies, 1974-1998, younger females	78
Figure 8.3	Iron by age, home food supplies, 1974-1998, older males	78
Figure 8.4	Iron by age, home food supplies, 1974-1998, older females	78
Figure 9.1	Vitamin D by age, home food supplies, 1974-1998, younger males	79
Figure 9.2	Vitamin D by age, home food supplies, 1974-1998, younger females	79
Figure 9.3	Vitamin D by age, home food supplies, 1974-1998, older males	79
Figure 9.4	Vitamin D by age, home food supplies, 1974-1998, older females	79
Figure 10.1	Folate by age, home food supplies, 1979-1998, younger males	80
Figure 10.2	Folate by age, home food supplies, 1979-1998, younger females	80

Section 5 Charts *continued*

		Page
Figure 10.3	Folate by age, home food supplies, 1979-1998, older males	80
Figure 10.4	Folate by age, home food supplies, 1979-1998, older females	80
Figure 11.1	Fruit and vegetables by age, home food supplies, 1974-1998, younger males	81
Figure 11.2	Fruit and vegetables by age, home food supplies, 1974-1998, younger females	81
Figure 11.3	Fruit and vegetables by age, home food supplies, 1974-1998, older males	81
Figure 11.4	Fruit and vegetables by age, home food supplies, 1974-1998, older females	81
Figure 12.1	Food eaten out 1994/98: energy	82
Figure 12.2	Food brought home 1994/98: energy	82
Figure 12.3	All food 1994/98: energy	82
Figure 13.1	Food eaten out 1994/98: percentage of energy from fat	83
Figure 13.2	Food eaten out 1994/98: percentage of energy from saturated fatty acids	83
Figure 13.3	Food brought home 1994/98: percentage of energy from fat	83
Figure 13.4	Food brought home 1994/98: percentage of energy from saturated fatty acids	83
Figure 13.5	All food 1994/98: percentage of energy from fat	83
Figure 13.6	All food 1994/98: percentage of energy from saturated fatty acids	83
Figure 14.1	Food eaten out 1994/98: Calcium 1994/98	84
Figure 14.2	Food eaten out 1994/98: Iron 1994/98	84
Figure 14.3	Food brought home 1994/98: Calcium 1994/98	84
Figure 14.4	Food brought home 1994/98: Iron 1994/98	84
Figure 14.5	All food 1994/98: Calcium 1994/98	84
Figure 14.6	All food 1994/98: Iron 1994/98	84
Figure 15.1	Food eaten out 1994/98: Vitamin D 1994/98	85
Figure 15.2	Food eaten out 1994/98: Folate 1994/98	85
Figure 15.3	Food brought home 1994/98: Vitamin D 1994/98	85
Figure 15.4	Food brought home 1994/98: Folate 1994/98	85
Figure 15.5	All food 1994/98: Vitamin D 1994/98	85
Figure 15.6	All food 1994/98: Folate 1994/98	85
Figure 16.1	Food eaten out 1994/98: Copper 1994/98	86
Figure 16.2	Food eaten out 1994/98: Zinc 1994/98	86
Figure 16.3	Food brought home 1994/98: Copper 1994/98	86
Figure 16.4	Food brought home 1994/98: Zinc 1994/98	86
Figure 16.5	All food 1994/98: Copper 1994/98	86
Figure 16.6	All food 1994/98: Zinc 1994/98	86
Figure 17.1	Food eaten out 1994/98: Fruit and vegetables (g per person per day)	87
Figure 17.2	Food eaten out 1994/98: Fruit and vegetables (g per 1,000 kcal)	87
Figure 17.3	Food brought home 1994/98: Fruit and vegetables (g per person per day)	87
Figure 17.4	Food brought home 1994/98: Fruit and vegetables (g per 1,000 kcal)	87
Figure 17.5	All food 1994/98: Fruit and vegetables (g per person per day)	87
Figure 17.6	All food 1994/98: Fruit and vegetables (g per 1,000 kcal)	87

Figure 1.1: Average energy in home food supplies

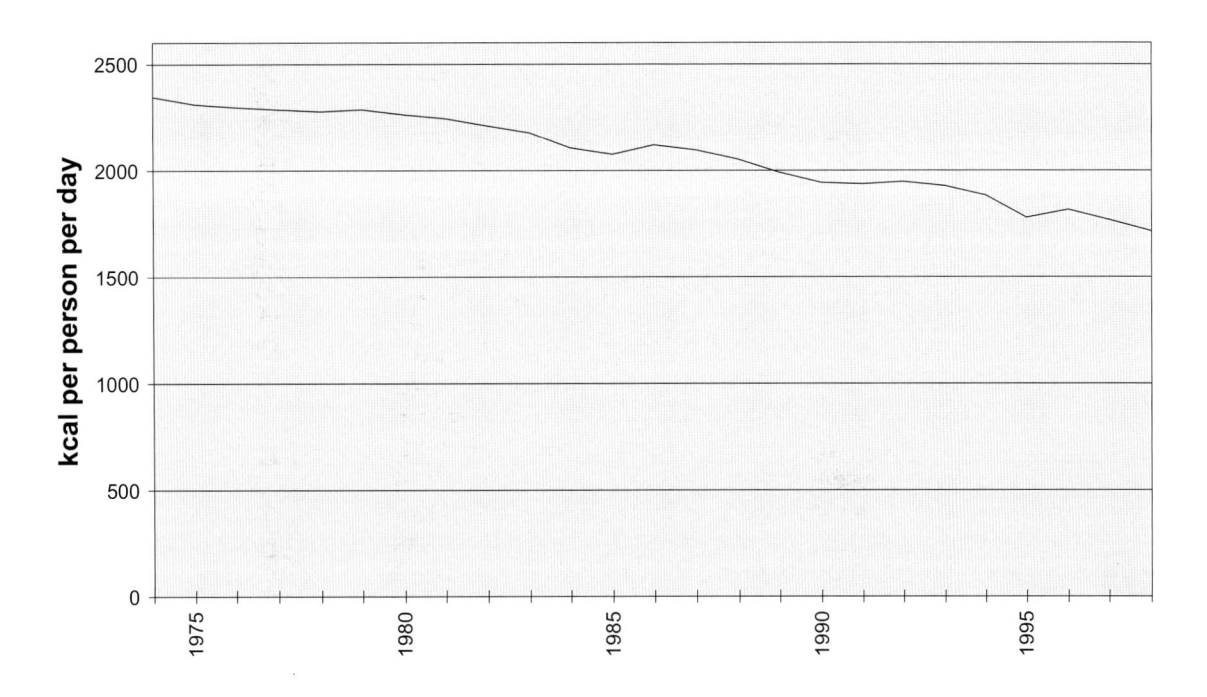

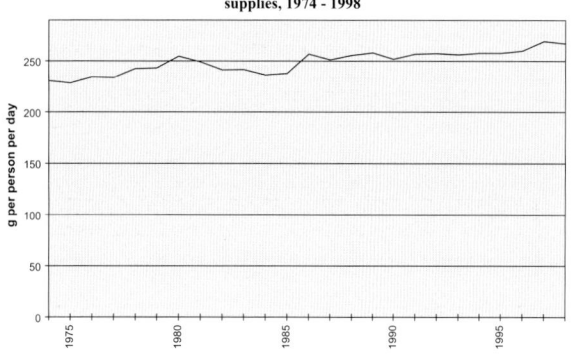

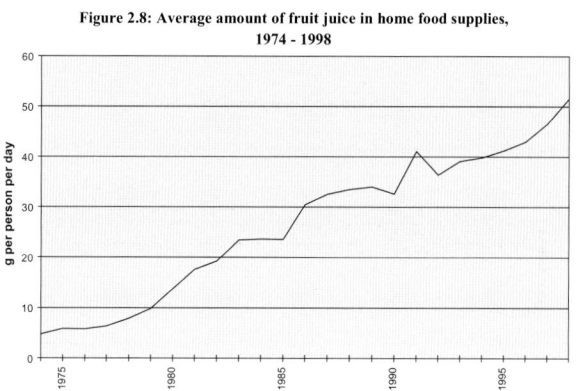

Figure 2.1: Average amount of fat in home food supplies, 1974 - 1998

Figure 2.2: Average amount of saturated fatty acids in home food supplies, 1974 - 1998

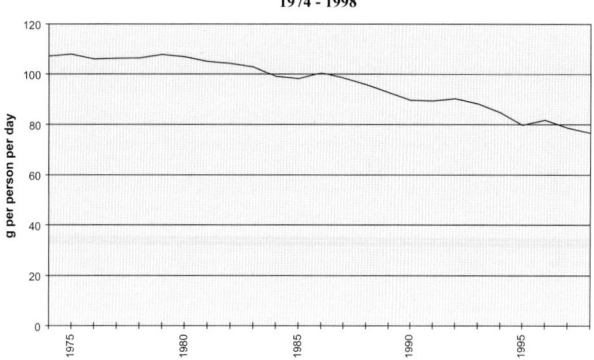

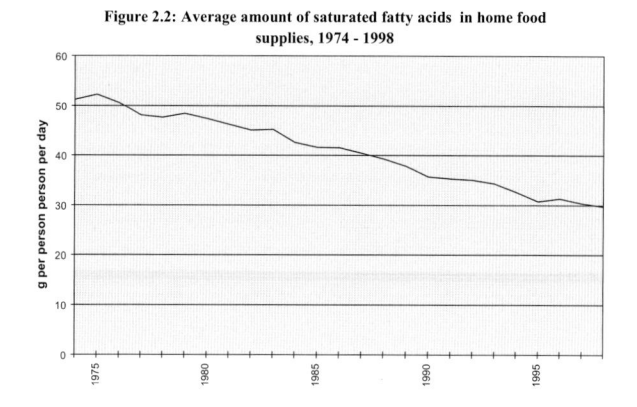

Figure 2.3: Average amount of calcium in home food supplies, 1974 - 1998

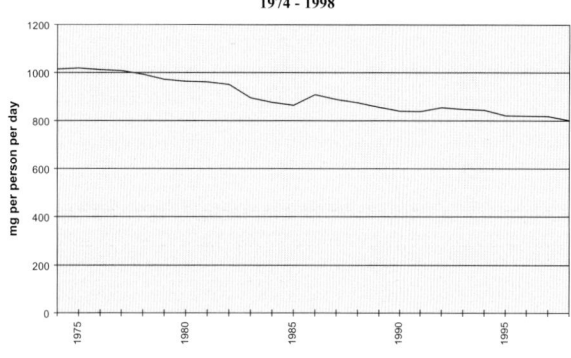

Figure 2.4: Average amount of iron in home food supplies, 1974 - 1998

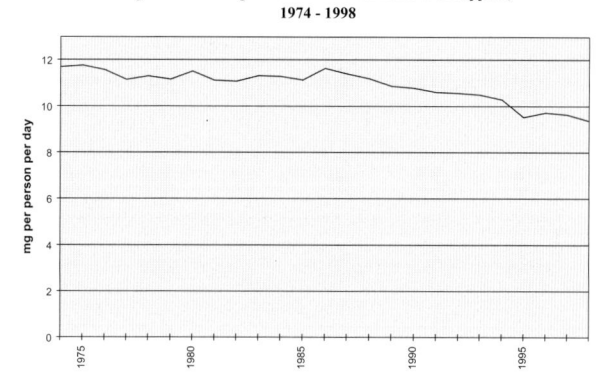

Figure 2.5: Average amount of vitamin D in home food supplies, 1974 - 1998

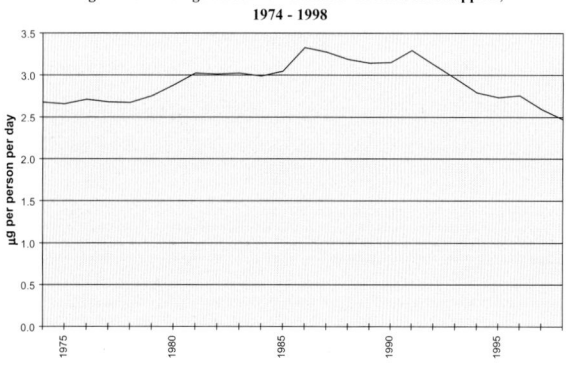

Figure 2.6: Average amount of folate in home food supplies, 1979 - 1998

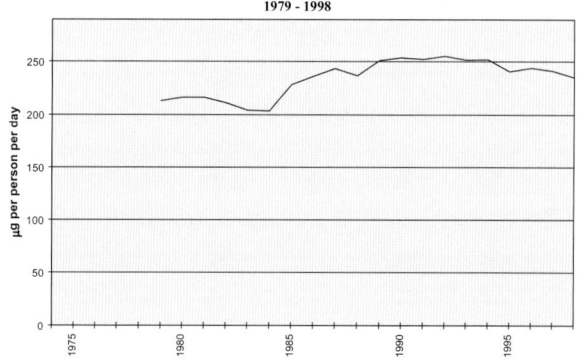

Figure 2.7: Average amount of fruit and vegetables in home food supplies, 1974 - 1998

Figure 2.8: Average amount of fruit juice in home food supplies, 1974 - 1998

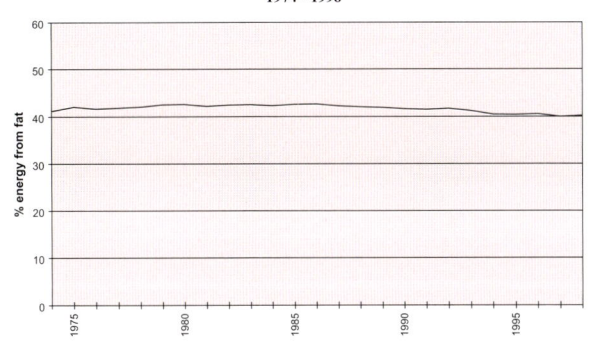

Figure 3.1: Percentage of energy from fat in home food supplies, 1974 - 1998

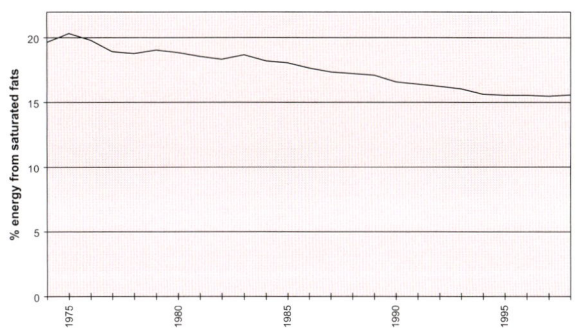

Figure 3.2: Percentage of energy from saturated fatty acids in home food supplies, 1974 - 1998

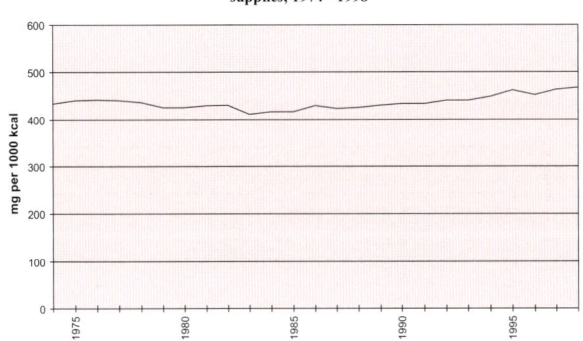

Figure 3.3: Calcium (mg) per 1,000 kcal of food energy in home food supplies, 1974 - 1998

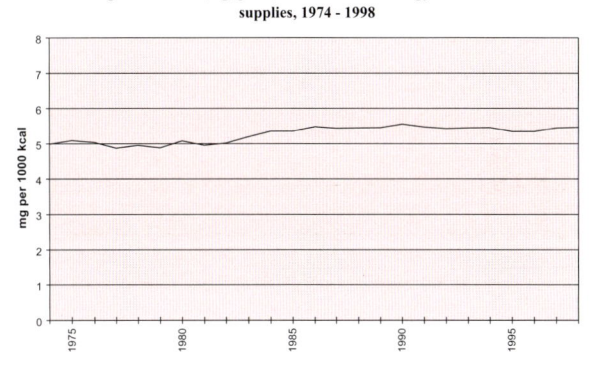

Figure 3.4: Iron (mg) per 1,000 kcal of food energy in home food supplies, 1974 - 1998

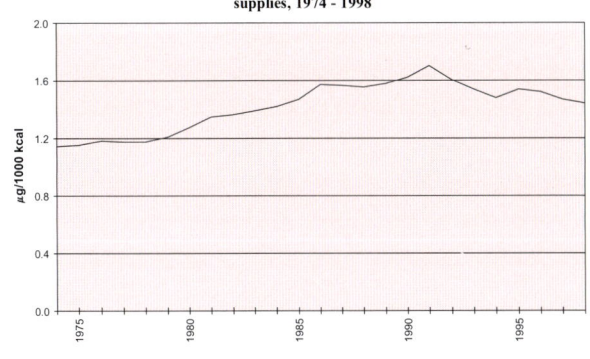

Figure 3.5: Vitamin D (µg) per 1,000 kcal of food energy in home food supplies, 1974 - 1998

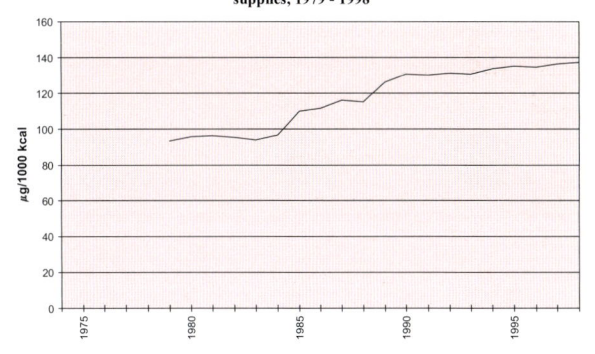

Figure 3.6: Folate (µg) per 1,000 kcal of food energy in home food supplies, 1979 - 1998

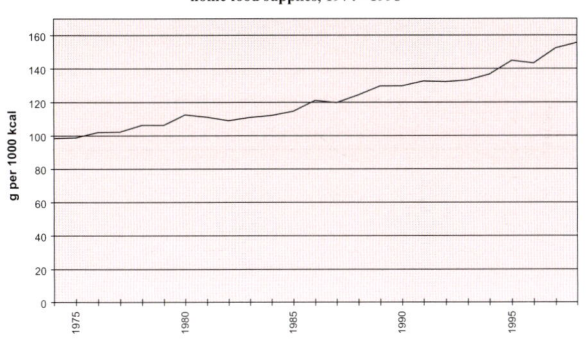

Figure 3.7: Fruit and vegetables (g) per 1,000 kcal of food energy in home food supplies, 1974 - 1998

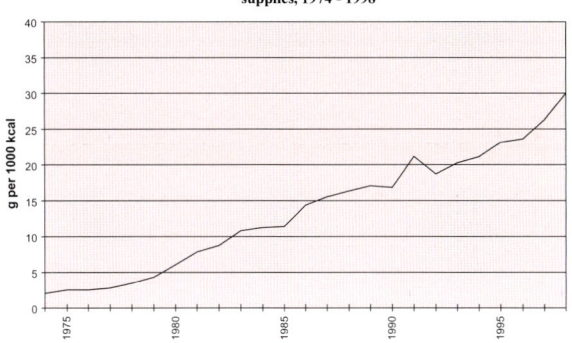

Figure 3.8: Fruit Juice (g) per 1,000 kcal of food energy in home food supplies, 1974 - 1998

Figure 4.1 Energy from home food supplies, males, 1974 - 1998

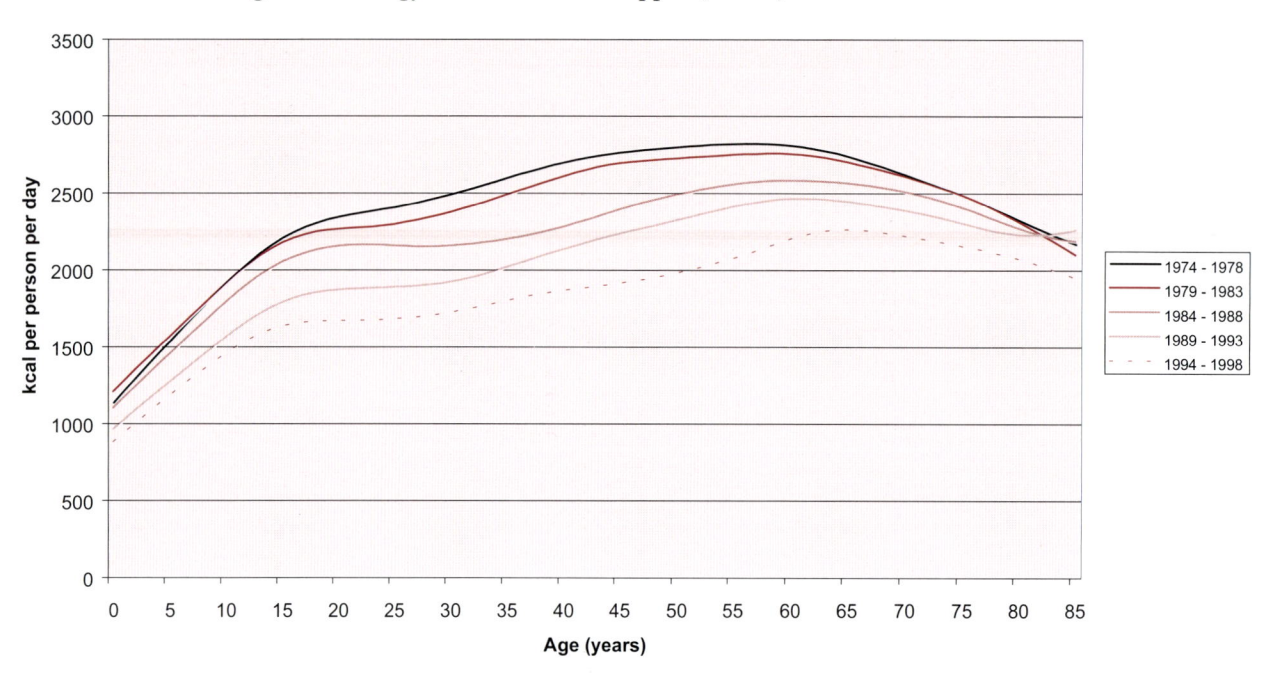

Figure 4.2. Energy from home food supplies, females, 1974 - 1998

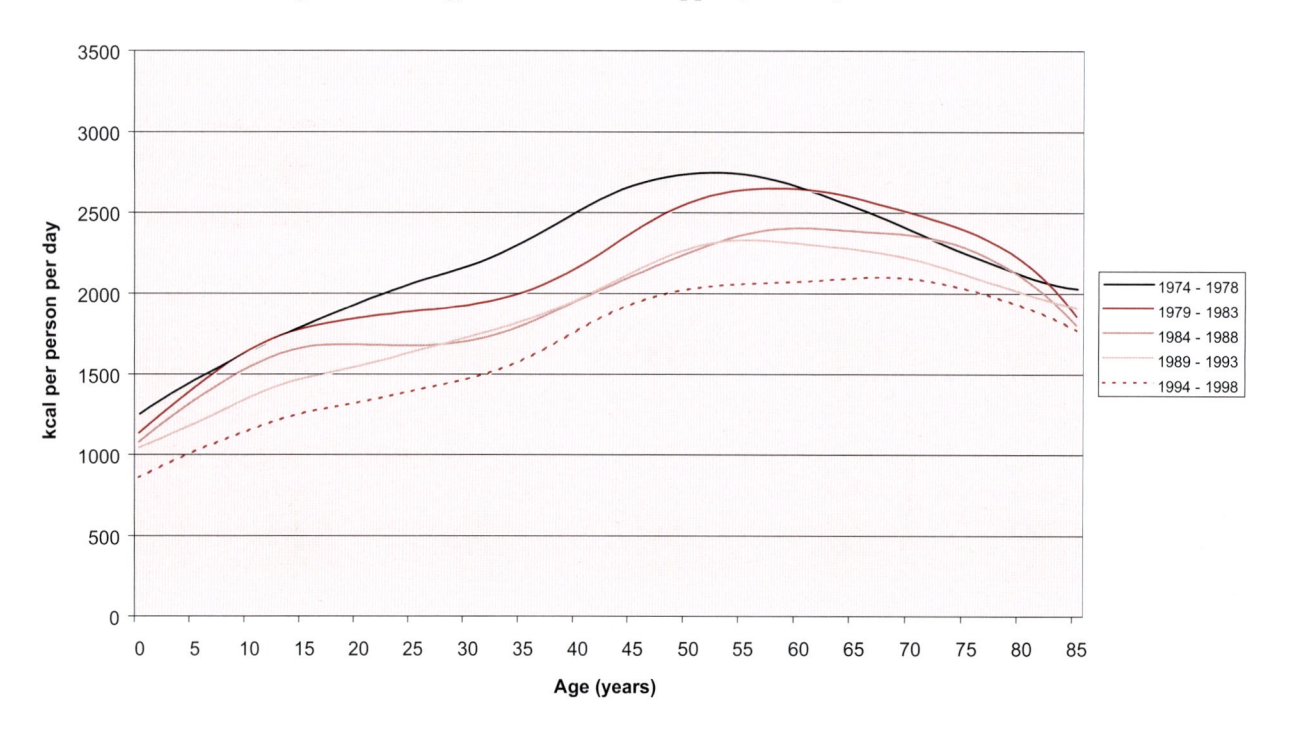

Figure 5.1. Percentage of energy from fat by age, home food supplies 1974 - 1998, younger males

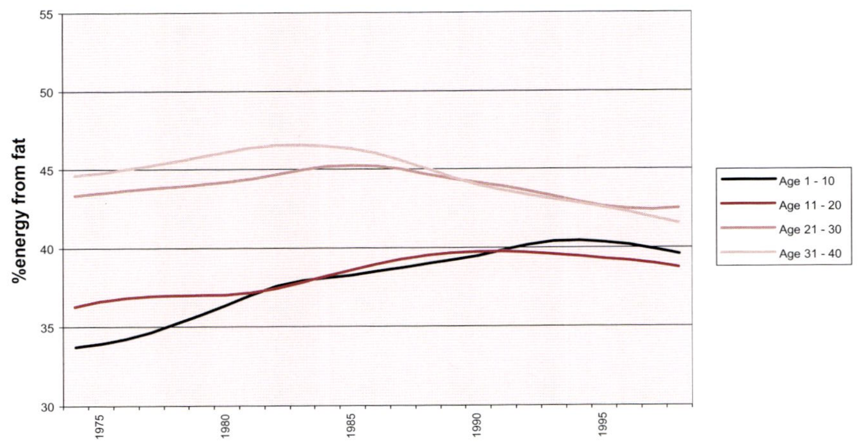

Figure 5.2. Percentage of energy from fat by age, home food supplies 1974 - 1998, younger females

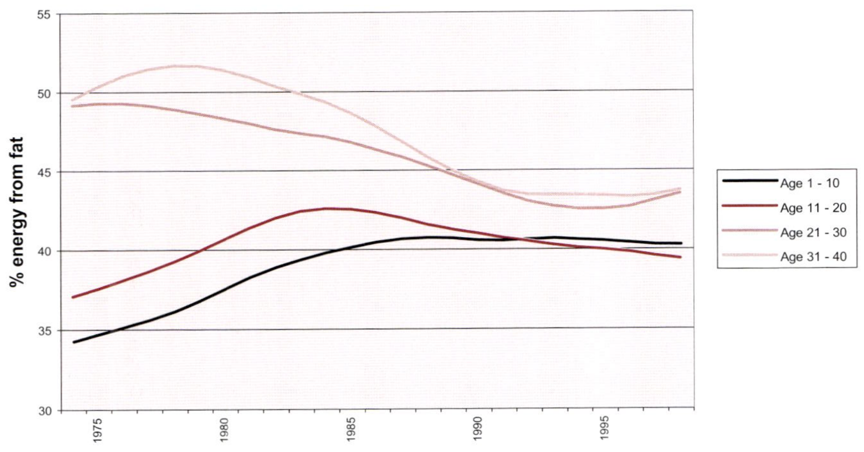

Figure 5.3. Percentage of energy from fat by age, home food supplies 1974 - 1998, older males

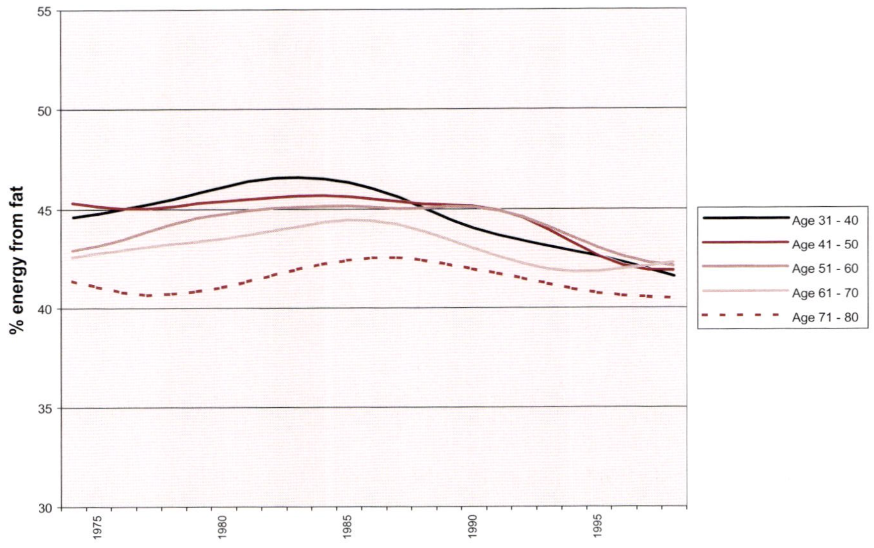

Figure 5.4. Percentage of energy from fat by age, home food supplies 1974 - 1998, older females

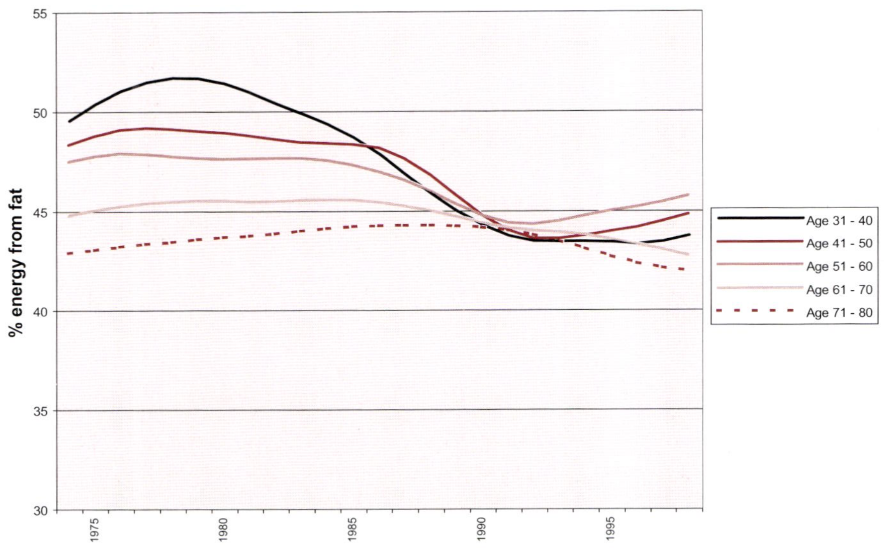

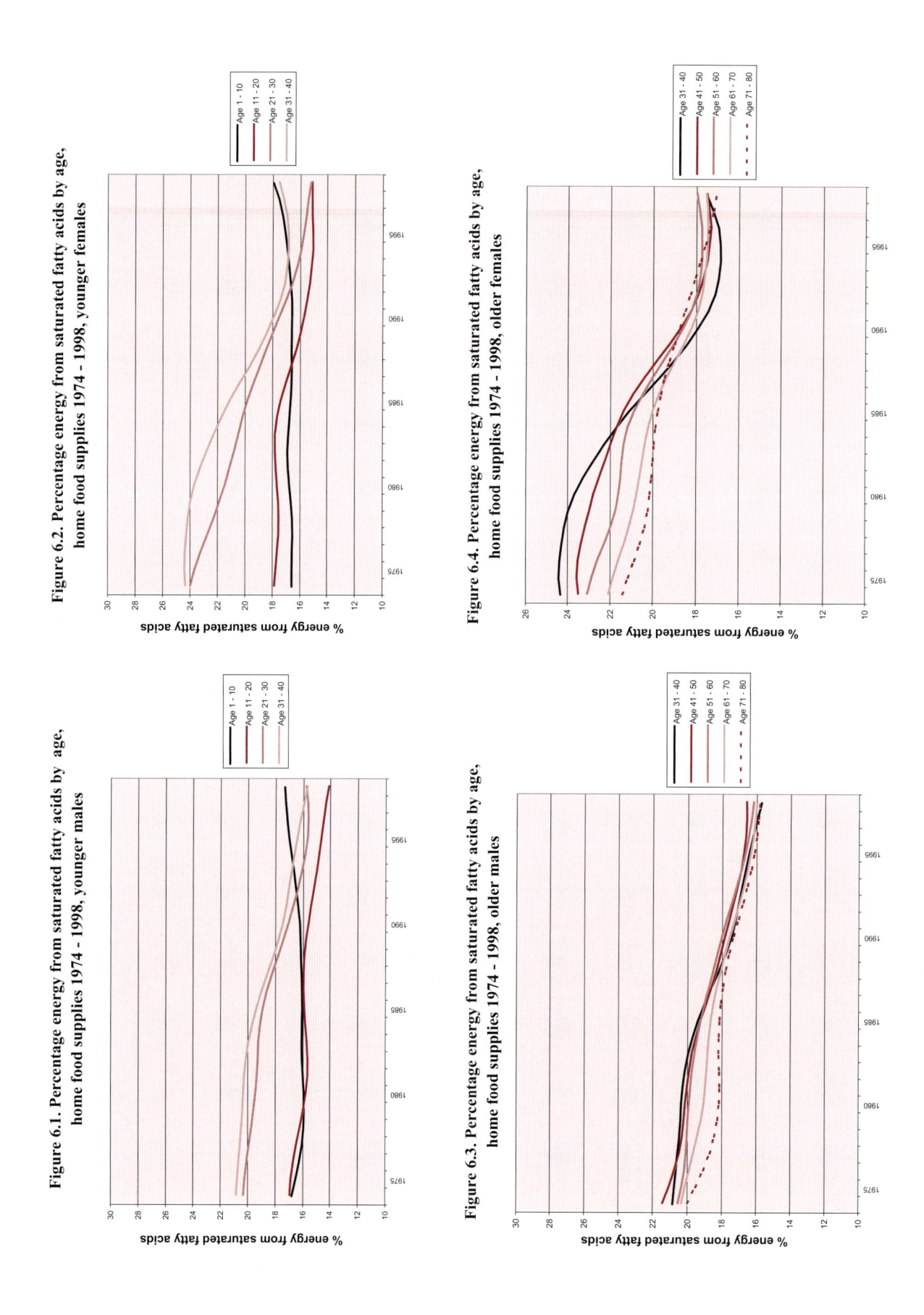

Figure 6.1. Percentage energy from saturated fatty acids by age, home food supplies 1974 - 1998, younger males

Figure 6.2. Percentage energy from saturated fatty acids by age, home food supplies 1974 - 1998, younger females

Figure 6.3. Percentage energy from saturated fatty acids by age, home food supplies 1974 - 1998, older males

Figure 6.4. Percentage energy from saturated fatty acids by age, home food supplies 1974 - 1998, older females

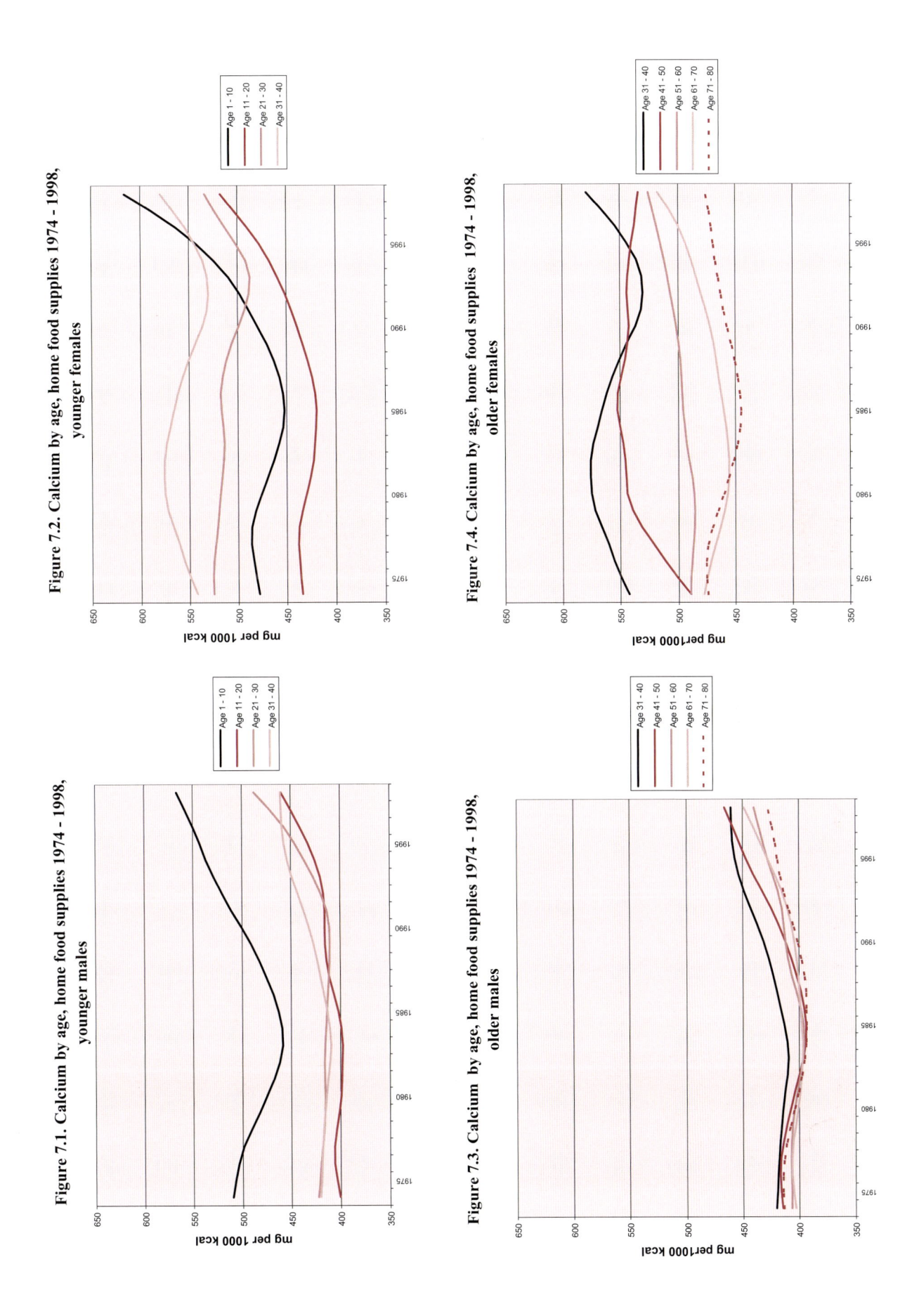

Figure 7.1. Calcium by age, home food supplies 1974 - 1998, younger males

Figure 7.2. Calcium by age, home food supplies 1974 - 1998, younger females

Figure 7.3. Calcium by age, home food supplies 1974 - 1998, older males

Figure 7.4. Calcium by age, home food supplies 1974 - 1998, older females

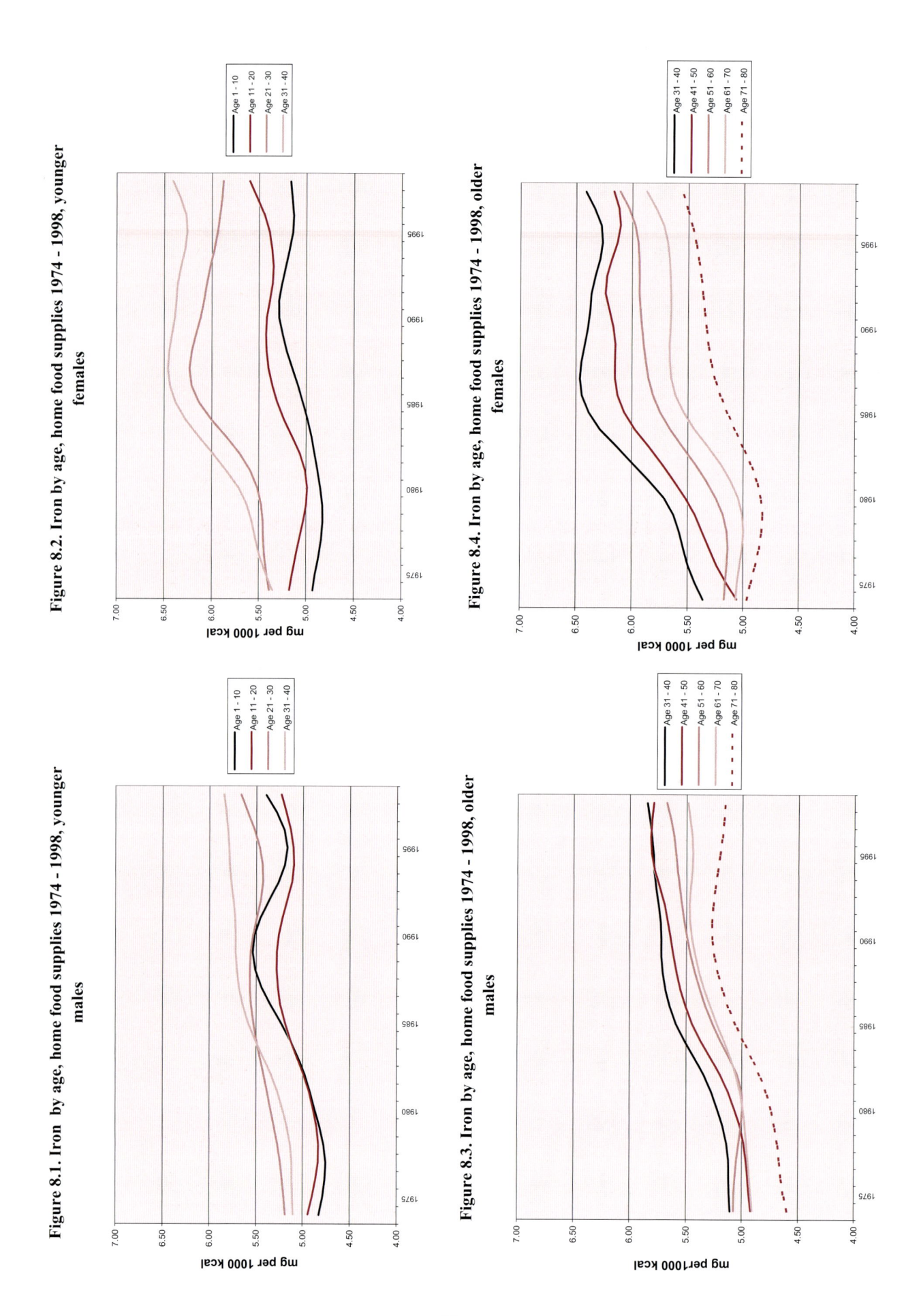

Figure 8.1. Iron by age, home food supplies 1974 - 1998, younger males

Figure 8.2. Iron by age, home food supplies 1974 - 1998, younger females

Figure 8.3. Iron by age, home food supplies 1974 - 1998, older males

Figure 8.4. Iron by age, home food supplies 1974 - 1998, older females

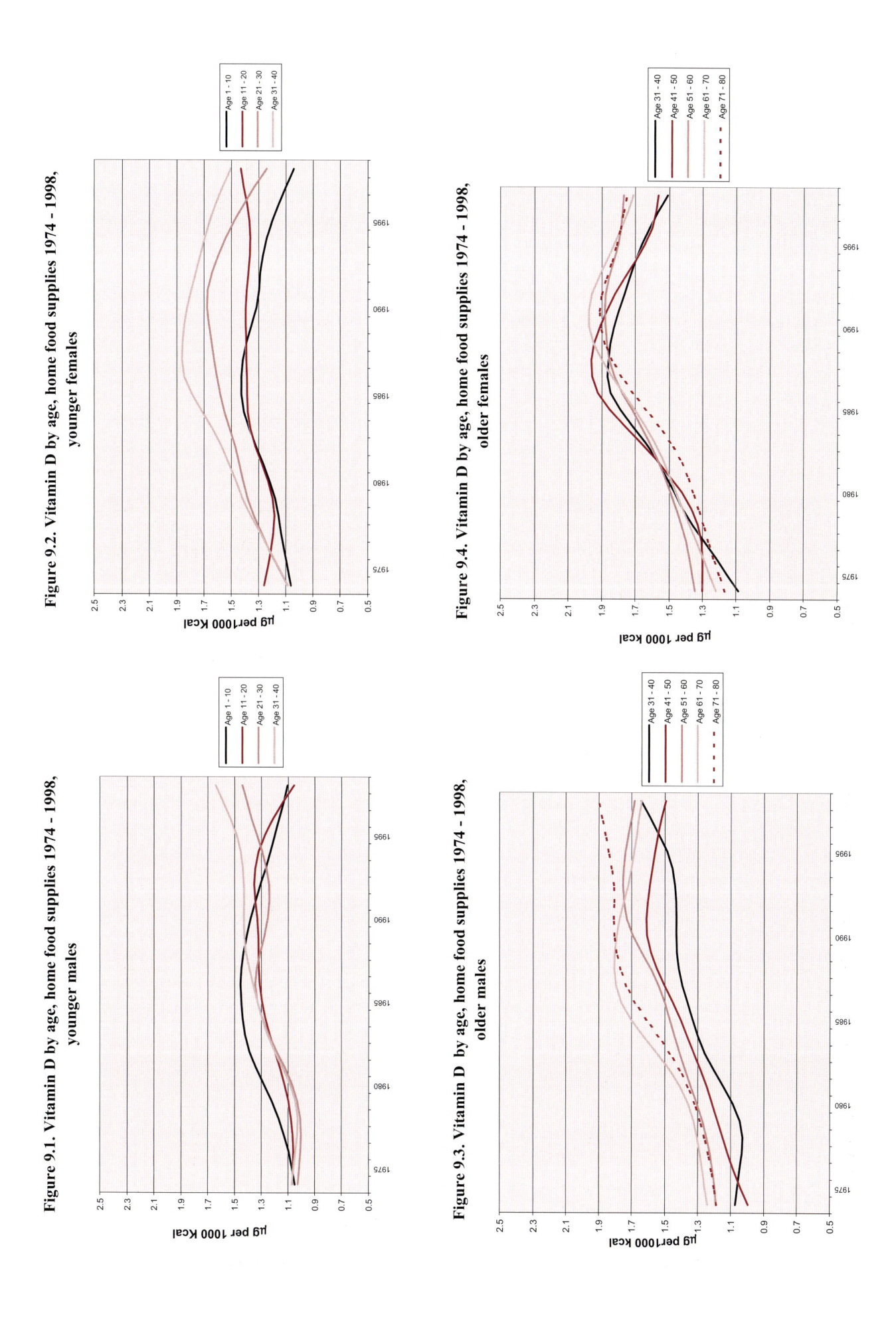

Figure 9.1. Vitamin D by age, home food supplies 1974 - 1998, younger males

Figure 9.2. Vitamin D by age, home food supplies 1974 - 1998, younger females

Figure 9.3. Vitamin D by age, home food supplies 1974 - 1998, older males

Figure 9.4. Vitamin D by age, home food supplies 1974 - 1998, older females

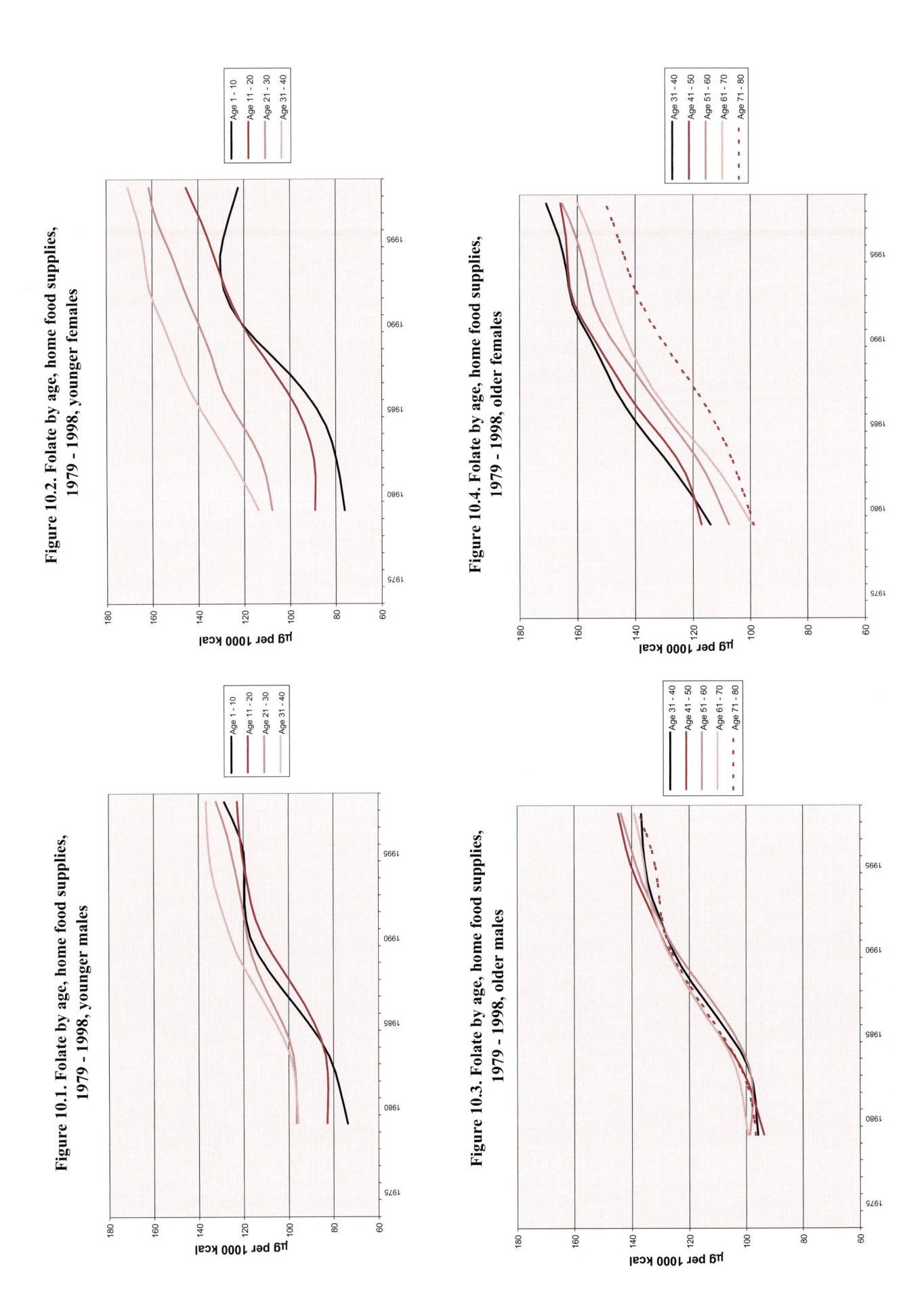

Figure 10.1. Folate by age, home food supplies, 1979 - 1998, younger males

Figure 10.2. Folate by age, home food supplies, 1979 - 1998, younger females

Figure 10.3. Folate by age, home food supplies, 1979 - 1998, older males

Figure 10.4. Folate by age, home food supplies, 1979 - 1998, older females

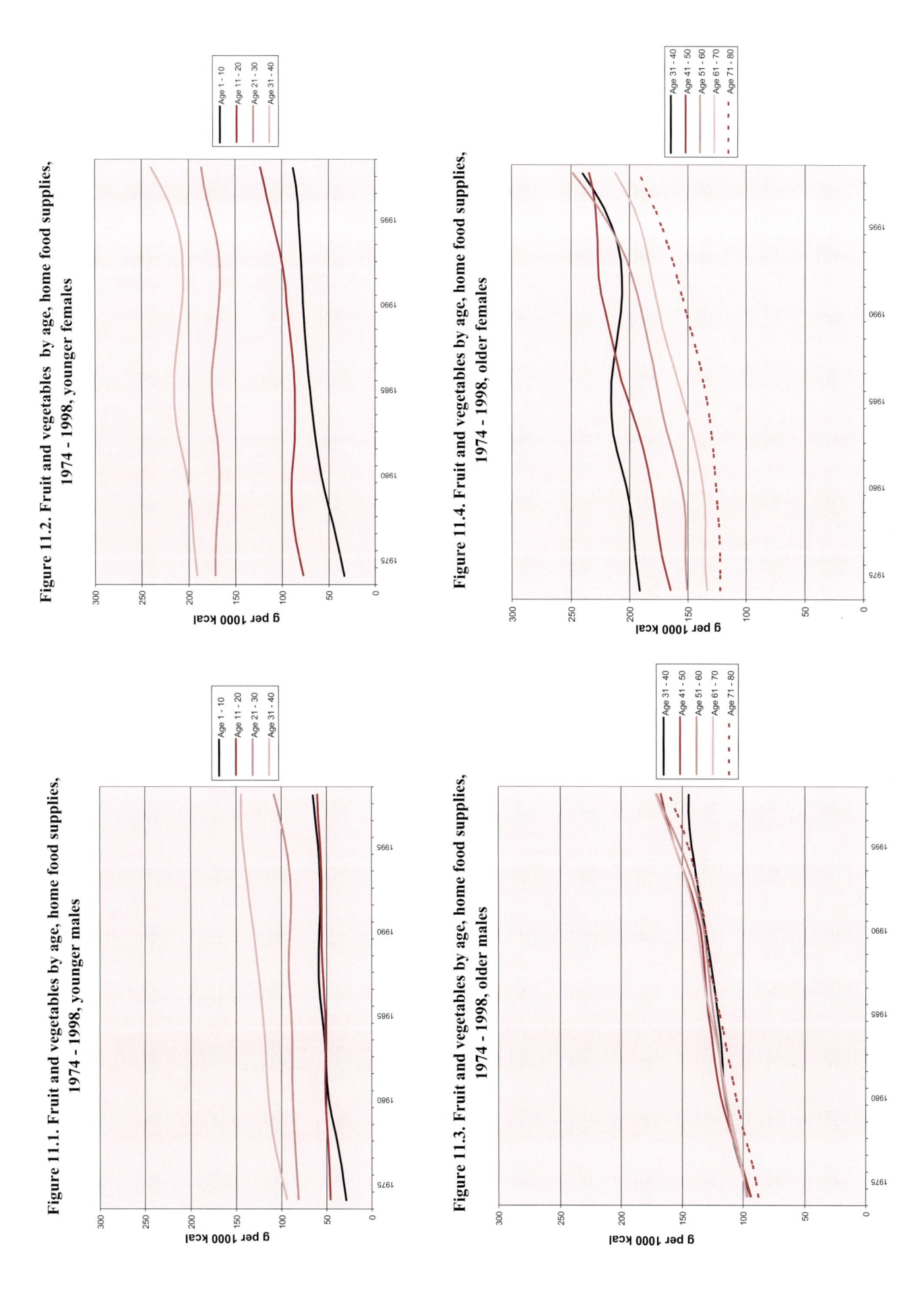

Figure 11.1. Fruit and vegetables by age, home food supplies, 1974 - 1998, younger males

Figure 11.2. Fruit and vegetables by age, home food supplies, 1974 - 1998, younger females

Figure 11.3. Fruit and vegetables by age, home food supplies, 1974 - 1998, older males

Figure 11.4. Fruit and vegetables by age, home food supplies, 1974 - 1998, older females

Figure 12.1. Food eaten out 1994/98: energy

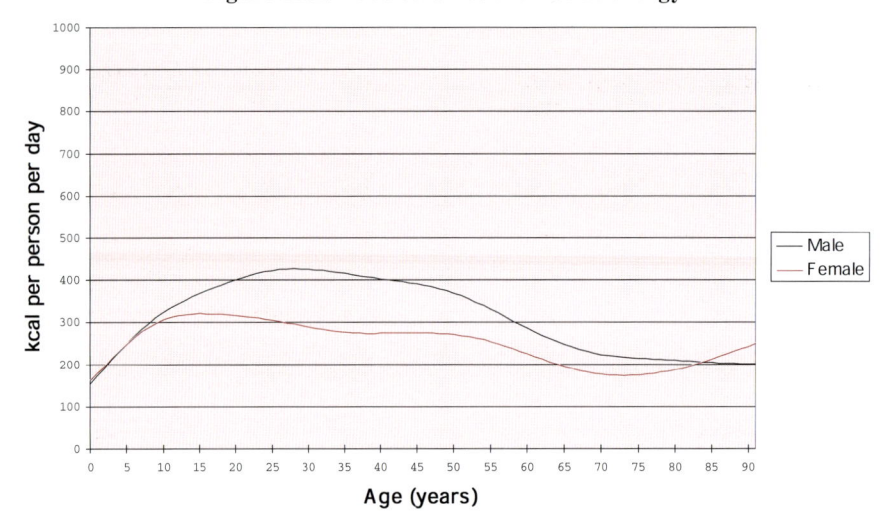

Figure 12.2. Food brought home 1994/98: energy

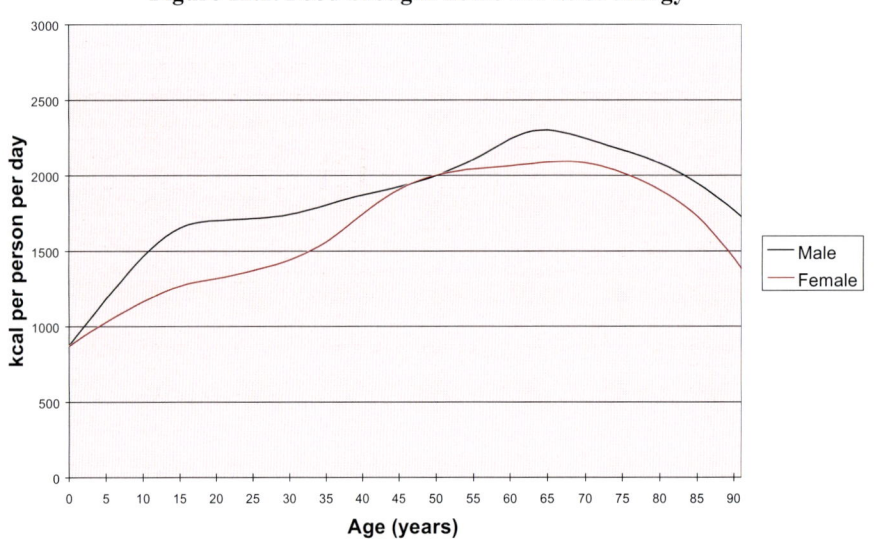

Figure 12.3. All food 1994/98: energy

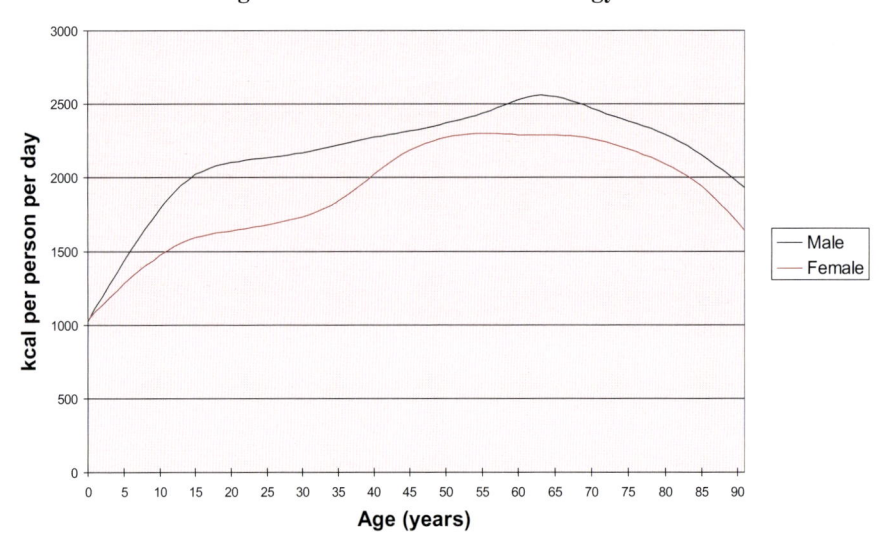

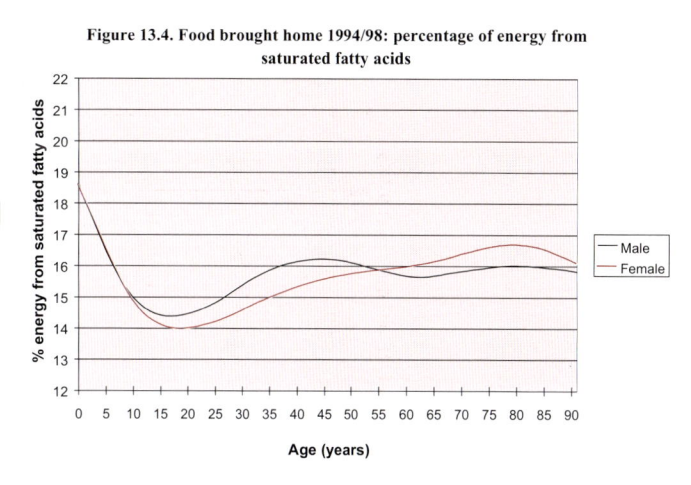

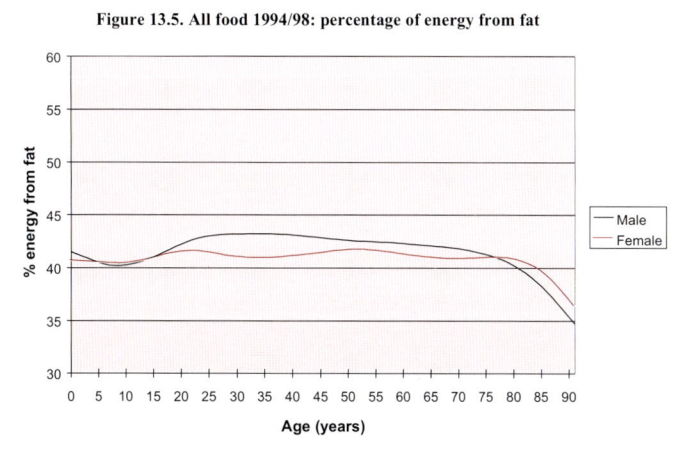

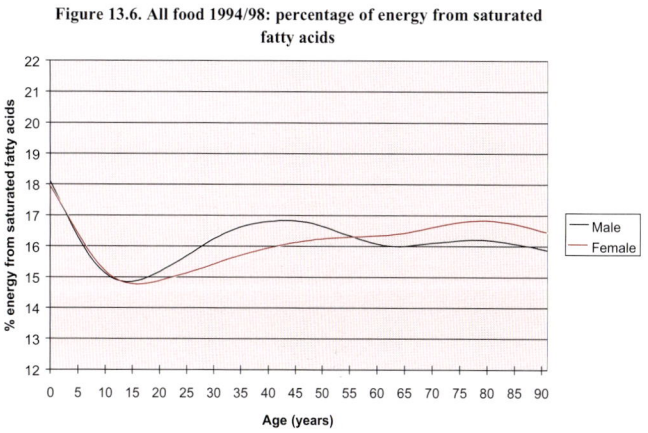

Figure 13.1. Food eaten out 1994/98: percentage of energy from fat

Figure 13.2. Food eaten out 1994/98: percentage of energy from saturated fatty acids

Figure 13.3. Food brought home 1994/98: percentage of energy from fat

Figure 13.4. Food brought home 1994/98: percentage of energy from saturated fatty acids

Figure 13.5. All food 1994/98: percentage of energy from fat

Figure 13.6. All food 1994/98: percentage of energy from saturated fatty acids

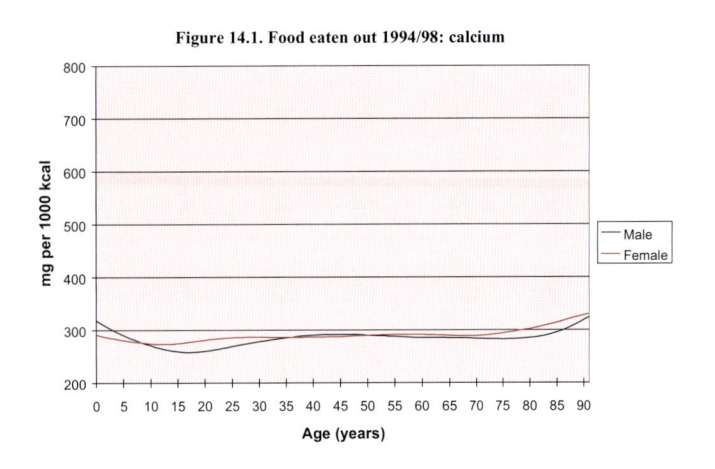

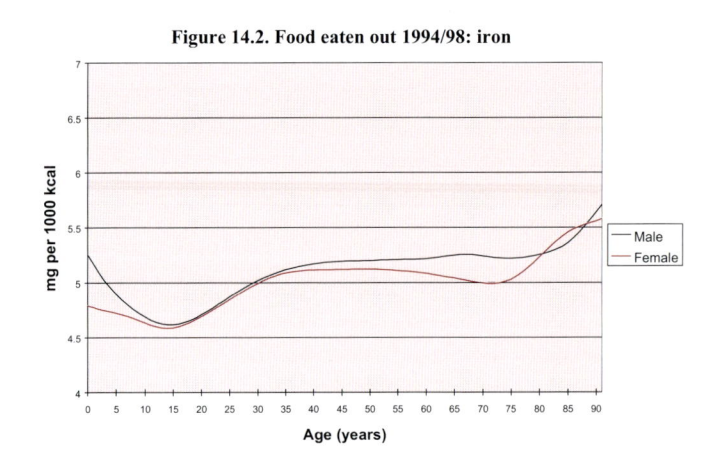

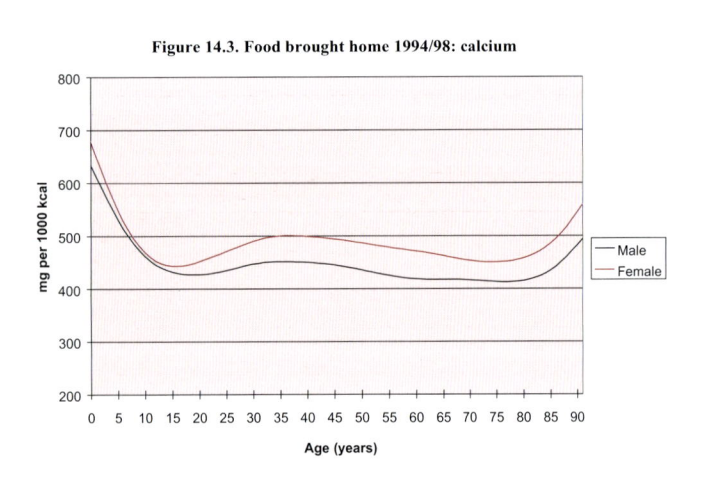

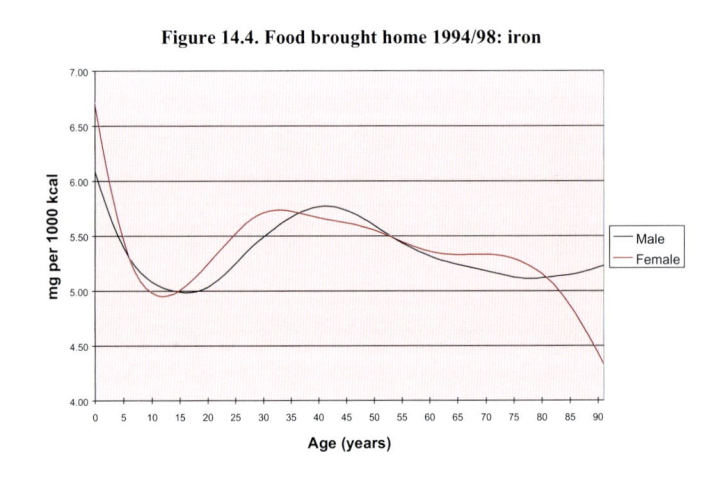

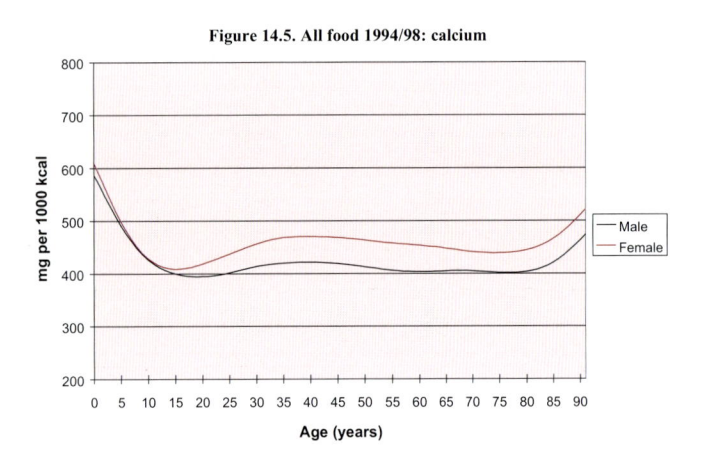

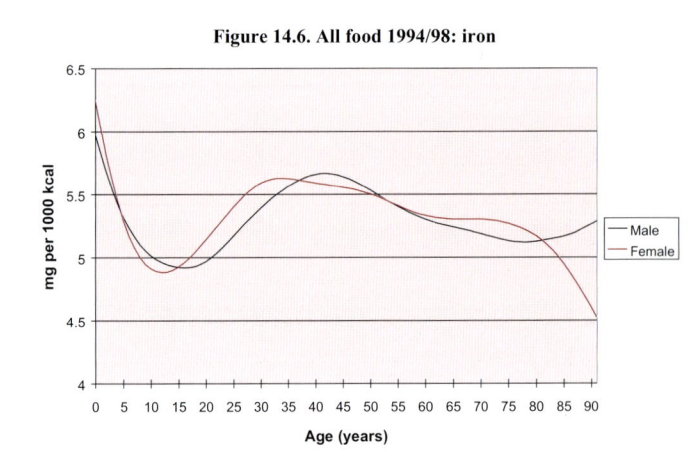

Figure 14.1. Food eaten out 1994/98: calcium

Figure 14.2. Food eaten out 1994/98: iron

Figure 14.3. Food brought home 1994/98: calcium

Figure 14.4. Food brought home 1994/98: iron

Figure 14.5. All food 1994/98: calcium

Figure 14.6. All food 1994/98: iron

Figure 15.1. Food eaten out 1994/98: Vitamin D

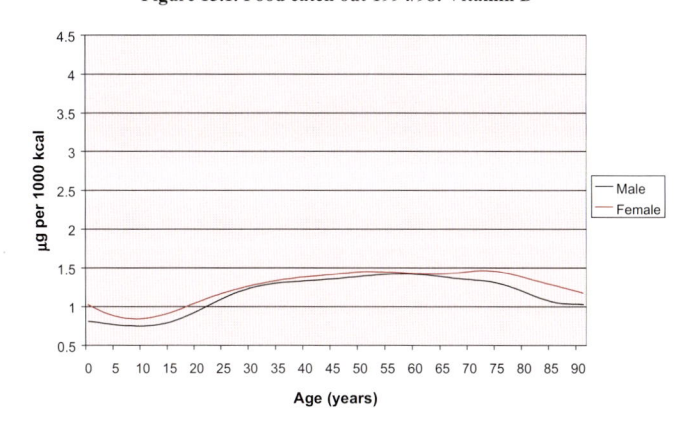

Figure 15.2. Food eaten out 1994/98: Folate

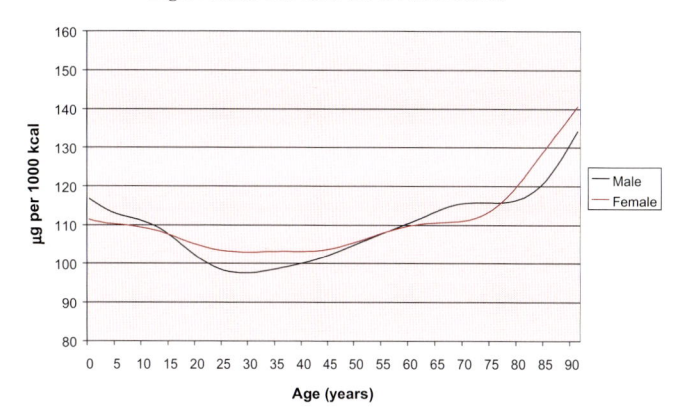

Figure 15.3. Food brought home 1994/98: Vitamin D

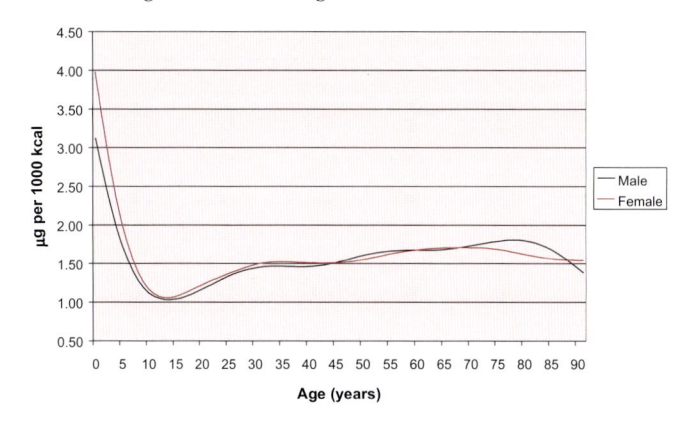

Figure 15.4. Food brought home 1994/98: Folate

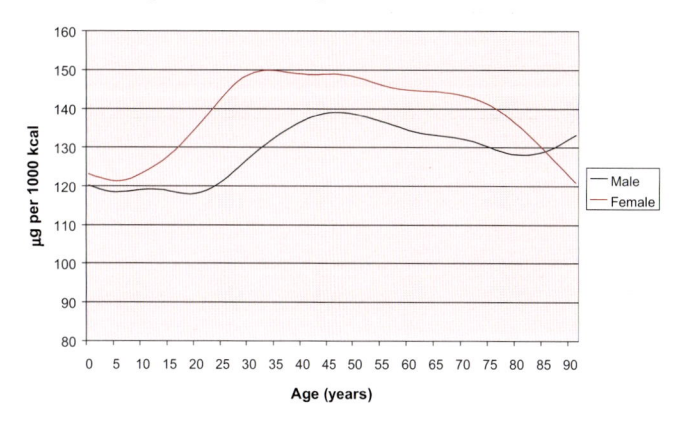

Figure 15.5. All food 1994/98: Vitamin D

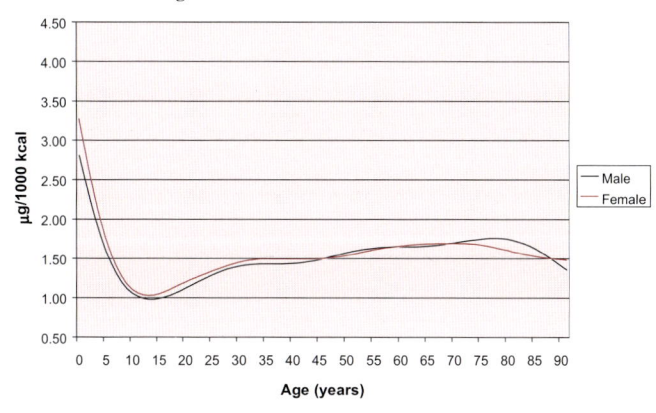

Figure 15.6. All food 1994/98: Folate

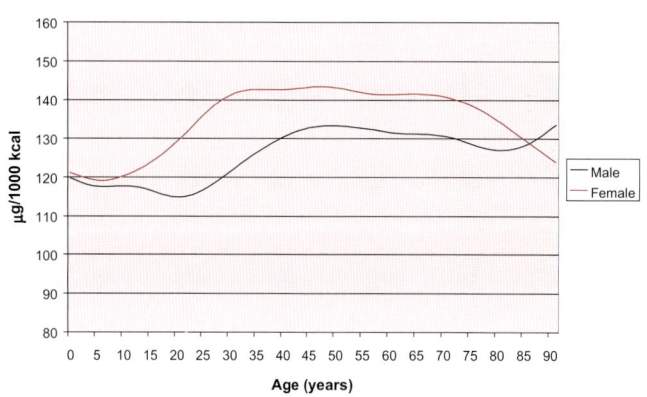

Figure 16.1. Food eaten out 1994/98: Copper

Figure 16.2. Food eaten out 1994/98: Zinc

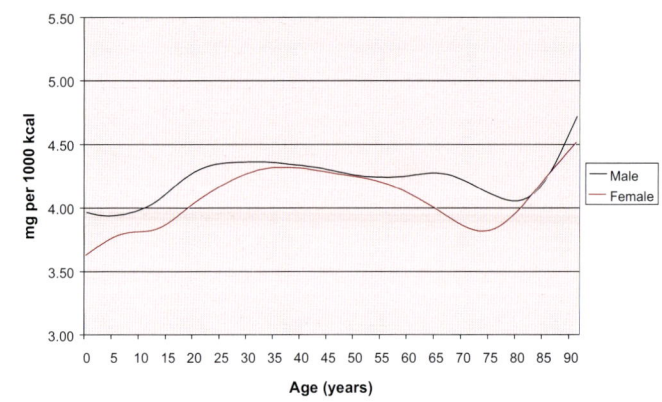

Figure 16.3. Food brought home 1994/98: Copper

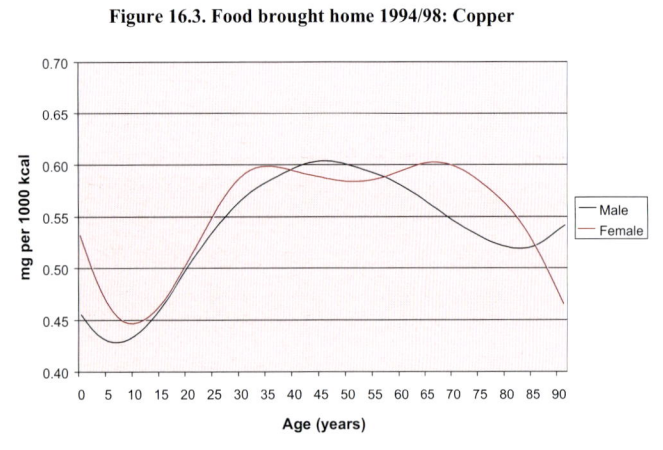

Figure 16.4. Food brought home 1994/98: Zinc

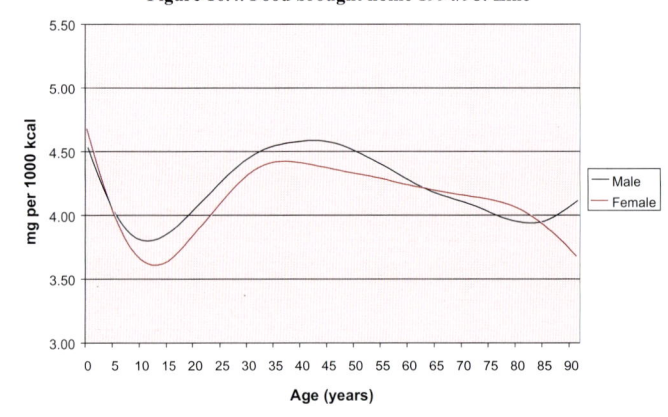

Figure 16.5. All food 1994/98: Copper

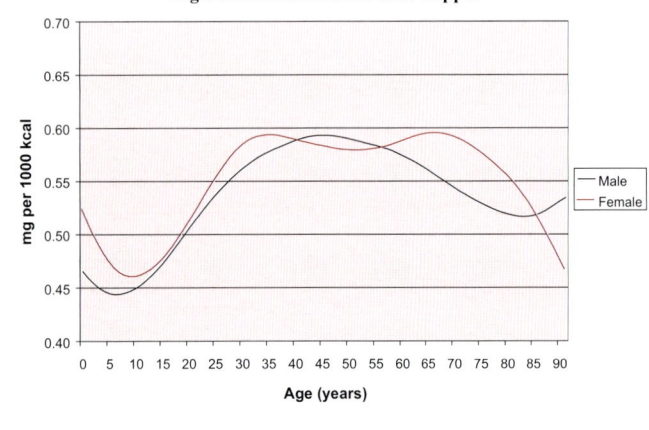

Figure 16.6. All food 1994/98: Zinc

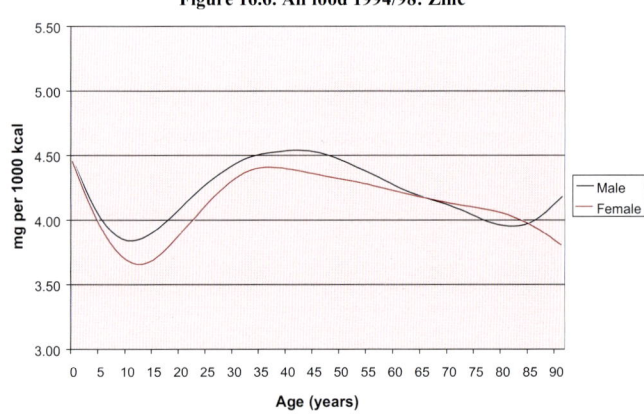

Figure 17.1. Food eaten out 1994/98: Fruit and vegetables (g per person per day)

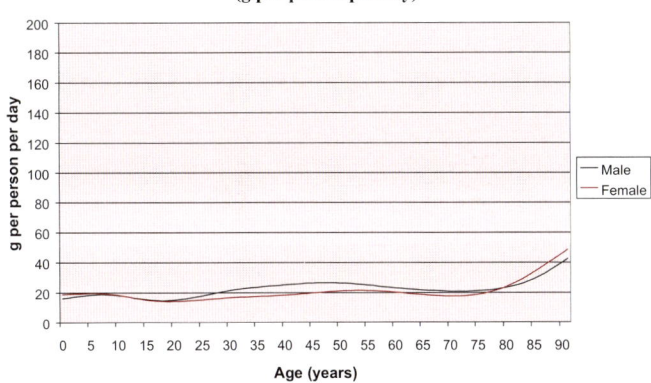

Figure 17.2. Food eaten out 1994/98: Fruit and vegetables (g per 1,000 kcal)

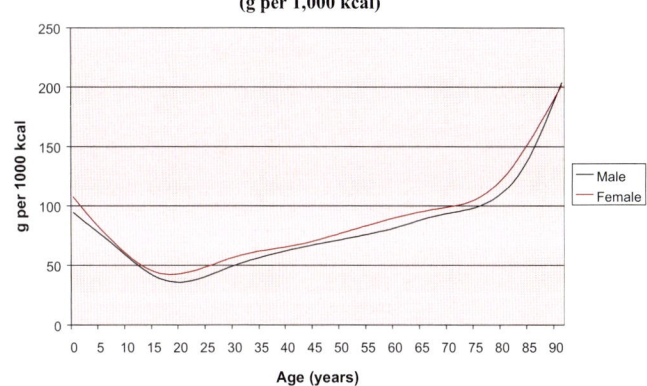

Figure 17.3. Food brought home 1994/98: Fruit and vegetables (g per person per day)

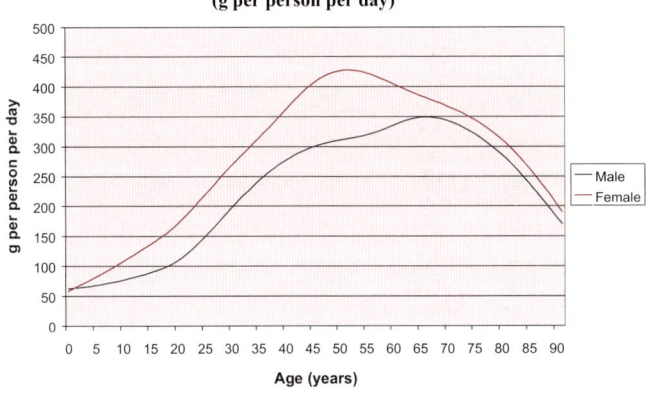

Figure 17.4. Food brought home 1994/98: Fruit and vegetables (g per 1,000 kcal)

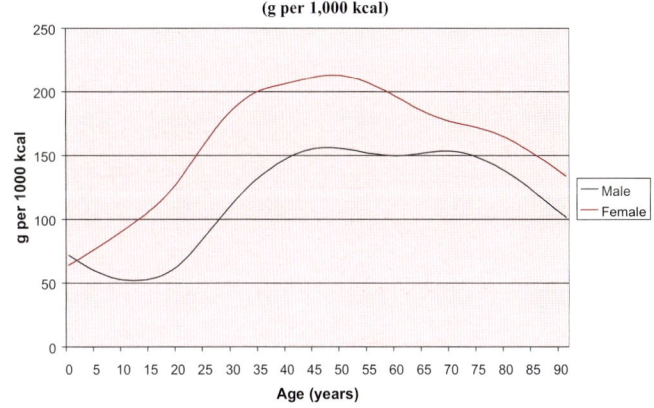

Figure 17.5. All food 1994/98: Fruit and vegetables (g per person per day)

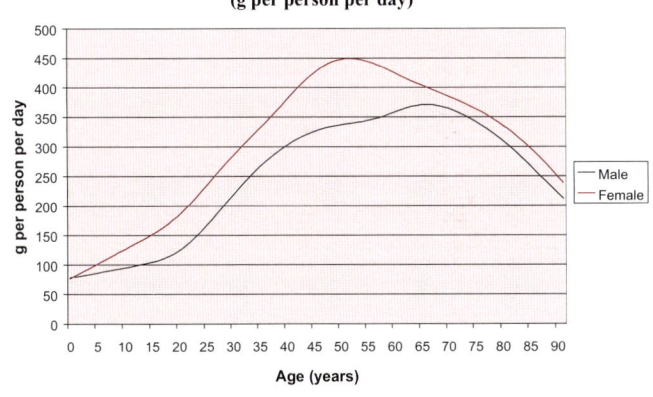

Figure 17.6. All food 1994/98: Fruit and vegetables (g per 1,000 kcal)

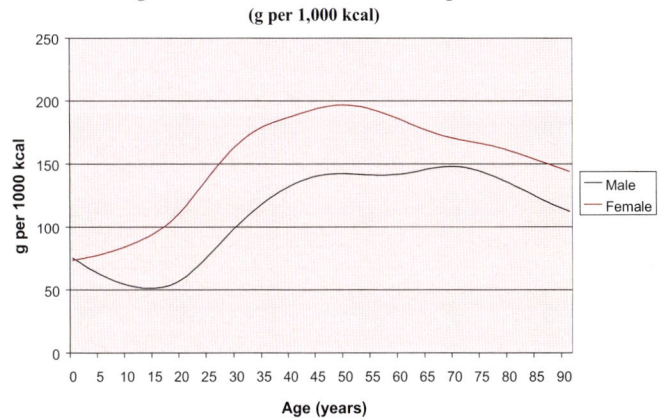

Comparison with other sources

The main alternative modern sources of information on British diet are the detailed National Diet and Nutrition Surveys (NDNS) which are the joint responsibility of the Ministry of Agriculture, Fisheries and Food and the Department of Health.

In this final part of this Section the estimated intakes obtained using NFS data are compared with the estimated intakes produced in the NDNS.

Method

Each NDNS survey focuses on people in a particular age range. At present there are published reports on NDNS surveys of: adults aged 16 to 64 years, [5], conducted in 1986/7; children aged 1½ to 4½ years, [6], conducted in 1992/3; and adults aged 65 years and over, [7], conducted in 1994/5. Field-work on a NDNS survey of young people aged 4 to 18 years [8] conducted in 1997/8 has been completed and early results from this survey are reported here.

The NDNS surveys collect weighed intake records of food consumed by respondents. The recording period varies from four to seven days with results weighted to give estimates of average daily intakes over a one-week period. Food consumed inside and outside the home is covered in the surveys but food consumed outside the home is not weighed.

To obtain NFS figures as comparable as possible with the NDNS results, the following procedure was employed. For each NDNS survey, NFS data for a period spanning the period of the NDNS survey was isolated and subjected to the sort of statistical analysis reported earlier. These statistical methods require large amounts of data to produce accurate estimates, so in each case a period extending a year or two each side of the NDNS survey period was used.

The result of the NFS analysis is a set of estimated nutrient intakes for males and females at each completed year of age from 0 to 90. The published NDNS reports give average intakes by age range (e.g. for children aged 4 to 6 years, adults aged 16 to 24 years). To produce NFS based figures for comparison, simple averages of the NFS estimates for each relevant completed year of age were produced.

Results

The NFS and NDNS estimated intakes are shown in four sets of tables, 5.1 to 5.4. In each set Table (a) gives NFS based estimates and Table (b) gives NDNS estimates. All estimates are reported as per person per day intakes. Results are given, where available, for energy, total fats, saturated fatty acids, calcium, iron, vitamin D, folate, copper and zinc[17].

The comparison of NFS and NDNS results must be done with care as there are a number of important differences in the surveys. Shortly each NDNS survey will be considered in turn but first some general comments are in order.

The main difference between the surveys is of course that the NDNS collects weighed intake records of consumption from individuals while the NFS collects household totals of food purchases and other acquisitions except in the Eating Out Survey where consumption is estimated from records of consumption expressed in terms of standard portion sizes. There are a number of consequences of this difference.

First, the NFS data are, record for record, in one way less informative than the NDNS data. Relatively complex statistical methods are required to infer individual age-specific average intakes from household totals and they are demanding of data.

To set against this, it is possible that the relatively unobtrusive NFS data collection method results in less under-reporting bias. Among NFS respondents, individuals in multi-person households may be less likely to feel that their personal eating habits are being scrutinised than they would if they were taking part in a recorded intake survey. In single-person households, because the NFS records purchases which may be for additions to food stores or for visitors, respondents may feel relatively comfortable about yielding up information about large purchases.[18]

Another consequence of this fundamental difference in methodology is that the NFS-based results make no allowance for wastage of edible food whereas the NDNS results relate to food actually consumed.

A further difference is that until 1992 the NFS results presented here are based on data that excluded confectionery and soft and alcoholic drinks and all food from non-home supplies. The NDNS results are based on records of consumption of all food and drinks. This means that in general the NFS based figures are somewhat less accurate than the NDNS.

---

[17] NFS results for copper and zinc are not reported for the 1986/7 period (adults aged 16 to 64) because nutrient conversion factors are not present in the NFS data base for this period

[18] As argued earlier, one can expect the main effect of purchasing for visitors to cancel out across households, but see [3] for some caveats to this remark

Comparisons: children and young people

Turning now to a comparison of the results obtained with these two types of data, consider first the estimated intakes for young people aged 4 to 18 years shown in Table 1a (NFS) and Table 1b (NDNS). Both sets of results relate to nutrients from foods consumed in and out of the home. Generally there is remarkably good agreement once the inevitable sampling inaccuracy in the two sets of estimates is taken into account. The levels of intakes estimated using the two surveys are generally close. Both sets of results show the same pattern of age and gender related variation, with boys having higher estimated intakes than girls, and older children higher estimated intakes than younger ones.

Agreement is also quite good for the estimated intakes of young children (aged 1½ to 4½ years) shown in Tables 2a and 2b. The general change with age in calcium intakes is similarly recorded by the two surveys. The NFS results do not include food from non-home food supplies, whereas the NDNS results do.

Comparisons: adults

There are more substantial differences between the NFS and NDNS estimates for adults. Tables 3a (NFS) and 3b (NDNS) compare results for the mid-1980s for adults in four age ranges from 16 to 64 years. Note that the NFS results presented here do not include food from non-home food supplies, whereas the NDNS results do[19]. So we would expect the NFS results to lie below those from the NDNS and indeed they do for younger males. Recall the age dependence in amounts eaten out discussed in the previous sub-section. However for younger females (16 to 24 years) the NDNS figures are close to the NFS-based figures which is unexpected given the likely amount of eating out done by women in this age group (see sub-section *Variations in energy and nutrients from food eaten out and from home supplies*). For older women the NFS figures are much higher.

There is no clear explanation for this difference at this time but two factors may be involved. First it is likely (see [1]) that the method applied to the NFS data results in some upward bias in estimated intakes for older women and men. This is because this age group tends to receive more visits than it makes visits to others. Second, it is possible that under-reporting and non-response in the NDNS causes

---

[19] The Eating Out extension to the NFS did not start until 1993. Here and elsewhere in this Section, the NFS results, in contrast to the NDNS results, exclude energy intakes from confectionery and soft and alcoholic drinks

downward bias in its estimates. This issue is recognised in a number of the NDNS reports[20].

The results for older adults shown in Table 4a (NFS) and Table 4b (NDNS) display patterns similar to those found for younger adults. Here both sets of results relate to nutrients from foods consumed in and out of the home.

The estimated levels of intakes obtained from the NFS are substantially higher than those from the NDNS especially for women. However the NFS results for those aged 85 to 90 are based on *very* small numbers of such people in NFS households, the NFS estimates for this group are quite imprecise, and the comparison is with NDNS respondents aged 85 and over which includes a few people over 90 who may have very low intakes, people not included in the NFS results presented here. In addition there was some evidence of under-reporting in the NDNS by people aged 65 years and over, particularly amongst women.

The two sets of results are in good agreement on the decline in intakes with age and in many cases on the extent of lower intakes by women than men.

Here and in the other surveys considered, if nutrients amounts are re-scaled to a common level of energy intake by age and gender then there is good general agreement between the NFS data, treated as it has been here, and the NDNS data. Both sets of data and approaches therefore convey similar messages about the composition of diet.

Remarks

The National Food Survey does not contain the wealth of detail captured by the National Diet and Nutrition Surveys. However it is relatively inexpensive per respondent, and unobtrusive - and perhaps, in consequence, less prone to under-recording. It has the major advantage that it is conducted virtually every week of the year and has been for over 50 years, giving an unparalleled source of information on the changing diet in Great Britain.

The analysis of the NFS reported in this Section has hardly scratched the surface of this unique resource. The method employed does require refinement and the interpretation of the results requires continuing careful study.

For children and young people, there is good agreement between NDNS estimates of energy and nutrient intakes and the NFS-based estimates given here. For adults, the NFS estimates generally suggest higher intakes than the NDNS, particularly for middle-aged and older women

---

[20] See Section 7.2.2 in [5] and Section 5.2.2 in [5]

but there is no clear explanation of this difference. Both surveys suggest similar patterns of variation in intakes with age and gender and convey similar messages about the composition of diet.

There are many issues left unstudied. Here are two examples.

The time and age variation in nutrient intakes revealed here partly reflect (a) cohort-specific differences arising from early habit formation, and (b) calendar time related events such as appearance of new food technology, for example the introduction of low saturated fat spreads. Disentangling these influences is an interesting avenue for research which may lead to improved understanding of the impact of public health policies on behaviour.

The long time series of nutrient intakes shown here can be produced by cohort, region, and by other classifications of households and people. There is then the exciting prospect of linking these disaggregated time series to similarly disaggregated time series of mortality and morbidity, adding to the epidemiological evidence on the links between British diet and health.

For these and other purposes the National Food Survey is a most valuable resource.

References

[1] Department of Health, *Nutrition and Bone Health*. Report on Health and Social Subjects: 49. London: The Stationery Office, 1998.

[2] Department of Health. *Dietary Reference Values for Food Energy and Nutrients for the United Kingdom*. Report on Health and Social Subjects: 41. London: HMSO, 1991.

[3] Chesher, A.D. Diet Revealed? Semiparametric Estimation of Nutrient Intake - Age Relationships (with discussion). *Journal of the Royal Statistical Society, A*, 1997; 160: 389-428.

[4] Chesher, A.D. Individual Demands from Household Aggregates: Time and Age Variation in the Composition of Diet. *Journal of Applied Econometrics*, 1998; 13: 505-524.

[5] Gregory, J., Foster, K., Tyler, H., and Wiseman, M. *The Dietary and Nutritional Survey of British Adults*. London, HMSO: 1990.

[6] Gregory, J.R., Collins, D.L., Davies, P.S,W., Hughes, J.M., and Clarke, P.C. *National Diet and Nutrition Survey: children aged 1½ to 4½ years, Volume 1: Report of the diet and nutrition survey*. London, HMSO: 1995.

[7] Finch, S., Doyle, W., Lowe, C., Bates, C.J., Prentice, A., Smithers, G., and Clarke, P.C. *National Diet and Nutrition Survey: people aged 65 years and over, Volume 1: Report of the diet and nutrition survey*. London, The Stationery Office: 1998.

[8] *National Diet and Nutrition Survey: young people aged 4 to 18 years, Volume 1: Report of the diet and nutrition survey (in preparation)*.

Table 5.1a National Food Survey based estimates of average nutrient intakes per person per day. Children and young people aged 4 to 18, 1995 - 1998. All food excluding confectionery, soft and alcoholic drinks.

Nutrient	Gender	Age in years 4 - 6	7 - 10	11 - 14	15 - 18
Energy (kcal)	M	1425 *41*	1719 *38*	1998 *38*	2103 *41*
	F	1292 *40*	1423 *39*	1564 *38*	1634 *41*
Total fats (g)	M	63 *2.4*	76 *2.2*	89 *2.2*	96 *2.4*
	F	59 *2.4*	64 *2.3*	70 *2.2*	75 *2.4*
Saturated fatty acids (g)	M	25.6 *0.77*	28.8 *0.73*	32.5 *0.72*	33.8 *0.78*
	F	23.8 *0.77*	24.4 *0.74*	25.7 *0.73*	26.6 *0.77*
Calcium (mg)	M	670 *17*	730 *16*	809 *16*	840 *17*
	F	615 *16*	610 *16*	643 *16*	677 *17*
Iron (mg)	M	7.4 *0.22*	8.7 *0.21*	10.0 *0.21*	10.3 *0.23*
	F	6.27 *0.22*	6.82 *0.21*	7.58 *0.21*	7.94 *0.22*
Vitamin D (µg)	M	1.80 *0.11*	1.67 *0.11*	1.98 *0.11*	2.25 *0.11*
	F	1.56 *0.11*	1.40 *0.11*	1.67 *0.11*	2.00 *0.11*
Folate (µg)	M	166 *5.6*	204 *5.3*	240 *5.3*	246 *5.7*
	F	148 *5.6*	165 *5.4*	186 *5.3*	198 *5.6*
Copper (mg)	M	0.62 *0.03*	0.76 *0.03*	0.92 *0.03*	1.03 *0.03*
	F	0.57 *0.03*	0.63 *0.03*	0.72 *0.03*	0.78 *0.03*
Zinc (mg)	M	5.5 *0.16*	6.4 *0.16*	7.6 *0.15*	8.3 *0.17*
	F	4.9 *0.16*	5.2 *0.16*	5.6 *0.16*	6.0 *0.16*

Figures in italics are estimated standard errors.

Table 5.1b National Diet and Nutrition Survey estimates of average nutrient intakes per person per day. Children and young people aged 4 to 18, January 1997 – January 1998. All food.

Nutrient	Gender	Age in years			
		4 - 6	7 - 10	11 - 14	15 - 18
Energy (kcal)	M	1520 *22*	1777 *22*	1968 *29*	2285 *42*
	F	1397 *21*	1598 *19*	1672 *24*	1622 *29*
Total fats (g)	M	60 *1.1*	70 *1.1*	77 *1.4*	89 *1.8*
	F	56 *1.1*	64 *0.9*	67 *1.1*	64 *1.4*
Saturated fatty acids (g)	M	25.1 *0.5*	28.3 *0.5*	30.3 *0.6*	34.7 *0.8*
	F	23.8 *0.5*	25.7 *0.4*	26.2 *0.5*	24.7 *0.6*
Calcium (mg)	M	706 *19*	741 *15*	799 *19*	878 *23*
	F	657 *17*	656 *13*	641 *16*	653 *17*
Iron (mg)	M	8.2 *0.2*	9.7 *0.2*	10.8 *0.2*	12.5 *0.3*
	F	7.3 *0.2*	8.4 *0.2*	8.8 *0.2*	8.7 *0.2*
Vitamin D (µg)	M	2.1 *0.09*	2.4 *0.07*	2.6 *0.08*	3.2 *0.13*
	F	1.8 *0.07*	2.1 *0.08*	2.2 *0.08*	2.1 *0.08*
Folate (µg)	M	191 *4.5*	212 *3.7*	245 *5.2*	305 *8.9*
	F	169 *4.2*	188 *3.6*	205 *4.7*	210 *5.3*
Copper (mg)	M	0.70 *0.02*	0.81 *0.01*	0.90 *0.02*	1.06 *0.02*
	F	0.64 *0.02*	0.74 *0.01*	0.79 *0.02*	0.80 *0.02*
Zinc (mg)	M	5.5 *0.13*	6.1 *0.10*	7.1 *0.13*	8.7 *0.20*
	F	4.9 *0.10*	5.7 *0.09*	5.9 *0.11*	6.1 *0.14*

Figures in italics are estimated standard errors.

Table 5.2a National Food Survey based estimates of average nutrient intakes per person per day. Children aged 1½ years to 4½ years, 1991 - 1994. Home food supplies excluding confectionery, soft and alcoholic drinks.

Nutrient	Gender	Age in years		
		1½ - 2½	2½ - 3½	3½ - 4½
Energy (kcal)	M	993 *54*	1043 *46*	1093 *43*
	F	1019 *55*	1065 *47*	1106 *43*
Total fats (g)	M	46 *3*	48 *3*	49 *2*
	F	49 *3*	50 *3*	51 *2*
Saturated fatty acids (g)	M	20.3 *1.0*	20.3 *0.9*	20.4 *0.8*
	F	20.4 *1.1*	20.6 *0.9*	20.7 *0.8*
Calcium (mg)	M	624 *21*	612 *18*	600 *16*
	F	576 *21*	568 *18*	561 *17*
Iron (mg)	M	5.8 *0.3*	5.8 *0.3*	5.9 *0.2*
	F	5.6 *0.3*	5.6 *0.3*	5.7 *0.2*
Vitamin D (μg)	M	2.54 *0.16*	2.16 *0.14*	1.85 *0.13*
	F	2.28 *0.16*	2.02 *0.14*	1.80 *0.13*
Folate (μg)	M	120 *7.4*	125 *6.4*	130 *5.9*
	F	120 *7.6*	126 *6.5*	133 *6.0*
Copper (mg)	M	0.29 *0.04*	0.31 *0.04*	0.32 *0.03*
	F	0.35 *0.04*	0.37 *0.04*	0.38 *0.03*
Zinc (mg)	M	3.15 *0.27*	3.18 *0.24*	3.22 *0.22*
	F	3.22 *0.28*	3.28 *0.24*	3.33 *0.22*

Figures in italics are estimated standard errors.

Table 5.2b National Diet and Nutrition Survey estimates of average nutrient intakes per person per day. Children aged 1½ years to 4½ years, July 1992 - June 1993. All food.

Nutrient	Age in years			
			Male	Female
	1½ - 2½	2½ - 3½	3½ - 4½	3½ - 4½
Energy (kcal)	1045 *10.2*	1160 *9.8*	1273 *16.8*	1183 *15.6*
Total fats (g)	42.5 *0.52*	46.3 *0.50*	50.1 *0.85*	47.2 *0.87*
Saturated fatty acids (g)	19.7 *0.27*	20.8 *0.26*	21.9 *0.41*	20.6 *0.42*
Calcium (mg)	663 *11.4*	635 *10.5*	625 *14.3*	595 *13.6*
Iron (mg)	4.9 *0.07*	5.4 *0.07*	6.1 *0.11*	5.6 *0.10*
Vitamin D (µg)	1.2 *0.05*	1.2 *0.04*	1.4 *0.07*	1.3 *0.05*
Folate (µg)	120 *1.8*	133 *2.0*	143 *3.0*	138 *2.9*
Copper (mg)	0.4 *0.01*	0.5 *0.01*	0.5 *0.01*	0.5 *0.01*
Zinc (mg)	4.3 *0.06*	4.4 *0.06*	4.7 *0.09*	4.4 *0.09*

Figures in italics are estimated standard errors.

Table 5.3a National Food Survey based estimates of average nutrient intakes per person per day. Adults aged 16 to 64, 1985 - 1988. Home food supplies, excluding confectionery, soft and alcoholic drinks.

Nutrient	Gender	\multicolumn{4}{c}{Age in years}			
		16-24	25-34	35-49	50-64
Energy (kcal)	M	2158 *34*	2136 *45*	2337 *51*	2604 *52*
	F	1663 *35*	1695 *52*	2140 *54*	2592 *49*
Total fats (g)	M	99 *1.9*	105 *2.5*	114 *2.8*	124 *2.9*
	F	78 *2.0*	82 *2.9*	105 *3.0*	125 *2.7*
Saturated fatty acids (g)	M	40.6 *0.7*	42.9 *1.0*	46.8 *1.1*	51.8 *1.1*
	F	31.5 *0.8*	34.2 *1.1*	44.3 *1.2*	53.0 *1.0*
Calcium (mg)	M	861 *13*	876 *17*	934 *19*	1000 *19*
	F	681 *13*	797 *19*	1009 *20*	1118 *18*
Iron (mg)	M	11.3 *0.19*	11.8 *0.25*	12.8 *0.28*	13.5 *0.28*
	F	9.0 *0.19*	10.2 *0.28*	12.4 *0.30*	13.9 *0.27*
Vitamin D (µg)	M	3.01 *0.10*	2.91 *0.13*	3.25 *0.14*	3.96 *0.15*
	F	2.10 *0.10*	2.39 *0.15*	3.53 *0.16*	4.23 *0.14*
Folate (µg)	M	215 *4*	238 *6*	266 *6*	291 *6*
	F	179 *4*	218 *6*	283 *7*	323 *6*

Figures in italics are estimated standard errors.

Table 5.3b Dietary and Nutritional Survey of British Adults aged 16 to 64 years. Estimates of average nutrient intakes per person per day. Adults aged 16 to 64 years, October 1986 - August 1987. All food.

Nutrient	Gender	Age in years				
		16-24	25-34	35-49	50-64	16-64
Energy (kcal)	M	2460 *47*	2440 *38*	2500 *32*	2380 *31*	2450 *18*
	F	1700 *32*	1670 *29*	1730 *23*	1610 *23*	1680 *13*
Total fats (g)	M	103.5 *2.1*	103.1 *1.8*	103.3 *1.5*	99.4 *1.5*	102.3 *0.9*
	F	73.6 *1.6*	73.6 *1.5*	75.5 *1.2*	70.9 *1.2*	73.5 *0.7*
Saturated fatty acids (g)	M	41.6 *0.97*	41.7 *0.86*	42.0 *0.70*	42.7 *0.77*	42.0 *0.40*
	F	30.4 *0.74*	30.9 *0.73*	31.7 *0.57*	30.8 *0.59*	31.1 *0.32*
Calcium (mg)	M	894 *23*	931 *20*	960 *17*	949 *16*	937 *9*
	F	675 *19*	699 *17*	760 *14*	739 *13*	726 *8*
Iron (mg)	M	12.6 *0.29*	13.8 *0.36*	14.2 *0.26*	13.9 *0.28*	13.7 *0.15*
	F	9.8 *0.28*	10.2 *0.25*	11.0 *0.25*	10.6 *0.23*	10.5 *0.13*
Vitamin D (µg)	M	2.81 *0.14*	3.16 *0.15*	3.71 *0.14*	3.80 *0.17*	3.43 *0.08*
	F	2.10 *0.09*	2.30 *0.10*	2.61 *0.09*	2.82 *0.12*	2.51 *0.05*
Folate (µg)	M	302 *7.6*	317 *6.4*	321 *5.6*	300 *5.7*	311 *3.1*
	F	198 *4.7*	206 *4.4*	220 *3.7*	218 *3.9*	213 *2.1*

Figures in italics are estimated standard errors.

Table 5.4a National Food Survey based estimates of average nutrient intakes per person per day - Adults aged 65 and over, 1993 - 1996. All food excluding confectionery, soft and alcoholic drinks.

Nutrient	Gender	Age in years		
		65-74	75-84	85+
Energy (kcal)	M	2485 *52*	2287 *69*	2112 *168*
	F	2300 *47*	2160 *56*	1939 *132*
Total fats (g)	M	115 *2.9*	103 *3.9*	88 *9.5*
	F	105 *2.6*	99 *3.1*	87 *7.5*
Saturated fatty acids (g)	M	44.4 *0.9*	41.5 *1.3*	38.0 *3.2*
	F	42.7 *0.9*	41.3 *1.0*	36.8 *2.5*
Calcium (mg)	M	995 *20*	928 *27*	880 *66*
	F	1006 *18*	944 *22*	863 *52*
Iron (mg)	M	12.9 *0.28*	11.7 *0.38*	10.9 *0.92*
	F	12.0 *0.26*	11.0 *0.30*	9.5 *0.72*
Vitamin D (µg)	M	4.0 *0.15*	4.1 *0.19*	3.8 *0.47*
	F	3.9 *0.13*	3.4 *0.16*	2.7 *0.37*
Folate (µg)	M	320 *7*	290 *9*	278 *23*
	F	320 *6*	284 *8*	241 *18*
Copper (mg)	M	1.38 *0.04*	1.23 *0.05*	1.13 *0.12*
	F	1.37 *0.03*	1.19 *0.04*	0.99 *0.09*
Zinc (mg)	M	10.4 *0.2*	9.3 *0.3*	8.3 *0.7*
	F	9.4 *0.2*	8.7 *0.2*	7.7 *0.5*

Figures in italics are estimated standard errors.

Table 5.4b National Diet and Nutrition Survey estimates of average nutrient intakes per person per day. Free living adults aged 65 and over, October 1994 - September 1995. All food.

Nutrient	Gender	65-74	75-84	85+
Energy (kcal)	M	1954 *28*	1843 *27*	1713 *46*
	F	1445 *21*	1399 *23*	1374 *27*
Total fats (g)	M	76.1 *2*	72.4 *1*	69.2 *2*
	F	58.2 *1*	57.8 *1*	57.6 *1*
Saturated fatty acids (g)	M	30.8 *0.7*	30.0 *0.7*	31.1 *1.2*
	F	24.7 *0.6*	24.5 *0.6*	26.0 *0.8*
Calcium (mg)	M	852 *17*	813 *18*	764 *26*
	F	704 *15*	680 *17*	647 *19*
Iron (mg)	M	11.1 *0.2*	10.8 *0.2*	10.4 *0.4*
	F	9.0 *0.2*	8.4 *0.2*	7.7 *0.2*
Vitamin D (µg)	M	4.25 *0.21*	3.81 *0.16*	3.18 *0.22*
	F	2.96 *0.16*	3.03 *0.17*	2.31 *0.12*
Folate (µg)	M	282 *6*	249 *6*	234 *9*
	F	215 *5*	201 *5*	184 *6*
Copper (mg)	M	1.17 *0.04*	1.04 *0.04*	0.87 *0.04*
	F	0.91 *0.03*	0.83 *0.04*	0.79 *0.04*
Zinc (mg)	M	9.0 *0.15*	8.4 *0.17*	8.1 *0.26*
	F	7.0 *0.12*	6.7 *0.15*	6.4 *0.18*

Figures in italics are estimated standard errors.

Appendix A

Structure of the Survey

Introduction

The National Food Survey is a continuous sampling enquiry into the domestic food consumption and expenditure of private households in the United Kingdom (since the introduction of Northern Ireland into the Survey in January 1996). Each household, which participates, does so voluntarily, and without payment, for one week only. By regularly changing the households surveyed, information is obtained continuously throughout the year, apart from a short break over the Christmas period.

Household food and drink

Structure of the sample for Great Britain

The sample for the National Food Survey in Great Britain is selected so as to be representative of mainland Britain (including Anglesey and the Isle of Wight, but not the Scilly Isles, the area north of the Caledonian Canal nor the islands of the Scottish mainland). The size of the sample was reduced in January 1997 but, with an improved design, standard errors were relatively unaffected. From January 1997 the primary sampling unit has been postcode sectors with addresses being drawn from the Small Users Postcode Address File (PAF). The sample is stratified by three variables: the 24 regions that comprise the Government Office Regions Metropolitan split; the proportions of heads of household in Socio-Economic Groups 1 - 5 or 13 (in 3 bands); and the proportions of households with no car. Three hundred and seventy two postcode sectors (or groups of postcode sectors) are selected annually with probability proportional to size of the sector (measured as the number of addresses in England and Wales, and by multiple occupancy indicator, which gives the number of households at an address, in Scotland) and allocated equally to months. Each year half of the selected sectors are retained from the previous year's sample and half replaced by a new selection from the same stratum. The Local Authority Districts containing the 372 sectors used in 1998 are shown in Table A2.

Within each selected postcode sector, 28 addresses are sampled. At multi-household addresses in England and Wales, up to two extra households are selected per address, with a maximum of four extra households in any one postcode sector. In Scotland the 28 addresses are selected with probability proportional to the multiple occupancy indicator and then one household is selected at each address. The field periods used by the interviewers are calendar months. Interviewers are instructed to spread the diary periods evenly throughout the field period.

In 1998, 10,416 addresses were selected at the second stage of sampling. When visited, a few of these addresses were found to be institutions or other establishments not eligible for inclusion in the survey; others were found to be unoccupied or demolished. In addition, some addresses were found to contain more than the allowable number of households (see above). After allowing for these factors, the estimated number of eligible households in the survey was 9,226. In some households, the prospective diary keeper was interviewed but refused to give any information; a number of other diary keepers answered a questionnaire, relating to the household composition, occupation, etc. but declined to keep a week's record; a further group were lost or rejected at the editing stage. The result was a responding sample of 5,973 individual households, representing 64.7 per cent of the eligible sample. In 1997 there were 6,065 households in the sample (a response rate of 65.4 per cent). Details for 1998 are as follows:

Table A1 Responding sample to the Main Survey in Great Britain[a], 1998

	Households	Household selected (%)
Number of households at the addresses selected in the sample	9226	100
Non-contact	403	4
Interview refused or not practicable	2212	24
Diary keeper answered a questionnaire but declined to keep a week's record	638	7
Total non-productive	3253	35
Number of responding households	5973	64.7

(a) the sample in Northern Ireland consisted of 735 responding households

Table A3 shows how the achieved sample of 5,973 households in Great Britain was distributed according to various characteristics recorded in the Survey. In terms of the percentage breakdowns of the sample, it shows:

(a) more low income heads of household (groups C and D) in 1998 than in 1997; fewer higher income heads of household (groups A1, B and E1).

(b) the percentage in various categories being more extreme than in any year since 1992. These include:

> (i) more single-parent households; fewer households with 3 or more adults with children.

> (ii) more households owning accommodation outright; fewer owning with a mortgage.

> (iii) more in furnished rented accommodation; fewer in non-council unfurnished rented accommodation.

> (iv) more main diary keepers aged 35-44; fewer heads of household under 25.

None of these differences in sample profiles has had much effect on the final results except the first (income). The sample for 1998 shows expenditure on food and drink as £16.94 per person per week compared with £16.71 in 1997; an increase of 1.4 per cent. Although having fewer high-income households in the 1998 sample (relative to the 1997 sample) would have tended to reduce expenditure, having more low-income and pensioner households would have tended to offset the reduction. In fact, the offset was only partial and based on the 1997 sample profile expenditure in 1998 would have been £17.10. Thus it could be argued that a better estimate of the increase in 1998 was 2.3 per cent, not 1.4 per cent. However, these two estimates are consistent with each other once sampling variability is taken into account. The standard error of total expenditure is 1.0 per cent (Table A5). Thus the 1998 estimate is more likely than not (i.e. 50 per cent confidence) to lie in the range £16.75 to £17.13 and 1997 in the range £16.52 to £16.90.

Information collected

The person, male or female, principally responsible for domestic food arrangements provides information about each household. That person is referred to as the main "diary keeper". The main diary keeper keeps a record, with guidance from an interviewer, of all food, intended for human consumption, entering the home each day for seven days. The Main Survey therefore excludes pet food and any meals out except those based on food from the household supply, e.g. picnics, packed lunches, etc and school milk. The inclusion of school milk in the Main Survey rather than in the Eating Out Survey is to preserve continuity with household food as defined before the latter Survey was introduced. The Main Survey also covers soft and alcoholic drinks and chocolate and sugar confectionery brought home, although these are items which are typically likely to be purchased by individual household members for their own consumption without coming to the attention of the main diary keeper.

The following details are noted for each food item: the description, quantity (in either imperial or metric units) and – in respect of purchases – the cost. Food items obtained free from a farm or other business owned by the household member or from the hedgerow, a garden or allotment is recorded only at the time it is used. To avoid the double counting of purchases, gifts of food and drink are excluded if a donating household bought them.

As well as the details about foods entering the household, the diary keeper also notes which persons (including visitors) are present at each meal together with a description of the type (but not the quantities) of food served. This enables an approximate check to be made between the foods served and those acquired during the week. Records are also kept of the number and nature (whether lunch, dinner, etc.) of the meals obtained outside the home by each member of the household; this is used in the nutritional calculations – see below. The quantity of school milk consumed by children is also recorded.

On a separate questionnaire, details are entered of the characteristics of the family and its members. However names are not collected and the identities of both the persons and the addresses are strictly confidential; only those who were involved respectively with selecting the sample and carrying out the fieldwork know them. They are not divulged to the Ministry of Agriculture, Fisheries and Food who are responsible for analysing and reporting the Survey results.

As the main part of the Survey records only the quantities of food entering the household, and not the amount actually consumed by individuals, it cannot provide meaningful frequency distributions of households classified according to levels of food eaten or of nutrient intake. However, averaged over sufficient households, the quantities recorded should equate to consumption (in the widest sense, including waste food that is discarded or fed to pets) provided purchasing habits are not disturbed by participation in the Survey and there is no net accumulation or depletion of household food stocks.

Nutritional analysis

The energy value and nutrient content of food obtained for consumption in the home[1] are evaluated using special tables of food composition. The nutrient conversion factors are mainly based on values given in The Composition of Foods[2] and its supplements. The conversion factors are revised each year to reflect changes as a result of any new methods of food production, handling and fortification, and also to take account of changes in the structure of the food categories used in the Survey e.g. changes in the relative importance of the many products grouped under the heading of "reduced fat spreads". The nutrient factors used make allowance for inedible materials such as the bones in meat and the outer leaves and skins of vegetables. For certain foods, such as potatoes and carrots, allowance is also made for seasonal variations in the wastage and/or nutrient content. Further allowances are made for the expected cooking losses of thiamin and vitamin C; average thiamin retention factors are applied to appropriate food items within each major food group and the (weighted) average loss over the whole diet is estimated to be about 20 per cent. The losses of vitamin C are set at 75 per cent for green vegetables and 50 per cent for other vegetables. However, no allowance is made for wastage of edible food, except when the adequacy of the diet is being assessed in comparison with recommended intakes (see below). In that context, the assumption is made that, in each type of household, 10 per cent of all foods and hence of all nutrients available for consumption is either lost through wastage or spoilage in the kitchen or on the plate, or is fed to domestic pets/live-stock[3].

The energy content of the food is calculated from the protein, fat, available carbohydrate (as monosaccharide) and alcohol contents using the respective conversion factors (4, 9, 3.75 and 7 kcal per gram). It is expressed both in kilocalories and MegaJoules (1,000 kcal = 4.184 MJ). Niacin is expressed as niacin equivalent, which includes one-sixtieth of the tryptophan content of the protein in the food. Vitamin A activity is expressed as micrograms of retinol equivalent, that is the sum of the weights of retinol and one-sixth of the β-carotene. Fatty acids are grouped according to the number of double bonds present, that is into saturated, monounsaturated (both cis and trans) and polyunsaturated fatty acids. For the diet as a whole, the fatty acids constitute about 95 per cent of the weight of the fat. This proportion varies slightly for individual

---

[1] See Glossary

[2] B Holland, A. A Welch, I D Unwin, D H Buss, A A Paul and D A T Southgate, *McCance and Widdowson's The Composition of Foods* 5th edition, Royal Society of Chemistry and Ministry of Agriculture, Fisheries and Food, Royal Society of Chemistry, 1991

[3] An enquiry into the amounts of potentially edible food which are thrown away or fed to pets in Great Britain recorded an average wastage of about 6 per cent of household food supplies (see R W Wenlock, D H Buss, B J Derry and E J Dixon, *British Journal of Nutrition,*, 43, 1980, pp 53 - 70). However, this was considered likely to be a minimum estimate, and the conventional Survey deduction of 10 per cent was retained thereby preserving continuity with previous years.

foods, being lower for dairy fats with their greater content of short-chain acids and a little higher for most other foods.

The nutritional results are tabulated in two main ways for each category of households in the Survey:

a) Per person (per day). This presentation is directly comparable to the per person (per week) presentation in Section 2 of this Report of the amounts of food obtained. However, it has some drawbacks where the interpretation of nutrient intakes is concerned. It does not take into account contributions made by meals consumed outside the home or by foods outside of the diary keepers' purview (e.g. confectionery or drinks bought for household consumption without the knowledge of the diary keeper). Nor is any allowance made for the wastage of edible food. The average per person can also be misleading. For example, average per capita energy intakes in families with small children are invariably less than those for wholly adult households but this does not by itself indicate that the former are less well nourished because, on average, children have a smaller absolute need for energy.

b) As a proportion of Dietary Reference Values published by the Department of Health[4]. Some of the above drawbacks are overcome in this presentation. It involves comparing intakes with household needs after the age, sex and possible pregnancy of each member have been taken into account. Allowance is also made for meals eaten outside the home and for the presence of visitors by re-defining, in effect, the number of people consuming the household food – not by adding or subtracting estimates of the nutrient content of the meals in question. Moreover, for these comparisons, the estimated energy and nutrient contents are reduced throughout by 10 per cent to allow for wastage of edible food. This difference should be borne in mind when comparing these results with the nutritional intakes per person.

---

[4] Department of Health. *Dietary Reference Values for Food Energy and Nutrients for the United Kingdom.* Report on Health and Social Subjects No 41, HMSO, 1991

Table A2 Districts surveyed in 1998

Government Office Region	Coverage of regions by county/unitary authority	Districts containing postcode sectors selected for the 1998 sample
North East	Hartlepool UA, Middlesborough UA, Redcar & Cleveland UA, Stockton-on-Tees UA, Durham, Northumberland, Tyne-and-Wear	Alnwick, Chester-le-Street, Darlington, Derwentside, Gateshead, Langbaugh, Newcastle-Upon-Tyne, North Tyneside, Sedgefield, Stockton-on-Tees, Sunderland, Tynedale, Wansbeck,
North West (incl. Merseyside)	Cumbria, Cheshire, Lancashire, Greater Manchester, Merseyside	Allerdale, Blackburn, Blackpool, Bolton, Carlisle, Chester, Congleton, Crewe, Ellesmere Port, Hyndburn, Lancaster, Macclesfield, Oldham, Salford, South Lakeland, South Ribble, Stockport, Tameside, Trafford, Wigan, Knowsley, Liverpool, Sefton, St Helens, Wirral
Yorkshire and the Humber	City of Kingston-upon-Hull UA, East Riding of Yorkshire UA, North East Lincolnshire UA, North Lincolnshire UA, York UA, North Yorkshire, South Yorkshire, West Yorkshire	Barnsley, Booth Ferry, Bradford, Calderdale, Cleethorpes, Doncaster, Glanford, Grimsby, Hambleton, Harrogate, Kingston-upon-Hull, Kirklees, Leeds, Rotherham, Sheffield
East Midlands	Derby UA, Derbyshire, Leicester UA, Rutland UA, Leicestershire, Lincolnshire, Northamptonshire, Nottinghamshire	Bassetlaw, Bolsover, Charnwood, Chesterfield, Daventry, Derby, East Lindsey, Gedling, Harborough, Hinchley, Leicester, Mansfield, Melton, Northampton, Nottingham, Oadby & Wigston, Rotherham, South Kesteven, Wellingborough, West Derbyshire
West Midlands	Hereford and Worcester, Shropshire, Stoke-on-Trent UA, Staffordshire, Warwickshire, West Midlands	Birmingham, Bridgnorth, Bromsgrove, Cannock Chase, Coventry, Dudley, Lichfield, North Warwickshire, Nuneaton, Sandwell, Solihull, South Staffordshire, Stafford, Staffordshire Moorland, Stoke-on-Trent, Stratford-on-Avon, The Wrekin, Walsall, Warwick
East	Cambridgeshire, Norfolk, Suffolk, Luton UA, Bedfordshire, Essex, Hertfordshire	Babergh, Basildon, Cambridge, Chelmsford, Colchester, Dacorum, East Cambridgeshire, Epping Forest, Fenland, Great Yarmouth, Harlow, Huntingdon, Ipswich, Luton, Mid Suffolk, North Norfolk, Norwich, Rochford, South Bedfordshire, South Cambridgeshire, Southend-on-Sea, St Albans, St Edmundsbury, Stevenage, Suffolk Coastal, Tendring, Watford, Welwyn Hatfield

London	London	Barking, Barnet, Bexley, Brent, Bromley, Camden, Croydon, Ealing, Enfield, Greenwich, Hackney, Hammersmith, Haringey, Havering, Hillingdon, Hounslow, Islington, Kensington & Chelsea, Kingston Upon Thames, Lambeth, Lewisham, Merton, Redbridge, Sutton, Tower Hamlets, Waltham Forest, Wandsworth
South East	Berkshire, Milton Keynes UA, Buckinghamshire, Brighton and Hove UA, East Sussex, Portsmouth UA, Southampton UA, Hampshire, Isle of Wight UA, Kent, Oxfordshire, West Sussex, Surrey	Arun, Ashford, Aylesbury Vale, Bracknell, Brighton, Canterbury, Cherwell, Chichester, Crawley, Dartford, Eastbourne, Eastleigh, Gillingham, Gosport, Guildford, Havant, Lewes, Maidstone, Medina, Mole Valley, New Forest, Portsmouth, Reading, Reigate, Runnymede, S. Bucks – Beaconsfield, Sevenoaks, Shepway, South Oxfordshire, South Wight, Southampton, Surrey Heath, Tonbridge, Wealden, Woking, Wycombe
South West	Bath and North East Somerset UA, City of Bristol UA, North Somerset UA, South Gloucestershire UA, Cornwall, Devon, Bournemouth UA, Poole UA, Dorset, Gloucestershire, Somerset, Swindon UA, Wiltshire	Bath, Bournemouth, Bristol, Caradon, Carrick, Christchurch, Cotswold, Gloucester, Plymouth, Poole, Restormel, South Hams, Taunton Deane, Teignbridge, Wansdyke, West Dorset, West Somerset, Weymouth, Wimbourne, Woodspring, Yeovil
Wales	The whole of Wales	Aberconwy, Alyn and Deeside, Cardiff, Delyn, Dinefwr, Islwyn, Llanelli, Montgomery, Neath, Newport, Preseli, Rhondda, Swansea, Taff Ely, Torfaen, Vale of Glamorgan, Wrexham Maelor
Scotland	The whole of Scotland excluding the area north of the Caledonian Canal and the islands off the Scottish mainland	Aberdeen, Argll & Bute, Dumbarton, Dundee, Dunfermline, East Lothian, Edinburgh, Falkirk, Glasgow, Gordon, Hamilton, Inverclyde, Kirkcaldy, Mid Lothian, Monklands, Moray, Perth & Kinross, Renfrew, Strathkelvin, Tweeddale, Wigtown

Table A3 Composition of the sample responding to the Main Survey, 1998

	Households Number	Households %	Persons Number	Persons %	Average number of persons per household	% owning Deep-freezer	% owning Micro-wave
All Households (GB)	5973	100	14735	100	2.47	94	80
Analysis by Government Office Region							
North East	350	5.9	891	6.0	2.55	93	86
North West	713	11.9	1784	12.1	2.50	94	83
Yorkshire and the Humber	497	8.3	1233	8.4	2.48	94	81
East Midlands	407	6.8	997	6.8	2.45	95	78
West Midlands	525	8.8	1395	9.5	2.66	95	82
East	523	8.8	1294	8.8	2.47	93	80
London	618	10.3	1474	10.0	2.39	92	71
South East	873	14.6	2135	14.5	2.45	95	80
South West	567	9.5	1353	9.2	2.39	94	81
England	5073	84.9	12556	85.2	2.48	94	80
Wales	359	6.0	838	5.7	2.33	93	83
Scotland	541	9.1	1341	9.1	2.48	93	84
Northern Ireland[a]	735	12.3	2100	14.3	2.86	82	79
Analysis by income group of head of household[b]							
A1	147	2.5	456	3.1	3.10	99	90
A2	269	4.5	811	5.5	3.01	97	89
B	1543	25.8	4476	30.4	2.90	96	88
C	1608	26.9	4448	30.2	2.77	95	85
D	403	6.7	1000	6.8	2.48	92	79
E1	599	10.0	1058	7.2	1.77	94	74
E2	723	12.1	1524	10.3	2.11	91	72
OAP	681	11.4	962	6.5	1.41	86	63
Analysis by household composition[c]							
No of Adults / No of children							
1 / 0	1510	25.3	1510	10.2	1.00	85	67
1 / 1 or more	350	5.9	966	6.6	2.76	93	83
2 / 0	1960	32.8	3920	26.6	2.00	96	80
2 / 1	484	8.1	1452	9.9	3.00	97	88
2 / 2	622	10.4	2488	16.9	4.00	99	91
2 / 3	209	3.5	1045	7.1	5.00	100	88
2 / 4 or more	78	1.3	499	3.4	6.40	100	83
3 / 0	393	6.6	1179	8.0	3.00	98	89
3 or more / 1 or 2	218	3.6	1009	6.8	4.63	99	90
3 or more / 3 or more	18	0.3	127	0.9	7.06	100	78
4 or more / 0	131	2.2	540	3.7	4.12	98	92
Analysis by ownership of dwelling							
Unfurnished, council	1181	19.8	2821	19.1	2.39	89	72
Unfurnished, other, rented	223	3.7	512	3.5	2.30	90	76
Furnished, rented	278	4.7	537	3.6	1.93	84	68
Rent free	62	1.0	133	0.9	2.15	95	82
Owns outright	1673	28.0	3363	22.8	2.01	95	76
Owns with mortgage	2534	42.4	7319	49.7	2.89	97	89
Shared ownership	22	0.4	50	0.3	2.27	95	95
Analysis by age of main diary keeper							
Age under 25	284	4.8	658	4.5	2.32	92	81
25 - 34	1181	19.8	3327	22.6	2.82	94	84
35 - 44	1212	20.3	4056	27.5	3.35	95	85
45 - 54	1092	18.3	2897	19.7	2.65	96	86
55 - 64	876	14.7	1746	11.8	1.99	95	82
65 - 74	772	12.0	1278	8.7	1.66	92	73
75 and over	550	9.2	764	5.2	1.39	87	57
Age unrecorded	6	0.1	9	0.1	1.50	67	83

(a) Northern Ireland is not included elsewhere in this table. The sample size for Northern Ireland is proportionally bigger than that for Great Britain. This is allowed for when compiling the estimates for the United Kingdom shown in some tables in Section 2 of this report
(b) for definition of income groups see Table A4 of this Appendix and Glossary
(c) see 'adult' and 'child' in the Glossary

Table A4 Distribution of the 1998 sample responding to the Main Survey according to income group of the head of household

Income Group	Gross weekly income of head of household (a)	Number of households	% in whole sample	percentage of households in groups A1 to D realised	target
Households with one or more earner (b)					
A1	£910 or more	147	2.5	3.7	3
A2	£640 but less than £910	269	4.5	6.8	7
B	£330 but less than £640	1543	25.8	38.9	40
C	£160 but less than £330	1608	26.9	40.5	40
D	Less than £160	403	6.7	10.2	10
Total A to D		3970	66.5		
Households without an earner (b)					
E1	£160 or more	599	10.0		
E2	Less than £160	723	12.1		
Pensioner households (c)					
OAP		681	11.4		
Total all households		5973	100		

(a) or of the principle earner if the head of the household was below £160 (the upper limit for group D)
(b) by convention, the short-term unemployed are classified as 'earners', until they have been out of work for more than a year
(c) see Glossary

Table A5 Standard errors by household food group, 1998

		Expenditure (pence) Mean	Standard error	SE(%)	Consumption (grams unless otherwise stated) Mean	Standard error	SE(%)
Milk and cream	(ml)	134.4	1.3	1.0	2045	18.1	0.9
Cheese		51.7	0.9	1.8	104	1.8	1.8
Carcase meat		104.2	2.2	2.1	244	6.2	2.6
Beef and veal		52.7	1.4	2.7	109	2.9	2.7
Mutton and lamb		24.6	1.1	4.6	59	3.9	6.5
Pork		27.0	0.9	3.2	76	2.7	3.6
Bacon and ham, uncooked		35.9	1.2	1.9	76	2.5	2.2
Poultry, uncooked		65.8	1.6	2.0	217	5.7	2.3
Other meat and meat products		139.3	2.5	1.8	697	5.5	1.7
Fish		77.3	1.8	2.3	146	3.3	2.3
Eggs	(no)	17.0	0.3	2.0	1.74	0	1.9
Fats and oils		36.2	0.7	1.9	195	4.3	2.2
Sugar and preserves		16.8	0.4	2.5	156	3.9	2.5
Vegetables		227.8	2.5	1.1	2365	24.1	1.2
Fruit		131.5	2.0	1.5	1090	16.2	1.5
Cereals (incl. bread)		267.9	2.8	1.1	1480	13.9	0.9
Beverages		48.9	1.9	2.2	58	1.3	2.9
Other foods		81.7	1.4	1.7	434	0.4	10.7
Total food (£)		**14.79**	**0.13**	**0.9**	na	na	na
Soft drinks	(ml)	51.9	1.0	2.0	1384	17.8	2.0
Alcoholic drinks	(ml)	120.3	9.1	6.8	388	14.7	3.8
Confectionery		30.3	0.9	3.0	56	1.5	2.7
Total food and drink (£)		**16.94**	**0.17**	**1.0**	na	na	na

Food and drink eaten out

The eating out (EO) part of the National Food Survey aims to collect information on expenditure and consumption of food and drink eaten outside the home, to supplement the information on household food and drink collected in the Main Survey. The results complete the assessment of all food and drink consumed by households in Great Britain (and expenditure, although only that by persons and not purchased on business). It is not run in Northern Ireland.

Structure of the sample

The Eating Out Survey is conducted on a sub-sample of half of the households selected for the main sample in Great Britain. For the main part (as described above), the primary sampling units are postcode sectors, with 28 addresses being sampled within these sectors, and up to four extra households where multi-household addresses are discovered. The households selected for inclusion in the Eating Out sample are the even-numbered addresses from the 28 (and any extra) households in the postcode sectors, i.e. address numbers 2, 4, 6, etc. Before the new sample design was introduced in January 1997, the Eating Out Survey was conducted on 26 of the 52 Local Authority Districts selected for the main sample. The response to the Eating Out Survey is shown in Table A6. No eating out data is accepted unless the household diary has been completed satisfactorily, in order to cross check certain entries and emphasise the completeness of records taken together. Households where one or more members initially decline to keep an eating out diary are excluded from the Eating Out Survey, although those households may still keep a household diary. Those households that complete the household diary and eating out diary for each member are said to have responded fully (55 per cent of the eligible sample). Households that complete a main diary and return satisfactory eating out records for some, but not all, members are partial respondents. These records have been included in the analysis, giving a total response rate to the Eating Out Survey of 58 per cent of eligible households. The composition of the sample is given in Tables A8 and A9. Standard errors for expenditure and consumption estimates in 1997 and 1998 are given in Table A10. For expenditure on all food and drink, the percentage standard error was 3.1 per cent in 1998.

Information collected

Participating households are asked to carry out the Main Survey in the normal way, with the main diary keeper recording household food. Each member of the household over the age of 11, including visitors staying with the household, is additionally given a diary to record all personal consumption of, and expenditure on, snacks, meals, confectionery and drinks eaten outside the home (not from household supplies). The diaries cover both food eaten by the respondent and food paid for by the respondent but consumed by others. The eating out of children under 11 is recorded and separately identified in the main diary keeper's diary.

Table A6 Responding sample to the Eating Out Survey, 1998

	Households	Households selected (%)
Number of households at the addresses selected in the sample	4568	100
Number that could not be visited for operational reasons	-	-
Number visited but no contact made	208	5
Main Survey requirements		
Interview refused or not practicable	1137	25
Diary keeper answered a questionnaire but declined to keep a week's record	326	7
Number of responding households for Main Survey data	2897	63
Eating Out requirements		
Main Survey diary and interview complete: some valid EO diaries	136	3
Main Survey diary and interview complete: all valid EO diaries	2531	55
Total responding EO households	2663	58

The following details are recorded in the eating out diary for each food item; the description, the number and size of certain items (where possible), the cost (where the respondent paid), the type of outlet where it was bought, and whether it was consumed on or off the premises. In addition, respondents also note for themselves each day which meals were eaten out, and which eaten at home or at another home, so as to provide a check for the eating out record in the main (household) diary.

The scheme for analysing the types of food eaten out is necessarily much more complex than that for the Main Survey, since many more foods comprise a number of ingredients and quantities are not collected. There are approximately 1600 individual food codes for eating out, compared with around 230 for household food, many meals and snacks contain items that must be coded separately in order to allow an accurate estimate of consumption and nutrient intakes to be made, for example chicken, gravy, roast potatoes and one or more types of vegetable in a roast chicken dinner. However, it may not be possible to put a cost on every item, so the expenditure may be attributed to a complete dish (course) or to a whole meal or snack code. Where prices are given for individual or component items, these are generally attributed to the item.

For estimating consumption and nutrient intakes, each food code is assigned both a portion size and values for energy and nutrients. Portion sizes were obtained from a variety of sources including catering outlets, MAFF's Food Portion Size book, the Dietary and Nutritional Survey of British Adults and package weights. For those foods obtained from a chain outlet or fast food outlet, or other foods with a fairly standard portion size, it is possible to be reasonably confident of the data used. For foods from other restaurants and eating places, the best estimates of portion sizes are made and these are reviewed annually.

The variety of types of foods and drink that are obtained for eating out causes some problems when estimating consumption and nutrient intakes. Estimated portion sizes and nutrient values may vary significantly for similar products. Some foods have a range of codes according to the approximate size of the portion, e.g. a small, standard or large chocolate bar or portion of chips, although others have a single average portion size which is applied in all cases (regardless of the age or gender of the consumer). Interviewers often need to probe for more precise details, such as whether a food was 'low fat' or whether a beverage had sugar added. Such probing is not always possible, or may not provide the detail desired, so some assumption must be made in coding the item.

A number of efforts are made to reduce the possibility of expenditure or consumption being overlooked or omitted by respondents, including the completion of a daily summary grid indicating where main meals and snacks were eaten, if at all. Some respondents record no eating out at all over the survey week and these records are accepted unless there is a reason to suspect under-recording or it appears strongly inconsistent with the meal record kept by the main diary keeper in the household diary. Table A7 shows the percentage of people in the Eating Out Survey for whom no expenditure was recorded classified by the income group of the head of household. Generally, those in lower income groups were more likely to record no expenditure on eating out, particularly for food and soft drinks. Forty three per cent of all respondents spent no money on food and drink eaten out.

Table A7 Percentage of people in the EO Survey with no EO expenditure in the survey week, by income group of the head of household, 1998

Income group	Percentage with no EO spending on:				
	Food	Soft drinks	Confectionery	Alcohol	Any food or drink
A1	35	74	79	76	31
A2	35	71	85	83	32
B	38	74	84	81	34
C	44	76	84	84	38
D	56	80	85	87	49
E1	58	89	96	84	54
E2	67	87	92	91	63
OAP	73	98	100	93	70
Total	48	79	87	85	43

The Eating Out Survey was conducted for two years on a trial basis before results were first published in the 1994 annual report. In that time it underwent a number of methodological changes to improve data quality. The Family Expenditure Survey conducted by the Office for National Statistics provides an alternative source of information on the eating out expenditure of households and this appears to record higher levels of spending, particularly on alcoholic drinks. The results of the Eating Out Survey are monitored on a quarterly basis and further improvements in data quality and completeness are being sought.

Nutritional analysis

A separate nutrient database has been created for the Eating Out Survey, based largely on MAFF's Nutrient Databank for the National Diet and Nutrition Survey (NDNS) programme, with additional composite or recipe dishes being created where necessary. Each food code is assigned both a portion size and a total of 44 nutrients, including energy, protein, carbohydrates, fat and fatty acids, alcohol and a range of vitamins and minerals. These values are estimated using The Composition of Foods and its supplements, together with information gained from manufacturers and fast food and restaurant chains for specific products. The nutrient values used make allowance for inedible materials such as bones in meat but no allowance has been made for food wastage since there is as yet no reliable information on the proportion of food wasted when eaten out. Both the nutrient information and the portion size assigned to each food are reviewed annually and updated as appropriate.

The nutritional results have been tabulated by region, income group of head of hosehold and household composition in the same way as for the Main Survey. In addition they have also been tabulated by age and gender since, unlike the Main Survey, the eating out information is collected by individuals. The nutritional results from the Eating Out Survey have been added to the nutritional results from the Main Survey (plus soft and alcoholic drinks and confectionery) for households completing the Eating Out Survey, in order to express the total nutrient intakes as a proportion of the Dietary Reference Values (Table 4.14). For this analysis the Reference Nutrient Intakes (RNIs) for the individual nutrients and the Estimated Average Requirement (EAR) for energy were weighted for the sample in the Eating Out Survey. These weighted reference values will differ from those used in the analysis of the Main Survey because of the difference in composition of the two samples. For the comparisons between total intakes and the RNIs, the estimated intakes of energy and nutrients in the component coming from the Main Survey (excluding soft and alcoholic drinks and confectionery) are reduced by 10 per cent to allow for wastage of edible food.

Table A8 Composition of the sample responding to the Eating Out Survey by age and gender, 1998

Age	Male	Female	Total
Unknown	2	1	3
0-4	189	198	387
5-14	452	413	865
15-24	282	346	628
25-34	391	490	881
35-44	418	474	892
45-54	383	444	827
55-64	344	349	693
65-74	267	317	584
75+	159	246	405
Total	2887	3278	6165

Table A9 Composition of the sample of households responding to the Eating Out Survey, 1998

	Households [a] Number	%	Persons [b] Number	%	Average number [b] of persons per household
All Households	2663	100	6165	100	2.32
Analysis by Government Office Region					
North East	156	5.6	382	6.2	2.45
North West	340	12.8	827	13.4	2.43
Yorkshire and the Humber	192	7.2	408	6.6	2.13
East Midlands	178	6.7	406	6.6	2.28
West Midlands	221	8.3	524	8.5	2.37
East	219	8.2	497	8.1	2.27
London	262	9.8	572	9.3	2.18
South East	406	15.2	945	15.3	2.33
South West	270	10.1	637	10.3	2.36
England	2244	84.3	5198	84.3	2.32
Wales	167	6.3	384	6.2	2.30
Scotland	252	9.5	583	9.5	2.31
Analysis by income group of head of household					
A1	56	2.1	164	2.7	2.93
A2	126	4.7	381	6.2	3.02
B	667	25.0	1787	29.0	2.68
C	712	26.7	1863	30.2	2.62
D	179	6.7	424	6.9	2.37
E1	278	10.4	475	7.7	1.71
E2	321	12.1	628	10.2	1.96
OAP	324	12.2	443	7.2	1.37
Analysis by household composition					
Number of adults / Number of children					
1 / 0	709	26.6	709	11.5	1.00
1 / 1 or more	163	6.1	449	7.3	2.75
2 / 0	910	34.2	1788	29.0	1.96
2 / 1	207	7.8	607	9.8	2.93
2 / 2	262	9.8	1011	16.4	3.86
2 / 3	78	2.9	373	6.1	4.78
2 / 4 or more	28	1.1	162	2.6	5.79
3 / 0	157	5.9	448	7.3	2.85
3 or more / 1 or 2	95	3.6	401	6.5	4.22
3 or more / 3 or more	6	0.2	41	0.7	6.83
4 or more / 0	48	1.8	176	2.9	3.67
Analysis by ownership of dwelling					
Unfurnished, council	521	19.6	1149	18.6	2.22
Unfurnished, other, rented	109	4.1	249	4.0	2.28
Furnished, rented	107	4.0	204	3.3	1.91
Rent free	22	0.8	42	0.7	1.91
Owns outright	777	29.2	1500	24.3	1.96
Owns with mortgage	1118	42.0	3004	48.7	2.69
Joint ownership	9	0.3	17	0.3	1.89

(a) fully or partially responding households
(b) number of persons for whom satisfactory diaries completed

Table A10 Standard errors for selected Eating Out results, 1997 and 1998

	Mean	1997 Standard error (a)	SE (%)	Mean	1998 Standard error	SE (%)
Consumption (grams):						
Ethnic foods	38	2.1	5.5	41	2.2	5.4
Meat and meat products	107	2.9	2.7	110	2.9	2.6
Fish and fish products	23	0.9	3.9	25	1.1	4.4
Cheese and egg dishes and pizza	27	1.2	4.4	27	1.2	4.4
Potatoes and vegetables	192	5.8	3.0	197	6.1	3.1
Salads	22	1.1	5.0	21	1.3	6.2
Rice, pasta and noodles	27	1.4	5.2	27	1.5	5.6
Soup (ml)	16	1.0	6.3	16	1.2	7.5
Baby food	...	0.2	50.0	...	0.1	100.0
Breakfast cereal	1	0.1	10.0	1	0.1	10.0
Fruit (fresh and processed)	22	1.0	4.5	19	1.0	5.3
Yoghurt	6	0.5	8.3	6	0.6	10.0
Bread	14	0.5	3.6	15	0.6	4.0
Sandwiches	50	2.9	5.8	45	1.5	3.3
Rolls	31	1.3	4.2	28	1.2	4.3
Sandwich/roll extras	8	0.3	3.8	8	0.3	3.8
Miscellaneous foods (e.g. sauces, butter)	18	0.7	3.9	18	0.7	3.9
Other additions (e.g. sugar, salt, cream)	13	0.7	5.4	11	0.6	5.5
Beverages (ml)	406	18.5	4.6	395	18.3	4.6
Ice creams, desserts and cakes	56	1.6	2.9	51	1.5	2.9
Biscuits	11	0.9	8.2	11	0.8	7.3
Crisps, nuts and snacks	11	0.5	4.5	10	0.4	4.0
Soft drinks including milk (ml)	348	13.3	3.8	318	12.4	3.9
Alcoholic drinks (ml)	491	22.3	4.5	435	19.1	4.4
Confectionery	19	0.8	4.2	17	0.7	4.1
Expenditure (£)						
Total food and drink	6.61	0.15	2.3	6.73	0.21	3.1
of which:						
Alcoholic drink	1.58	0.02	1.3	1.52	0.03	2.0

(a) standard errors for 1997 are slightly different to those published in the 1997 report as they have been calculated to be comparable with those for 1998 which do not take the complex sample design into account

Appendix B

Supplementary Tables for the Main Survey

List of supplementary tables

		Page
B1	Household consumption of individual foods: quarterly and annual national averages, 1998	120
B2	Average prices paid for household foods, 1995 – 1998	128
B3	Average number of mid-day and total meals eaten per week outside the home, 1998	132
B4	Average number of mid-day meals per week by source, per child aged 5 – 14 years, 1998	133
B5	Household food consumption of main food groups by income group, 1998	134
B6	Household food expenditure on main food groups by income group, 1998	136
B7	Household food expenditure on main food groups by household composition, 1998	138
B8	Household food consumption by household composition groups within income groups: selected food items, 1998	140
B9	Nutritional value of household food: national averages, 1995 – 1998	142
B10	Nutritional value of household food by government office region, 1998	143
B11	Nutritional value of household food by income group, 1998	145
B12	Nutritional value of household food by household composition, 1998	146
B13	Contribution made by selected foods to the nutritional value of household food: national averages, 1998	147

Table B1 Household consumption of individual foods: quarterly and annual national averages, 1998

grams per person per week, unless otherwise stated

		Jan/March	April/June	July/Sept	Oct/Dec	Yearly Average (Consumption)	Yearly Average (Purchases)	Percentage of all households purchasing each type of food during survey week
MILK AND CREAM								
Liquid wholemilk, full price [a]	(ml)	645	733	641	649	667	658	37
Welfare milk	(ml)	5	26	10	12	13	…	…
School milk	(ml)	13	10	11	18	13	8	2
Skimmed milk [a]	(ml)	1167	1057	1136	1080	1110	1107	64
Condensed milks	(eq ml)	18	15	16	16	16	16	3
Infant milks	(eq ml)	37	33	14	16	25	21	1
Instant milks	(eq ml)	17	17	16	12	15	15	1
Other milks and dairy desserts [a]	(ml)	44	42	49	40	44	44	17
Yoghurt and fromage frais [a]	(ml)	135	129	119	120	126	125	38
Cream	(ml)	15	18	16	17	17	17	12
Total milk and cream		**2095**	**2080**	**2027**	**1980**	**2045**	**2010**	**92**
CHEESE								
Natural [a]		92	99	94	93	94	94	49
Processed		9	10	10	10	10	10	10
Total cheese		**101**	**110**	**104**	**103**	**104**	**104**	**53**
MEAT AND MEAT PRODUCTS								
Carcase meat								
Beef and veal [a]		116	100	105	114	109	108	31
Mutton and lamb [a]		52	61	61	62	59	57	14
Pork [a]		73	74	78	77	76	75	21
Total carcase meat		**242**	**236**	**243**	**254**	**244**	**240**	**48**
Liver [a]		5	3	5	4	4	4	3
Offal, other liver		2	1	1	1	1	1	1
Bacon and ham, uncooked [a]		82	73	71	76	76	75	36
Bacon and ham, cooked including canned		35	42	42	40	40	40	36
Cooked poultry, not canned [a]		27	35	37	31	33	33	19
Corned meat		12	12	13	9	11	11	10
Other cooked meat, not canned		6	6	7	7	7	7	8
Other canned meats and meat products		30	32	33	28	31	31	13
Broiler chicken, and parts uncooked, Including frozen		145	136	133	124	134	134	29
Other poultry, uncooked [a]		77	74	70	114	84	83	12
Rabbit and other meats		4	1	…	1	1	1	…
Sausages, uncooked, pork		48	53	44	45	47	47	20
Sausages, uncooked, beef		15	15	11	12	13	13	5
Meat pies and sausage rolls, ready to eat [a]		19	21	24	21	21	21	13
Frozen convenience meats and meat products [a]		76	82	75	78	78	77	24
Pate and delicatessen type sausage [a]		9	7	7	9	8	8	9
Other meat products [a]		109	113	105	105	108	108	39
Total other meat and meat products		**702**	**705**	**677**	**703**	**697**	**694**	**84**
Total meat and meat products		**944**	**941**	**920**	**957**	**941**	**934**	**86**
FISH								
White, filleted, fresh		19	16	12	13	15	15	7
White, unfilleted, fresh		8	1	2	1	3	3	…
White, uncooked, frozen		18	15	19	17	18	18	8
Herring, filleted, fresh		1	…	1	…	…	…	…
Herring, unfilleted, fresh		…	…	…	…	…	…	…
Fatty, fresh, other than herring		12	17	17	13	15	14	6
White, processed		5	4	5	5	5	5	3
Fatty, processed, filleted		3	2	1	1	2	2	1
Fatty, processed, unfilleted		2	2	3	3	2	2	2
Shellfish		4	5	4	7	5	5	4
Cooked fish		11	11	9	12	11	11	7
Canned salmon		7	8	6	6	6	6	5
Other canned or bottled fish		23	26	23	21	23	23	16
Fish products, not frozen [a]		10	14	14	10	12	12	9
Frozen convenience fish products		28	28	30	28	28	28	13
Total fish		**150**	**150**	**145**	**137**	**146**	**144**	**52**

Table B1 *continued*

grams per person per week, unless otherwise stated

	Consumption					Purchases	Percentage of all households purchasing each type of food during survey week
	Jan/March	April/June	July/Sept	Oct/Dec	Yearly Average	Yearly Average	
EGGS	1.75	1.80	1.73	1.68	1.74	1.68	41
FATS							
Butter [a]	35	41	35	42	39	39	22
Margarine [a]	25	25	30	22	26	25	9
Lard and compound cooking fat	9	8	7	8	8	8	4
Vegetable and salad oils	50	43	39	62	49	49	9
Other fats [a]	77	74	68	77	74	74	29
Total fats	**196**	**191**	**179**	**212**	**195**	**194**	**55**
SUGAR AND PRESERVES							
Sugar	114	124	112	125	119	119	23
Jams, jellies and fruit curds	16	18	14	19	17	16	9
Marmalade	14	11	14	15	14	13	7
Syrup, treacle	3	2	2	3	2	2	1
Honey	5	5	4	5	5	5	2
Total sugar and preserves	**152**	**160**	**147**	**166**	**156**	**155**	**34**
VEGETABLES							
Fresh potatoes [a]	723	716	684	737	715	690	54
Fresh green vegetables							
Cabbages, fresh	52	50	54	61	54	51	16
Brussels sprouts, fresh	29	2	5	36	18	17	8
Cauliflower, fresh	93	86	87	84	88	86	29
Leafy salads, fresh	44	66	66	37	53	52	31
Peas, fresh	3	7	10	4	6	5	4
Beans, fresh	9	12	44	14	20	12	7
Other fresh green vegetables	8	7	7	8	7	7	3
Total fresh green vegetables	**238**	**231**	**273**	**244**	**246**	**231**	**58**
Other fresh vegetables							
Carrots, fresh	122	108	105	114	112	109	37
Turnips and swedes, fresh	40	20	18	33	28	27	9
Other root vegetables, fresh	34	13	18	28	23	21	10
Onions, shallots, leeks, fresh	103	84	83	98	92	87	33
Cucumbers, fresh	27	41	46	22	34	33	21
Mushrooms, fresh	38	35	34	34	35	35	27
Tomatoes, fresh	85	101	120	79	96	90	41
Miscellaneous fresh vegetables	63	60	77	62	66	63	27
Total other fresh vegetables	**511**	**462**	**501**	**470**	**486**	**465**	**72**
Processed potatoes							
Chips, excluding frozen	26	30	24	27	27	27	15
Instant potato	2	2	1	2	2	2	1
Canned potato	5	10	8	5	7	7	2
Potato products, not frozen [a]	51	55	54	54	53	53	38
Frozen chips and other frozen convenience potato products	112	114	102	116	111	111	19
Total processed potatoes	**196**	**211**	**189**	**204**	**200**	**199**	**54**
Processed other vegetables							
Tomatoes, canned or bottled	41	38	43	47	42	42	14
Canned peas	34	31	30	28	31	31	13
Canned beans [a]	113	113	116	128	118	117	31
Canned vegetables other than pulses, potatoes or tomatoes	25	26	29	24	26	26	12
Dried pulses, other than air-dried	6	4	5	9	6	6	2
Air dried vegetables	...	2	1	1	1	1	1
Vegetable juices	11	8	6	6	8	8	4
Other vegetable products [a]	38	44	44	31	39	39	24
Frozen peas	37	32	33	34	34	34	9
Frozen beans	11	9	8	4	8	8	2
All frozen vegetables and frozen vegetable products, nse	56	43	46	40	46	46	12
Total processed other vegetables	**372**	**350**	**361**	**352**	**359**	**359**	**63**
Total potatoes	**919**	**927**	**873**	**941**	**915**	**889**	**76**
Total other vegetables	**1121**	**1043**	**1135**	**1066**	**1091**	**1054**	**86**

Table B1 continued

grams per person per week, unless otherwise stated

	Consumption					Purchases	Percentage of all households purchasing each type of food during survey week
	Jan/ March	April/ June	July/ Sept	Oct/ Dec	Yearly Average	Yearly Average	
FRUIT							
Fresh							
Oranges	80	66	61	46	63	63	13
Other citrus fruit	102	51	46	102	75	75	21
Apples	188	173	180	182	181	173	41
Pears	49	42	31	53	44	43	14
Stoned fruit	22	35	91	16	41	40	14
Grapes	45	30	49	37	40	40	16
Soft fruit, other than grapes	7	33	40	5	21	18	8
Bananas	195	198	206	192	198	197	49
Rhubarb	2	6	5	…	3	1	…
Other fresh fruit	30	46	96	28	50	50	11
Total fresh fruit	**718**	**681**	**806**	**662**	**716**	**701**	**70**
Other fruit and fruit products							
Canned peaches, pears and pineapple	19	20	14	16	17	17	7
Other canned and bottled fruit	19	21	18	21	20	20	8
Dried fruit and dried fruit products	14	17	13	27	18	18	7
Frozen fruit and fruit products	1	2	2	2	2	1	1
Nuts and nut products	9	10	10	25	14	14	9
Fruit juices (ml)	299	331	325	262	304	304	32
Total other fruit and fruit products	**361**	**401**	**381**	**354**	**374**	**373**	**46**
Total fruit	**1079**	**1081**	**1187**	**1016**	**1090**	**1074**	**77**
CEREALS							
White bread, standard loaves, unsliced	58	50	60	75	61	60	14
White bread, standard loaves, sliced	215	245	217	196	218	218	33
White bread premium loaves	135	141	153	151	145	145	24
White bread softgrain loaves	28	14	18	14	18	18	3
Brown bread	70	64	70	72	69	69	17
Wholemeal bread	90	83	78	71	81	81	18
Other bread [a]	138	174	149	140	150	149	48
Total bread	**735**	**770**	**745**	**719**	**742**	**742**	**88**
Flour	46	44	42	87	55	55	6
Buns, scones and teacakes	49	39	39	38	41	41	22
Crispbread	5	5	5	5	5	5	5
Cakes and pastries (not frozen)	78	84	92	97	88	87	38
Biscuits, other than chocolate biscuits [a]	81	81	83	81	81	81	34
Chocolate biscuits	49	51	49	53	51	50	28
Oatmeal and oatmeal products	12	10	9	12	11	11	4
Breakfast cereals [a]	138	133	138	133	136	135	38
Canned milk puddings	24	26	20	29	25	25	9
Other puddings	5	3	3	12	6	6	3
Rice [a]	76	56	57	54	61	61	17
Cereal based invalid foods (including 'slimming' foods)	…	…	…	…	…	…	…
Infant cereal foods	1	1	2	1	1	1	1
Frozen convenience cereal foods [a]	46	40	43	49	45	44	18
Cereal convenience foods, including canned, nse [a]	121	138	130	122	128	127	46
Other cereal foods	5	4	5	3	4	4	2
Total cereals	**1471**	**1485**	**1462**	**1495**	**1478**	**1475**	**94**
BEVERAGES							
Tea	35	34	36	36	35	35	25
Coffee, beans and ground	3	4	4	5	4	4	3
Coffee, instant	12	13	12	12	12	12	19
Coffee, essence (ml)	…	…	…	…	…	…	…
Cocoa and drinking chocolate	4	3	2	4	3	3	3
Branded food drinks	3	3	2	4	3	3	2
Total beverages	**57**	**56**	**57**	**62**	**58**	**58**	**41**

Table B1 *continued*

grams per person per week, unless otherwise stated

		Jan/March	April/June	July/Sept	Oct/Dec	Yearly Average (Consumption)	Yearly Average (Purchases)	Percentage of all households purchasing each type of food during survey week
MISCELLANEOUS								
Mineral water	(ml)	110	141	124	118	124	124	8
Baby food, canned and bottled		6	6	4	6	5	5	1
Soups, canned		91	55	53	87	71	71	20
Soups, dehydrated and powdered		4	2	2	4	3	3	5
Spreads and dressings [a]		17	25	26	19	22	22	13
Pickles and sauces		90	102	94	96	96	95	34
Meat and yeast extracts		3	3	3	4	3	3	7
Table jellies, squares and crystals		2	2	3	2	3	3	3
Ice cream, mousse	(ml)	37	53	53	36	45	45	7
Ice cream products and other frozen dairy foods [a]	(ml)	32	59	67	40	50	50	12
Salt		9	9	7	5	8	8	3
Novel protein foods		4	4	4	4	4	4	2
SOFT DRINKS								
Concentrated	(ml)	84	108	106	79	94	94	13
Ready to drink	(ml)	419	525	491	454	473	472	35
Low calorie, concentrated	(ml)	35	36	35	27	33	33	5
Low calorie, ready to drink	(ml)	244	287	306	267	276	276	19
Total soft drinks [b]	**(ml)**	**1258**	**1532**	**1502**	**1251**	**1384**	**1383**	**52**
ALCOHOLIC DRINKS								
Low alcohol beers, lagers and ciders	(ml)	2	3	2	...	2	2	...
Beers	(ml)	58	65	75	61	65	65	5
Lagers and continental beers	(ml)	92	169	127	123	128	128	8
Ciders and perry	(ml)	23	28	33	22	27	27	2
Wine	(ml)	114	156	120	148	135	134	16
LA wine, wine and spirit with additions	(ml)	5	7	4	4	5	5	1
Fortified wines	(ml)	9	10	5	13	9	9	2
Spirits	(ml)	13	10	14	21	15	15	4
Liqueurs	(ml)	1	1	1	4	2	2	1
Alcopops	(ml)	...	2	...	1	1	1	...
Total alcoholic drinks	**(ml)**	**317**	**451**	**383**	**398**	**388**	**387**	**28**
CONFECTIONERY								
Solid chocolate		11	13	11	14	12	12	13
Chocolate coated/filled bars/sweets		29	25	25	32	28	28	20
Chewing gum		1	1	1	1	1	1	3
Mints and boiled sweets [a]		11	13	14	13	13	13	12
Fudge, toffee, caramels		2	2	2	2	2	2	2
Total confectionery		**53**	**53**	**52**	**62**	**56**	**55**	**34**

(a) these foods are given in greater detail in this table under 'Supplementary classifications'
(b) converted to unconcentrated equivalent

Table B1 *continued*

grams per person per week, unless otherwise stated

Supplementary classification [c]		Consumption Jan/March	April/June	July/Sept	Oct/Dec	Yearly Average	Purchases Yearly Average	Percentage of all households purchasing each type of food during survey week
MILK AND CREAM								
Liquid wholemilk, full price:								
UHT	(ml)	6	16	9	18	13	13	1
Sterilised	(ml)	46	32	21	22	30	30	2
Other	(ml)	592	684	610	609	624	615	35
Total liquid wholemilk, full price	**(ml)**	**645**	**733**	**641**	**649**	**667**	**658**	**37**
Low fat milks:								
Fully skimmed	(ml)	169	144	189	155	164	164	12
Semi and other skimmed	(ml)	998	913	947	925	945	943	56
Total skimmed milks	**(ml)**	**1167**	**1057**	**1136**	**1080**	**1110**	**1107**	**64**
Other milks and dairy desserts:								
Dairy desserts	(ml)	26	29	28	27	27	27	14
Other milks	(ml)	18	13	21	14	16	16	3
Total other milks	**(ml)**	**44**	**42**	**49**	**40**	**44**	**44**	**17**
Yoghurt and fromage frais:								
Yoghurt	(ml)	119	109	105	105	109	109	34
Fromage frais	(ml)	16	20	14	15	16	16	7
Total yoghurt and fromage frais	**(ml)**	**135**	**129**	**119**	**120**	**126**	**125**	**38**
CHEESE								
Natural hard:								
Cheddar and cheddar type		60	65	62	62	62	62	35
Other UK varieties or foreign equivalents		12	11	13	12	12	12	9
Edam and other continental		6	8	7	7	7	7	7
Cottage		8	8	5	4	6	6	5
Other natural soft		7	7	6	9	7	7	8
Total natural cheese		**92**	**99**	**94**	**93**	**94**	**94**	**49**
CARCASE MEAT								
Beef: Joints (including sides) on the bone		1	...	...	...	...	...	...
Joints, boned		24	22	21	30	24	24	5
Steak, less expensive varieties		27	16	19	21	20	20	8
Steak, more expensive varieties		23	24	25	23	24	24	10
Minced		40	38	38	39	39	39	16
Other beef and veal		2	1	1	2	2	2	1
Total beef and veal		**116**	**100**	**105**	**114**	**109**	**108**	**31**
Mutton		...	...	1	1	1	1	...
Lamb: Joints (including sides)		28	38	36	34	34	32	6
Chops (including cutlets and fillets)		15	16	17	14	16	16	7
All other		10	7	7	13	9	9	3
Total mutton and lamb		**52**	**61**	**61**	**62**	**59**	**57**	**14**
Pork: Joints (including sides)		21	24	25	32	26	25	4
Chops		27	25	25	20	24	24	10
Fillets and steaks		11	11	12	10	11	11	5
All other		14	14	16	16	15	15	5
Total pork		**73**	**74**	**78**	**77**	**76**	**75**	**21**
OTHER MEAT AND MEAT PRODUCTS								
Liver: Ox		...	...	...	...	...	...	...
Lambs		3	2	3	2	3	3	2
Pigs		1	1	2	1	1	1	1
Other		...	...	...	...	...	...	...
Total liver		**5**	**3**	**5**	**4**	**4**	**4**	**3**

Table B1 *continued*

grams per person per week, unless otherwise stated

Supplementary classification [c]	Jan/March	April/June	July/Sept	Oct/Dec	Yearly Average (Consumption)	Yearly Average (Purchases)	Percentage of all households purchasing each type of food during survey week
OTHER MEATS AND MEAT PRODUCTS							
Bacon and ham, uncooked:							
Joints (including sides and steaks cut from the joint)	30	30	31	36	32	31	12
Rashers, pre-packed	37	34	29	28	32	32	20
Rashers, not pre-packed	16	10	12	11	12	12	7
Total bacon and ham, uncooked	**82**	**73**	**71**	**76**	**76**	**75**	**36**
Cooked poultry, not purchased in cans:	26	30	29	27	28	28	18
Takeaway cooked poultry	2	5	7	4	5	5	2
Total cooked poultry, not purchased in cans	**27**	**35**	**37**	**31**	**33**	**33**	**19**
Other poultry, uncooked, including frozen:							
Chicken other than broilers	43	42	51	47	46	46	5
Turkey	28	30	16	60	34	34	7
All other	6	2	2	7	4	4	1
Total poultry, uncooked, including frozen	**77**	**74**	**70**	**114**	**83**	**83**	**12**
Meat pies and sausage rolls, ready to eat:							
Meat pies	12	13	16	14	14	14	9
Sausage rolls, ready to eat	8	8	8	7	8	8	5
Total meat pies and sausage rolls, ready to eat	**19**	**21**	**24**	**21**	**21**	**21**	**13**
Frozen convenience meats or frozen convenience meat products:							
Burgers	16	22	15	13	17	17	7
Meat pies, pasties, puddings	11	14	12	17	13	13	5
Other frozen convenience meats	49	45	48	47	47	48	17
Total frozen convenience meats or frozen convenience meat products	**76**	**82**	**75**	**78**	**78**	**77**	**24**
Pate and delicatessen-type sausages:							
Pate	3	3	2	4	3	3	4
Delicatessen-type sausages	6	4	5	5	5	5	5
Total pate and delicatessen-type sausages	**9**	**7**	**7**	**9**	**8**	**8**	**9**
Other meat products:							
Meat pastes and spreads	1	1	1	1	1	1	2
Meat pies, pasties and puddings	28	25	30	33	29	29	14
Takeaway meat pies, pasties and puddings	1	2	1	2	1	1	1
Ready meals	29	31	25	27	28	28	12
Takeaway ready meals	31	33	29	27	30	30	11
Other meat products, not specified elsewhere	19	22	20	15	19	19	11
Total other meat products	**109**	**113**	**105**	**105**	**108**	**108**	**39**
FISH							
Fish products, not frozen:							
Fish products, not frozen	8	11	10	7	9	9	7
Takeaway fish products	2	2	4	4	3	3	2
Total fish products, not frozen	**10**	**14**	**14**	**10**	**12**	**12**	**9**

Table B1 *continued*

grams per person per week, unless otherwise stated

Supplementary classification [c]	Jan/ March	April/ June	July/ Sept	Oct/ Dec	Yearly Average (Consumption)	Yearly Average (Purchases)	Percentage of all households purchasing each type of food during survey week
FATS							
Butter: New Zealand	10	11	10	10	10	10	6
Danish	7	9	8	10	9	9	6
UK	8	12	7	10	9	9	5
Other	10	10	11	11	10	10	6
Total butter	35	41	35	42	39	39	22
Margarine: Soft	21	23	26	18	22	22	8
Other	4	2	4	4	3	3	2
Total margarine	25	25	30	22	26	26	9
Other fats:							
Reduced fat spreads	49	44	42	48	46	46	18
Low-fat spreads	24	23	20	24	23	23	10
Suet and dripping	1	1	1	2	1	1	1
Other fats	4	6	4	4	4	4	3
Total other fats	77	74	68	77	74	74	29
VEGETABLES							
Fresh potatoes:							
Previous years crop purchased Jan-Aug	617	461	174	...	311	304	na
Current years crop purchased Jan-Aug	106	255	260	...	155	146	na
Current years crop purchased Sept-Dec	...	...	249	737	250	240	na
Total fresh potatoes	723	716	684	737	715	690	54
Canned beans:							
Baked beans in sauce	104	103	104	117	107	107	28
Other canned beans and pulses	9	10	12	11	11	11	5
Total canned beans	113	113	116	128	118	117	31
Potato products, not frozen:							
Crisps and potato snacks	46	48	48	49	48	48	37
Other potato products, not frozen	4	7	6	5	6	6	3
Total potato products, not frozen	51	55	54	54	53	53	38
Other vegetable products:							
Other vegetable products	33	40	39	27	35	35	21
Other vegetables, takeaway	5	5	4	3	4	4	4
Total other vegetable products	38	44	44	31	39	39	24
CEREALS							
Other bread:							
Rolls (excluding starch reduced rolls)	61	80	71	66	70	70	27
Malt bread and fruit bread	7	9	7	5	7	7	4
Vienna bread and French bread	27	38	29	30	31	31	15
Starch reduced bread and rolls	7	6	6	5	6	6	2
Sandwiches	7	8	6	7	7	7	5
Other	28	31	31	26	29	29	14
Total other bread	138	174	149	140	150	149	49
Biscuits, other than chocolate:							
Sweet biscuits other than chocolate	70	70	71	70	70	70	39
Unsweetened biscuits	11	10	11	11	11	11	10
Total biscuits other than chocolate	81	81	83	81	81	81	49

Table B1 *continued*

grams per person per week, unless otherwise stated

Supplementary classification [c]	Consumption Jan/March	April/June	July/Sept	Oct/Dec	Yearly Average	Purchases Yearly Average	Percentage of all households purchasing each type of food during survey week
CEREALS							
Breakfast cereals:							
Muesli	16	9	13	11	12	12	3
Other high-fibre breakfast cereals	66	56	56	61	59	59	21
Sweetened breakfast cereals	24	29	32	24	27	27	11
Other breakfast cereals	33	40	37	38	37	37	14
Total breakfast cereals	**138**	**133**	**138**	**133**	**136**	**135**	**38**
Rice:							
Dried rice	56	40	41	40	44	44	10
Cooked rice	21	16	16	14	17	17	8
Total rice	**76**	**56**	**57**	**54**	**61**	**61**	**17**
Frozen convenience cereal foods:							
Cakes and pastries	14	10	11	14	12	12	5
Other	32	30	32	35	32	32	14
Total frozen cereal convenience foods, not specified elsewhere	**46**	**40**	**43**	**49**	**45**	**44**	**18**
Cereal convenience foods (including canned) not specified elsewhere:							
Canned pasta	34	30	28	20	28	28	11
Fresh and dried pasta	37	47	44	40	42	42	17
Cakes, puddings and dessert mixes	9	7	5	7	7	7	7
Cereal snacks	10	12	11	14	12	12	12
Pizza	12	18	16	18	16	16	7
Takeaway pizza	3	6	7	6	5	5	2
Other cereal convenience foods	16	18	19	17	18	18	15
Total cereal convenience foods, including canned, nse	**121**	**138**	**130**	**122**	**128**	**127**	**46**
MISCELLANEOUS							
Spreads and dressings:							
Salad dressings	15	24	24	16	20	20	12
Other spreads and dressings	2	1	2	3	2	2	2
Total spreads and dressings	**17**	**25**	**26**	**19**	**22**	**22**	**13**
Ice-cream products and other frozen dairy foods:							
Ice-cream products (ml)	28	50	57	37	43	43	10
Other frozen dairy foods (ml)	4	9	11	3	7	7	3
Total ice-cream products and other frozen dairy foods (ml)	**32**	**59**	**68**	**40**	**50**	**50**	**12**
CONFECTIONERY							
Mints and boiled sweets:							
Hard pressed mints	2	2	2	2	2	2	3
Boiled sweets	9	11	12	11	11	11	10
Total mints and boiled sweets	**11**	**13**	**14**	**13**	**13**	**13**	**12**

(c) supplementary data for certain foods in greater detail than shown elsewhere in the table; the totals for each main food are repeated for ease of reference

Table B2 Average prices paid[a] for household foods, 1995 – 1998

pence per kg, unless otherwise stated [b]

	\multicolumn{4}{c}{Average prices paid}
	1995	1996	1997	1998
MILK AND CREAM				
Liquid wholemilk, full price	54.4	52.9	52.4	50.9
Skimmed milks	52.0	51.5	50.7	50.1
Infant milks	92.9	82.2	93.1	98.1
Instant milks	40.1	52.6	50.0	45.6
Other milks	159.3	234.0	185.0	130.4
Yoghurt and fromage frais	199.8	203.9	210.1	208.1
Cream	286.2	284.3	276.9	270.7
CHEESE				
Natural	452.0	482.0	507.8	496.2
Processed	465.5	496.1	503.9	491.5
MEAT AND MEAT PRODUCTS				
Carcase meat:				
Beef and veal	487.9	484.8	496.8	487.3
Mutton and lamb	414.9	441.0	473.3	429.3
Pork	350.3	418.3	397.9	358.9
Other meat and meat products:				
Liver	239.8	232.5	255.0	271.7
Offals, other than liver	264.6	317.1	291.1	245.1
Bacon and ham, uncooked	427.0	493.1	500.7	476.7
Bacon and ham, cooked, including canned	587.9	612.4	635.4	630.6
Cooked poultry, not purchased in cans	524.1	541.1	521.0	536.3
Corned meat	302.1	309.1	291.2	291.7
Other cooked meat not purchased in cans	628.0	609.9	685.2	667.8
Other canned meat/canned meat products	191.6	195.0	177.1	202.8
Broiler chicken, uncooked, including frozen	267.2	313.4	336.9	340.5
Other poultry, uncooked, including frozen	216.8	273.6	275.1	242.7
Rabbit and other meats	275.7	472.1	440.0	326.9
Sausages, uncooked, pork	257.3	270.7	279.1	274.9
Sausages, uncooked, beef	203.0	233.9	228.1	221.1
Meat pies and sausage rolls, ready to eat	327.9	358.2	351.4	358.7
Other frozen convenience meats and meat products	354.5	369.4	381.7	419.0
Pate and delicatessen type sausages	518.8	519.4	545.9	534.1
Other meat products	589.8	564.5	602.0	612.7
FISH				
White, filleted, fresh	557.4	540.0	547.3	601.9
White, unfilleted, fresh	416.8	345.7	436.4	310.3
White, uncooked, frozen	462.4	466.9	493.0	509.3
Herring, filleted, fresh	184.8	346.6	327.4	337.3
Herring, unfilleted, fresh	296.6	271.8	272.0	327.1
Fatty, fresh, other than herring	583.0	573.5	617.2	583.0
White, processed	548.9	496.3	555.0	577.6
Fatty, processed, filleted	603.4	481.4	460.1	424.8
Fatty, processed, unfilleted	428.3	879.6	986.1	901.5
Shellfish	960.4	842.9	831.3	963.7
Cooked fish	780.3	751.7	757.0	814.6
Canned salmon	494.7	447.8	438.6	538.6
Other canned/bottled fish	279.3	278.7	284.2	298.8
Fish products, not frozen	725.7	689.5	732.3	646.4
Frozen convenience fish products	362.2	363.1	402.3	414.6
EGGS	9.6	10.1	10.1	10.1
FATS				
Butter	288.0	304.8	308.4	316.1
Margarine	109.7	107.8	109.6	114.0
Low fat and dairy spreads	83.8	182.6	187.2	187.5
Vegetable and salad oils	113.1	123.9	133.7	124.9
Other fats	190.7	214.3	162.6	194.0

Table B2 *continued*

pence per kg, unless otherwise stated [b]

	Average prices paid			
	1995	1996	1997	1998
SUGAR AND PRESERVES				
Sugar	70.4	77.2	74.9	71.4
Jams, jellies and fruit curd	188.4	201.1	205.5	230.3
Marmalade	172.7	188.6	188.0	194.9
Syrup, treacle	163.6	161.2	180.3	199.6
Honey	283.7	304.2	321.5	330.6
VEGETABLES				
Potatoes	49.0	40.3	35.4	49.4
Fresh vegetables:				
Cabbages	72.0	73.8	70.4	75.7
Brussels sprouts	99.6	94.2	93.7	101.5
Cauliflowers	112.7	105.0	102.5	101.9
Leafy salad	171.1	182.8	204.3	223.4
Peas	308.4	341.8	292.5	349.9
Beans	266.7	249.7	285.2	300.0
Other green vegetables	256.9	193.6	198.3	209.2
Carrots	54.2	57.1	52.1	58.2
Turnips and swedes	56.4	67.6	59.0	67.0
Other root vegetables	140.2	119.8	125.9	122.8
Onions, shallots, leeks	98.7	86.1	94.1	99.7
Cucumbers	139.4	130.3	125.3	127.8
Mushrooms	278.1	277.7	270.1	277.9
Tomatoes	130.8	141.5	134.0	147.5
Miscellaneous fresh vegetables	211.5	203.5	226.5	232.8
Processed vegetables:				
Tomatoes, canned/bottled	53.7	52.7	51.4	53.8
Canned peas	75.3	81.4	83.3	82.7
Canned beans	61.7	63.5	63.6	67.5
Canned vegetables, other than pulses	128.2	126.6	123.0	125.5
Dried pulses, other than air dried	124.9	136.7	129.5	110.4
Air-dried vegetables	336.6	396.7	434.7	443.7
Vegetable juices	154.0	176.4	183.6	156.2
Chips, excluding frozen	346.2	382.0	360.5	394.8
Instant potato	312.7	338.3	349.3	314.4
Canned potatoes	82.5	84.1	77.0	69.2
Potato products, not frozen	507.9	512.9	519.3	515.6
Other vegetable products	388.6	381.5	401.6	405.0
Frozen peas	120.4	137.7	133.0	132.3
Frozen beans	130.5	163.9	156.0	146.7
Frozen chips and other convenience potato products	125.4	117.4	103.0	110.1
All frozen vegetables/vegetable products, not specified elsewhere	169.8	180.3	192.6	190.4
FRUIT				
Fresh:				
Oranges	94.4	98.5	96.7	97.6
Other citrus fruit	114.0	125.1	120.1	123.4
Apples	103.4	111.3	112.3	110.6
Pears	106.3	106.9	102.1	113.2
Stone fruit	194.2	161.7	190.1	213.2
Grapes	236.8	221.0	247.7	247.4
Soft fruit, other than grapes	309.9	311.0	306.4	342.9
Bananas	87.2	91.7	100.1	105.8
Rhubarb	109.4	131.7	124.9	128.7
Other fresh fruit	105.3	111.8	119.5	123.6
Other fruit and fruit products:				
Canned peaches, pears and pineapple	97.4	106.3	103.5	110.0
Other canned or bottled fruit	141.2	155.5	155.1	156.1
Dried fruit and dried fruit products	235.3	248.0	256.7	251.2
Frozen fruits and frozen fruit products	395.8	240.4	350.9	330.3
Nuts and nut products	385.1	390.8	416.5	456.8
Fruit juices	73.9	77.5	78.2	74.9

Table B2 *continued*

pence per kg, unless otherwise stated [b]

	Average prices paid			
	1995	1996	1997	1998
CEREALS				
White bread, standard loaves, unsliced	98.0	86.2	87.4	85.9
White bread, standard loaves, sliced	52.7	57.2	55.1	52.8
White bread, sliced, premium	72.1	73.3	73.2	75.0
White bread, sliced, soft-grain	69.3	70.6	70.3	62.4
Brown bread	89.1	89.0	86.0	86.9
Wholemeal bread	81.8	81.5	80.6	82.3
Other bread	193.7	195.3	198.0	206.8
Flour	40.6	38.8	39.9	39.5
Buns, scones and teacakes	208.2	209.3	214.4	217.9
Cakes and pastries	324.5	332.1	334.6	347.7
Crisp-bread	283.2	277.4	298.1	303.9
Biscuits, other than chocolate	203.1	217.9	233.7	225.2
Chocolate biscuits	345.2	340.0	338.9	335.3
Oatmeal and oat products	109.0	125.7	113.5	129.2
Breakfast cereals	252.5	258.9	264.0	267.3
Canned milk puddings	104.2	119.0	116.3	116.4
Other puddings	380.2	387.3	408.3	423.0
Rice	212.1	171.7	196.6	229.9
Cereal based invalid foods (including 'slimming' foods)	1474.6	942.4	n/a	675.4
Infant cereal foods	911.5	619.1	983.1	1037.8
Frozen convenience cereal foods	340.1	347.0	364.0	379.9
Cereal convenience foods, including canned, not specified elsewhere	361.3	328.0	355.4	324.3
Other cereal foods	127.3	147.8	161.0	196.3
BEVERAGES				
Tea	462.5	471.7	489.9	549.0
Coffee, beans and ground	819.3	855.8	960.5	1001.4
Coffee, instant	1697.5	1577.9	1674.7	1797.5
Coffee, essences	496.4	452.8	556.5	671.6
Cocoa and drinking chocolate	344.2	388.6	437.1	552.2
Branded food drinks	516.4	509.8	531.6	521.3
MISCELLANEOUS				
Mineral water	41.9	42.7	41.5	44.4
Baby foods, canned/bottled	303.4	326.9	329.4	366.1
Soups, canned	112.3	119.3	128.8	135.5
Soups, dehydrated and powdered	741.2	671.4	763.4	774.1
Spreads and dressings	244.8	254.9	269.7	286.0
Pickles and sauces	218.4	230.9	240.1	252.1
Meat and yeast extracts	850.2	792.6	869.1	917.6
Table jellies, squares and crystals	274.2	259.4	264.5	278.9
Ice-cream, mousse	108.6	104.2	97.9	114.8
Ice-cream products and other frozen dairy foods	252.9	217.8	202.5	201.0
Salt	57.7	61.0	63.9	79.5
Novel protein foods	519.4	473.9	631.7	637.3
SOFT DRINKS				
Soft drinks, concentrated	87.0	93.3	93.8	91.0
Soft drinks, ready to drink	48.8	52.2	52.5	55.4
Low-calorie soft drinks, concentrated	78.0	78.7	89.8	94.8
Low-calorie soft drinks, ready to drink	48.1	50.6	51.4	51.5
ALCOHOLIC DRINKS				
Low alcohol beers, lagers and ciders	81.7	118.1	158.5	167.2
Beers	164.0	169.4	177.9	182.8
Lagers and continental beers	149.8	155.1	155.0	162.0
Ciders and perry	135.2	137.5	131.9	144.1
Wine	400.6	410.7	430.4	500.0
Low alcohol wine, wines and spirits with additions	343.2	268.1	289.5	273.3
Fortified wines	512.9	520.5	600.1	557.0
Spirits	1372.2	1330.9	1356.3	1379.2
Liqueurs	1427.2	1030.9	1094.2	1260.3
Alcopops	na	na	275.1	327.3

Table B2 *continued*

pence per kg unless otherwise stated [b]

	Average prices paid			
	1995	1996	1997	1998
CONFECTIONERY				
Solid chocolate	537.2	570.5	573.6	575.0
Chocolate coated and filled bars and sweets	530.0	527.2	563.1	565.8
Chewing gum	970.4	779.3	1001.7	1086.4
Mints and boiled sweets	433.6	421.4	441.8	461.8
Fudge, toffee and caramels	441.4	433.2	454.5	439.8

(a) it should be noted that since the results for household consumption presented in this Report include both purchases and 'free' food, average prices paid cannot in general be derived by dividing the expenditure on a particular food by average consumption.

(b) pence per kg, except for the following; per litre of milk, yoghurt, cream, vegetable and salad oils, vegetable and fruit juices, coffee essence, ice-cream, ice-cream products and other frozen dairy food, soft drinks, alcoholic drinks; per equivalent litre of condensed, dried and instant milk; per egg.

Table B3 Average number of mid-day and total meals per week eaten outside the home, 1998

per person per week

	Meals not from the household supply		Net balance [a]	
	Mid-day meals	All meals out [b]	Persons	Visitors
All households (GB)	1.83	3.01	0.86	0.05
Analysis by Government Office Region				
North East	2.01	3.05	0.86	0.05
North West	1.76	2.88	0.86	0.04
Yorkshire and the Humber	1.77	2.85	0.86	0.04
East Midlands	1.65	2.72	0.87	0.04
West Midlands	1.76	2.87	0.87	0.05
East	1.81	3.14	0.85	0.05
London	2.18	3.50	0.84	0.05
South East	1.85	3.12	0.85	0.05
South West	1.70	2.86	0.86	0.05
England	1.83	3.02	0.86	0.05
Wales	1.84	2.98	0.86	0.05
Scotland	1.77	3.00	0.86	0.05
Northern Ireland	1.89	3.11	0.85	0.05
Analysis by income group of HOH				
A1	2.93	4.74	0.77	0.10
A2	2.42	3.80	0.82	0.06
B	2.11	3.51	0.84	0.04
C	1.85	3.08	0.86	0.04
D	1.66	2.66	0.87	0.04
E1	1.10	1.91	0.91	0.06
E2	1.60	2.51	0.88	0.05
OAPs (all)	0.73	1.30	0.93	0.04
Analysis by household composition				
Number of adults / Number of children				
1 / 0	1.71	3.25	0.84	0.08
1 / 1 or more	2.65	4.10	0.81	0.06
2 / 0	1.43	2.51	0.88	0.06
2 / 1	2.02	3.24	0.85	0.04
2 / 2	2.00	3.15	0.85	0.03
2 / 3	1.74	2.63	0.88	0.03
2 / 4 or more	1.92	2.63	0.88	0.03
3 / 0	1.75	3.07	0.85	0.05
3 or more / 1 or 2	2.16	3.37	0.85	0.03
3 or more / 3 or more	1.74	2.27	0.89	0.03
4 or more / 0	1.92	3.26	0.85	0.03
Analysis by age of main diary-keeper				
Under 25	2.02	3.53	0.83	0.05
25 – 34	2.29	3.84	0.82	0.04
35 – 44	2.09	3.24	0.85	0.04
45 – 54	1.96	3.25	0.85	0.05
55 – 64	1.22	2.14	0.90	0.07
65 – 74	0.85	1.50	0.93	0.06
75 and over	0.82	1.40	0.93	0.03
Analysis by house tenure				
Unfurnished; council	1.66	2.62	0.88	0.04
Other rented	2.00	3.40	0.84	0.04
Furnished; rented	2.62	4.29	0.80	0.06
Rent free	1.56	2.77	0.87	0.05
Owned outright	1.24	2.15	0.90	0.06
Owned with mortgage	2.10	3.45	0.84	0.04
Shared ownership	1.14	1.70	0.92	0.05
Analysis by ownership of deep freezer/microwave				
Microwave only	2.15	3.88	0.81	0.04
Freezer only	1.64	2.60	0.88	0.04
Household with a deep freezer and microwave	1.85	3.06	0.86	0.05
Households owning neither	1.75	3.03	0.96	0.04

(a) see Glossary
(b) based on a pattern of three meals per day

Table B4 Average number of mid-day meals per week, by source, per child aged 5 – 14 years, 1998

per child per week

	Meals not from the household supply		Meals from the household supply	
	School meals	other meals out	Packed meals	Other
All households (GB)	1.74	0.33	1.79	3.14
Analysis by Government Office Region				
North East	1.86	0.45	1.51	3.18
North West	1.87	0.27	1.72	3.14
Yorkshire and the Humber	1.90	0.31	1.43	3.37
East Midlands	1.68	0.29	2.12	2.91
West Midlands	1.75	0.22	1.86	3.17
East	1.43	0.48	1.95	3.14
London	2.29	0.32	1.39	2.99
South West	1.50	0.32	1.96	3.22
South East	1.47	0.26	2.36	2.91
England	1.74	0.31	1.84	3.11
Wales	2.40	0.32	1.46	2.81
Scotland	1.41	0.50	1.58	3.51
Northern Ireland	1.86	0.36	1.89	2.89
Analysis by income group of HOH				
A1	2.32	0.44	1.45	2.79
A2	2.08	0.35	1.64	2.93
B	1.41	0.40	2.09	3.10
C	1.47	0.31	2.17	3.05
D	1.76	0.27	1.69	3.29
E1	2.45	0.06	1.11	3.38
E2	2.82	0.23	0.50	3.44
OAPs (all) [a]	na	na	na	na
Analysis by household composition				
Number of adults / Number of children				
1 / 1 or more	2.31	0.40	1.10	3.19
2 / 1	1.79	0.39	1.94	2.89
2 / 2	1.47	0.37	1.99	3.17
2 / 3	1.56	0.24	2.14	3.06
2 / 4 or more	1.90	0.15	1.84	3.11
3 or more / 1 or 2	1.64	0.45	1.47	3.45
3 or more / 3 or more	2.45	0.34	1.24	2.97
Analysis by age of main diary-keeper				
Under 25	1.97	0.33	1.33	3.36
25 – 34	1.88	0.25	1.78	3.09
35 – 44	1.61	0.34	1.91	3.14
45 – 54	1.88	0.53	1.55	3.04
55 – 64	1.67	0.63	0.52	4.19
65 – 74 [a]	na	na	na	na
75 and over [a]	na	na	na	na
Analysis by house tenure				
Unfurnished; council	2.09	0.30	1.20	3.42
Other rented	1.49	0.22	2.37	2.91
Furnished; rented	2.23	0.28	1.35	3.15
Rent free	na	na	na	na
Owned outright	1.92	0.18	1.52	3.39
Owned with mortgage	1.55	0.38	2.09	2.98
Shared ownership [a]	na	na	na	na
Analysis by ownership of deep freezer/microwave				
Microwave only	1.54	0.50	2.50	2.46
Freezer only	2.05	0.19	1.69	3.08
Household with a deep freezer and microwave	1.68	0.35	1.81	3.16
Households owning neither	2.73	0.86	1.05	2.36

(a) estimates are not shown as these household groups contain samples of fewer than 20 children aged 5 to 14 years

Table B5 Household food consumption of main food groups by income group, 1998

grams per person per week, except where otherwise stated

		Income group Gross weekly income of head of household								
		Households with one or more earners						Households without an earner		
		£910 and over	£640 and under £910	£640 and over	£330 and under £640	£160 and under £330	Under £160	£160 and over	Under £160	OAP
		A1	A2	All A	B	C	D	E1	E2	
MILK AND CREAM										
Liquid wholemilk, full price	(ml)	399	541	490	563	642	744	634	965	980
Welfare and school milk	(ml)	9	15	13	15	16	47	22	105	2
Skimmed milks	(ml)	1120	1200	1171	1091	1047	1018	1471	1009	1260
Yoghurt and fromage frais	(ml)	179	179	179	139	116	95	161	83	101
Other milks and dairy desserts	(ml)	95	158	136	86	88	96	120	123	126
Cream	(ml)	36	29	31	17	12	11	32	9	18
Total milk and cream	**(ml)**	**1839**	**2121**	**2020**	**1912**	**1919**	**2012**	**2440**	**2295**	**2487**
CHEESE										
Natural		102	123	115	96	95	72	122	77	78
Processed		4	9	7	12	10	8	10	10	7
Total cheese		**106**	**132**	**122**	**108**	**105**	**80**	**131**	**86**	**85**
MEAT										
Beef and veal		103	93	96	102	119	101	122	102	113
Mutton and lamb		95	41	61	49	57	33	94	65	95
Pork		56	76	69	73	78	59	89	77	88
Total carcase meat		**254**	**210**	**226**	**223**	**254**	**193**	**306**	**245**	**296**
Bacon and ham, uncooked		61	56	58	68	68	75	117	89	104
Bacon and ham, cooked		35	45	41	38	41	37	46	36	48
Poultry, uncooked		222	249	239	216	216	171	248	197	261
Poultry, cooked		58	33	42	30	35	31	41	24	29
Other meats and meat products		346	295	308	323	350	297	311	344	333
Total meat and meat products		**976**	**885**	**918**	**898**	**963**	**805**	**1066**	**934**	**1071**
FISH										
Fresh		62	39	47	34	18	17	65	21	74
Processed and shell		18	23	21	15	10	10	23	11	12
Prepared, including fish products		46	49	48	55	50	44	79	47	46
Frozen, including fish products		28	43	38	38	42	51	60	60	74
Total fish		**154**	**154**	**154**	**142**	**122**	**122**	**227**	**139**	**208**
EGGS	(no)	1.52	1.63	1.59	1.43	1.67	1.79	2.16	2.12	2.59
Eggs purchased	(no)	1.44	1.48	1.47	1.38	1.61	1.74	2.13	2.06	2.52
FATS										
Butter		49	47	47	33	31	38	70	28	67
Margarine		18	19	18	16	28	23	27	37	51
Low fat and dairy spreads		25	51	42	70	65	51	96	70	94
Vegetable and salad oils	(ml)	51	50	50	39	57	50	50	51	46
Other fats		10	10	10	8	9	18	22	20	37
Total fats		**152**	**177**	**168**	**167**	**190**	**181**	**264**	**207**	**294**
SUGAR AND PRESERVES										
Sugar		44	74	63	85	114	157	142	183	207
Honey, preserves, syrup and treacle		43	40	42	29	29	29	77	34	81
Total sugar and preserves		**87**	**115**	**105**	**114**	**143**	**187**	**218**	**217**	**288**
VEGETABLES										
Fresh potatoes		479	627	574	605	689	799	854	883	1028
Fresh green		285	274	278	229	216	181	405	216	363
Other fresh		678	588	621	497	432	355	704	405	531
Processed potatoes		160	166	164	204	228	205	165	194	147
Processed other vegetables		346	340	340	348	368	327	360	391	351
Total potatoes		**639**	**793**	**738**	**809**	**917**	**1004**	**1019**	**1077**	**1175**
Total other vegetables		**1309**	**1202**	**1239**	**1074**	**1016**	**863**	**1469**	**1012**	**1245**

Table B5 continued

grams per person per week, except where otherwise stated

		Households with one or more earners						Households without an earner		OAP
		£910 and over	£640 and under £910	£640 and over	£330 and under £640	£160 and under £330	Under £160	£160 and over	Under £160	
		A1	A2	All A	B	C	D	E1	E2	
FRUIT										
Fresh		960	965	964	704	606	505	1215	588	835
Other, including fruit products		100	73	82	58	52	47	158	71	125
Fruit juices	(ml)	629	478	533	359	252	235	355	192	184
Total fruit		**1690**	**1516**	**1579**	**1121**	**909**	**786**	**1728**	**851**	**1144**
CEREALS										
White bread, standard loaves		140	181	167	234	307	383	248	350	316
Softgrain and premium loaves		119	140	132	168	173	150	143	152	191
Brown bread		68	62	64	58	60	53	130	80	102
Wholegrain bread		82	97	91	71	64	66	154	82	121
Rolls		61	64	63	77	71	64	81	55	57
Other breads		151	101	119	89	73	50	100	56	65
Total bread		**622**	**645**	**637**	**699**	**748**	**766**	**856**	**775**	**854**
Flour		15	33	26	42	54	35	82	97	78
Cakes		138	134	135	118	121	108	197	107	191
Biscuits		117	130	124	130	132	130	188	134	159
Oatmeal and oat products		4	17	12	8	7	3	26	16	24
Breakfast cereals		158	171	166	137	126	109	161	140	125
Other cereals		373	330	345	293	266	231	217	249	200
Total cereals		**1425**	**1458**	**1446**	**1427**	**1453**	**1381**	**1726**	**1518**	**1631**
BEVERAGES										
Tea		19	27	24	26	33	34	50	40	76
Coffee		21	16	18	15	16	17	30	13	14
Cocoa and drinking chocolate		1	4	3	3	3	3	5	4	3
Branded food drinks		1	3	2	1	3	4	9	3	6
Total beverages		**41**	**50**	**47**	**46**	**55**	**58**	**96**	**60**	**99**
MISCELLANEOUS										
Soups, canned, dehydrated and powdered		76	65	68	66	69	61	115	87	98
Mineral water	(ml)	558	132	285	148	104	56	93	72	73
Ice-cream and other frozen dairy food	(ml)	93	126	114	97	85	92	122	91	93
Other foods		166	169	167	154	144	122	140	114	90
Total miscellaneous		**893**	**490**	**634**	**463**	**401**	**330**	**470**	**365**	**355**
SOFT DRINKS										
Concentrated	(ml)	63	109	92	102	100	91	63	103	62
Ready to drink	(ml)	317	417	381	496	524	474	413	479	302
Low calorie, concentrated	(ml)	52	33	40	38	31	32	26	36	14
Low calorie, ready to drink	(ml)	390	327	349	310	308	184	270	183	120
Total soft drinks[a]	**(ml)**	**1282**	**1454**	**1390**	**1506**	**1487**	**1273**	**1128**	**1357**	**802**
ALCOHOLIC DRINKS										
Lager and beer	(ml)	220	166	186	255	220	133	135	99	94
Wine	(ml)	725	280	440	152	88	39	185	55	41
Others	(ml)	49	63	57	65	47	55	107	44	65
Total alcoholic drinks	**(ml)**	**993**	**509**	**683**	**471**	**354**	**228**	**426**	**197**	**199**
CONFECTIONERY										
Chocolate confectionery		46	39	41	43	41	34	51	31	32
Mints and boiled sweets		13	14	13	11	12	9	17	14	18
Other		2	3	3	2	2	2	5	2	6
Total confectionery		**61**	**55**	**57**	**57**	**55**	**45**	**72**	**48**	**57**

(a) converted to unconcentrated equivalent.

Table B6 Household expenditure on main food groups by income group, 1998

pence per person per week

	Income group Gross weekly income of head of household								
	Households with one or more earners						Households without an earner		
	£910 and over	£640 and under £910	£640 and over	£330 and under £640	£160 and under £330	Under £160	£160 and over	Under £160	OAP
	A1	A2	All A	B	C	D	E1	E2	
MILK AND CREAM									
Liquid wholemilk, full price	21.5	25.2	23.8	28.7	31.6	35.4	33.7	46.8	55.2
Welfare and school milk	0.5	0.5	0.5	0.5	0.3	0.3	0.1	0.1	0.1
Skimmed milks	58.5	62.7	61.2	54.7	51.7	47.6	77.4	47.9	65.0
Yoghurt and fromage frais	39.9	40.6	40.3	30.1	22.7	19.1	33.3	16.8	18.9
Other milks and dairy desserts	20.6	26.4	24.3	13.6	13.5	13.4	16.2	11.3	12.6
Cream	10.0	7.9	8.7	5.0	3.0	3.0	8.3	2.6	4.5
Total milk and cream	**151.1**	**163.3**	**158.9**	**132.6**	**122.8**	**118.8**	**168.9**	**125.5**	**156.2**
CHEESE									
Natural	65.0	67.3	66.5	49.0	44.0	32.9	65.3	34.0	38.6
Processed	3.5	5.0	4.4	5.9	4.9	3.9	4.4	4.4	3.2
Total cheese	**68.5**	**72.2**	**70.9**	**54.9**	**48.8**	**36.8**	**69.7**	**38.4**	**41.8**
MEAT									
Beef and veal	64.4	55.4	58.6	50.6	54.9	43.8	65.7	43.1	54.7
Mutton and lamb	47.9	24.2	32.8	20.3	21.5	15.3	42.0	26.1	35.6
Pork	26.2	29.8	28.5	26.9	25.1	20.6	35.3	26.4	31.7
Total carcase meat	**138.5**	**109.3**	**119.9**	**97.8**	**101.6**	**79.6**	**143.0**	**95.6**	**121.9**
Bacon and ham, uncooked	38.9	32.0	34.5	33.2	33.4	29.3	58.0	35.2	45.6
Bacon and ham, cooked	29.8	32.0	31.2	24.4	24.1	20.5	31.4	20.6	30.1
Poultry, uncooked	90.8	93.1	92.2	71.7	62.2	40.7	79.4	44.8	64.8
Poultry, cooked	31.1	16.9	22.0	18.1	18.6	14.2	19.1	11.9	13.6
Other meats and meat products	203.8	155.9	173.1	148.9	143.1	112.3	137.5	105.2	116.6
Total meat and meat products	**532.8**	**439.3**	**472.9**	**394.1**	**382.9**	**296.7**	**468.4**	**313.2**	**392.6**
FISH									
Fresh	39.0	25.1	30.2	18.0	9.7	10.6	41.4	10.8	31.8
Processed and shell	17.4	21.6	20.1	12.1	7.8	5.1	19.5	7.0	6.7
Prepared, including fish products	33.1	29.5	30.8	29.1	26.2	23.1	43.3	22.6	26.4
Frozen, including fish products	12.7	25.4	20.9	18.0	17.4	18.9	30.3	22.9	36.0
Total fish	**102.2**	**101.6**	**101.8**	**77.1**	**61.1**	**57.7**	**134.5**	**63.3**	**100.8**
EGGS									
Eggs purchased	18.0	19.3	18.8	14.7	15.4	16.1	23.2	18.4	25.0
FATS									
Butter	15.9	14.3	14.9	10.7	9.4	11.8	23.4	9.0	21.4
Margarine	1.3	2.7	2.2	1.9	3.1	2.7	3.1	4.0	5.6
Low fat and dairy spreads	5.0	10.1	8.3	13.1	11.8	9.3	18.3	12.7	17.6
Vegetable and salad oils	16.3	8.4	11.2	5.6	5.7	5.0	6.1	5.3	5.3
Other fats	2.1	1.7	1.8	1.7	1.7	3.3	3.7	2.7	6.1
Total fats	**40.5**	**37.2**	**38.4**	**33.1**	**31.8**	**32.2**	**54.6**	**33.6**	**56.0**
SUGAR AND PRESERVES									
Sugar	3.7	5.8	5.1	6.3	7.7	11.2	10.9	12.4	14.9
Honey, preserves, syrup and treacle	12.7	10.7	11.4	6.4	6.0	5.4	18.7	6.8	17.0
Total sugar and preserves	**16.4**	**16.6**	**16.5**	**12.7**	**13.7**	**16.7**	**29.6**	**19.2**	**31.9**
VEGETABLES									
Fresh potatoes	36.6	35.1	35.7	32.6	31.1	30.4	45.5	34.7	43.0
Fresh green vegetables	63.7	44.5	51.4	32.8	27.0	21.0	56.5	25.4	34.8
Other fresh vegetables	120.8	87.5	99.5	66.6	51.8	38.1	87.0	43.2	53.0
Processed potatoes	47.9	47.4	47.6	56.7	58.3	47.1	37.7	43.5	31.0
Processed other vegetables	68.9	59.3	62.7	51.8	45.4	38.3	52.3	41.9	42.6
Total potatoes	**84.5**	**82.5**	**83.2**	**89.3**	**89.3**	**77.5**	**83.2**	**78.2**	**74.0**
Total other vegetables	**253.4**	**191.2**	**213.6**	**151.2**	**124.1**	**97.4**	**195.8**	**110.5**	**130.5**

Table B6 continued

pence per person per week

	\multicolumn{6}{c	}{Households with one or more earners}	\multicolumn{2}{c	}{Households without an earner}	
	£910 and over	£640 and under £910	£640 and over	£330 and under £640	£160 and under £330	Under £160	£160 and over	Under £160	OAP
	A1	A2	All A	B	C	D	E1	E2	
FRUIT									
Fresh	156.0	133.5	141.6	92.5	72.8	58.2	159.6	67.7	101.2
Other, including fruit products	32.6	19.7	24.3	15.2	11.4	10.0	37.6	12.4	17.9
Fruit juices	69.5	43.3	52.7	28.0	18.8	15.8	32.5	13.0	12.4
Total fruit	**258.0**	**196.4**	**218.6**	**135.8**	**103.0**	**84.0**	**229.7**	**93.0**	**131.5**
CEREALS									
White bread, standard loaves	10.3	12.4	11.7	14.2	17.5	20.8	17.9	18.8	22.1
Softgrain and premium loaves	9.6	10.7	10.3	12.2	12.1	11.2	11.3	11.6	15.3
Brown bread	6.3	5.8	6.0	5.2	4.8	4.6	11.8	6.4	9.6
Wholegrain bread	7.9	8.6	8.3	5.7	5.1	4.7	13.7	6.3	10.9
Rolls	12.0	11.9	12.0	12.9	11.4	9.3	14.5	8.7	9.9
Other breads	42.1	24.8	30.9	22.3	17.6	11.6	22.6	12.2	13.3
Total bread	**88.2**	**74.2**	**79.2**	**72.5**	**68.5**	**62.2**	**91.8**	**64.0**	**81.2**
Flour	1.1	1.2	1.2	1.5	2.2	1.3	3.6	3.6	3.1
Cakes	59.1	46.1	50.8	36.1	35.0	30.4	62.4	29.3	57.6
Biscuits	44.9	42.2	43.2	36.4	35.7	33.1	49.0	32.2	38.2
Oatmeal and oat products	0.8	2.0	1.6	1.2	1.0	0.4	3.1	2.0	2.4
Breakfast cereals	46.6	46.4	46.5	37.3	34.1	28.7	41.1	35.5	30.5
Other cereals	128.1	111.5	117.5	95.6	76.2	59.8	66.1	57.4	41.3
Total cereals	**368.8**	**322.4**	**339.9**	**280.5**	**252.7**	**215.7**	**317.1**	**224.1**	**254.3**
BEVERAGES									
Tea	11.6	17.1	15.2	14.9	17.7	19.0	29.3	19.7	40.5
Coffee	28.8	25.2	26.5	25.6	26.6	22.5	46.8	19.4	22.3
Cocoa and drinking chocolate	0.3	1.8	1.3	1.7	1.7	1.1	2.9	2.1	1.8
Branded food drinks	0.6	1.7	1.3	0.6	1.3	2.2	4.6	1.5	3.0
Total beverages	**41.4**	**45.8**	**44.2**	**42.8**	**47.3**	**44.9**	**83.6**	**42.7**	**67.5**
MISCELLANEOUS									
Soups, canned, dehydrated and powdered	17.6	12.8	14.6	10.8	10.2	9.0	20.1	12.5	15.7
Mineral water	34.4	5.2	15.7	6.2	4.2	2.7	4.6	2.9	3.2
Ice-cream and other frozen dairy foods	22.3	27.0	25.3	15.9	12.6	12.7	19.9	11.9	11.5
Other foods	69.7	64.9	66.6	56.2	47.0	37.2	53.7	35.7	32.9
Total miscellaneous	**144.0**	**109.9**	**122.2**	**89.0**	**73.9**	**61.5**	**98.4**	**62.9**	**63.2**
Total food	**£20.80**	**£17.99**	**£19.00**	**£15.08**	**£13.67**	**£11.56**	**£19.57**	**£12.23**	**£15.25**
SOFT DRINKS									
Concentrated	9.0	11.5	10.6	9.7	8.9	6.8	6.8	7.1	5.6
Ready to drink	22.4	27.3	25.5	29.7	27.4	23.6	23.4	22.1	16.6
Low calorie, concentrated	7.9	3.3	5.0	3.6	3.1	2.3	2.5	2.4	1.0
Low calorie, ready to drink	25.7	17.2	20.3	16.0	16.2	8.3	12.1	7.9	6.9
Total soft drinks	**65.0**	**59.3**	**61.4**	**59.0**	**55.6**	**41.2**	**44.7**	**39.5**	**30.0**
ALCOHOLIC DRINKS									
Lager and beer	50.0	31.8	38.4	43.0	36.4	19.6	24.8	14.3	14.8
Wine	574.1	141.9	297.4	66.4	35.9	17.8	84.2	21.9	15.8
Others	47.5	47.3	47.4	32.0	20.5	13.3	93.1	17.4	53.1
Total alcoholic drinks	**671.5**	**221.0**	**383.1**	**141.4**	**92.8**	**50.8**	**202.1**	**53.6**	**83.7**
CONFECTIONERY									
Chocolate confectionery	29.2	22.1	24.7	23.9	22.6	19.8	31.6	16.8	17.8
Mints and boiled sweets	8.5	6.1	7.0	5.4	5.2	3.9	7.7	5.9	8.9
Other	1.3	1.6	1.5	1.6	1.3	1.1	2.6	1.3	2.9
Total confectionery	**39.1**	**29.9**	**33.2**	**30.9**	**29.0**	**24.8**	**41.9**	**23.9**	**29.6**
Total food and drink	**£28.55**	**£21.09**	**£23.78**	**£17.39**	**£15.44**	**£12.73**	**£22.43**	**£13.40**	**£16.69**

Table B7 Household food expenditure on main food groups by household composition, 1998

pence per person per week

Number of adults	1	1	2	2	2	2	2	3	3 or more	3 or more	4 or more	All households
Number of children	0	1 or more	0	1	2	3	4 or more	0	1 or 2	3 or more	0	
MILK AND CREAM												
Liquid wholemilk, full price	42.4	35.9	28.9	36.8	33.3	34.1	41.3	26.9	37.6	55.5	25.0	33.6
Welfare and school milk	0.1	0.6	-	0.3	1.1	0.7	1.1	-	-	0.3	-	0.4
Skimmed milks	68.0	39.2	67.9	47.0	47.3	39.3	31.1	66.8	53.2	33.0	57.5	55.5
Yoghurt and fromage frais	28.4	16.8	28.5	30.6	29.8	26.2	14.9	23.3	18.4	15.5	23.1	26.1
Other milks and dairy desserts	17.1	10.3	14.3	23.2	13.9	13.4	9.5	12.0	11.5	4.2	12.2	14.4
Cream	5.3	1.5	6.9	3.3	4.2	3.3	1.7	4.6	3.0	0.4	3.5	4.5
Total milk and cream	**161.2**	**104.3**	**146.6**	**141.0**	**129.7**	**117.0**	**99.6**	**133.6**	**123.8**	**109.0**	**121.3**	**134.4**
CHEESE												
Natural	55.0	32.8	59.7	46.0	38.0	34.7	24.9	52.9	37.4	14.9	54.2	46.8
Processed	3.4	5.6	4.0	6.3	5.9	5.0	4.1	4.7	5.1	3.1	7.0	4.9
Total cheese	**58.4**	**38.4**	**63.7**	**52.3**	**43.9**	**39.7**	**29.0**	**57.6**	**42.5**	**18.0**	**61.2**	**51.7**
MEAT												
Beef and veal	52.6	31.7	70.8	52.6	39.0	27.8	21.7	74.2	47.0	6.5	74.8	52.7
Mutton and lamb	31.4	11.6	36.1	17.6	16.3	12.0	16.8	30.2	20.0	35.2	26.9	24.6
Pork	25.9	17.0	36.6	27.8	19.9	18.5	11.6	36.4	26.7	4.6	24.1	26.9
Total carcase meat	**109.8**	**60.3**	**143.4**	**98.0**	**75.1**	**58.3**	**50.1**	**140.7**	**93.6**	**46.3**	**125.8**	**104.2**
Bacon and ham, uncooked	38.6	18.6	54.2	32.6	22.7	20.4	15.3	44.5	27.5	10.4	48.8	35.9
Bacon, cooked	29.7	18.0	30.8	26.0	22.1	17.4	13.6	27.8	19.6	17.2	26.9	25.1
Poultry, uncooked	61.1	44.7	80.3	71.0	59.1	46.9	39.4	79.1	62.3	53.6	69.7	65.8
Poultry, cooked	21.0	14.5	18.1	16.0	17.2	12.4	14.5	22.8	13.9	6.6	22.6	17.4
Other meats and meat products	161.3	107.1	148.6	155.8	130.5	105.5	80.2	167.0	125.8	51.9	169.6	139.3
Total meat and meat products	**421.6**	**263.2**	**475.4**	**399.3**	**326.7**	**260.8**	**213.1**	**482.0**	**342.7**	**186.0**	**463.3**	**387.8**
FISH												
Fresh	20.9	4.5	31.8	13.2	9.0	7.7	2.7	24.0	11.7	13.7	17.9	17.9
Processed and shell	10.0	4.4	16.7	8.7	8.1	5.8	4.4	16.3	6.1	10.0	7.9	10.6
Prepared, including fish products	36.8	18.0	37.8	25.9	20.6	14.9	17.8	36.4	19.3	9.7	30.4	28.1
Frozen, including fish products	34.8	11.5	24.7	19.4	16.9	16.0	10.0	25.0	13.4	4.8	16.9	20.7
Total fish and fish products	**102.6**	**38.3**	**111.0**	**67.2**	**54.6**	**44.5**	**34.9**	**101.7**	**50.5**	**38.1**	**73.1**	**77.3**
EGGS (purchased)	22.9	12.0	22.2	15.2	12.1	9.4	11.3	20.3	12.5	15.4	21.1	17.0
FATS												
Butter	19.1	4.0	18.0	10.0	8.0	5.7	4.5	15.9	7.1	4.8	13.9	12.2
Margarine	3.4	3.0	3.1	3.0	1.8	2.8	2.7	3.7	2.7	2.7	3.6	2.9
Low fat and reduced fat spreads	16.1	9.9	16.4	10.6	10.2	8.0	5.5	16.3	9.5	1.0	14.3	12.7
Vegetable and salad oils	6.8	3.8	8.3	5.1	3.7	3.6	2.2	7.5	7.2	4.1	9.0	6.1
Other fats	3.3	1.4	3.9	2.0	1.1	1.1	1.1	2.5	0.8	2.5	2.5	2.3
Total fats	**48.6**	**22.1**	**49.7**	**30.7**	**24.9**	**21.2**	**16.0**	**45.9**	**27.3**	**15.0**	**43.4**	**36.2**
SUGAR AND PRESERVES												
Sugar	11.6	6.9	11.2	6.8	5.6	5.9	4.6	9.3	8.6	4.1	8.4	8.5
Honey, preserves, syrup and treacle	14.8	3.1	12.3	6.7	5.9	3.8	2.3	7.1	4.8	1.3	9.9	8.3
Total sugar and preserves	**26.4**	**10.0**	**23.5**	**13.5**	**11.5**	**9.7**	**6.9**	**16.4**	**13.4**	**5.4**	**18.2**	**16.8**
VEGETABLES												
Fresh potatoes	39.9	27.2	44.1	30.9	26.3	20.3	18.6	39.8	29.5	17.6	43.0	34.1
Fresh green	45.2	18.5	49.3	28.8	21.9	15.5	9.2	38.5	23.8	13.7	31.6	32.9
Other fresh	72.4	35.4	85.6	56.6	47.7	40.8	26.1	69.7	42.0	47.3	65.4	61.2
Processed potatoes	43.0	57.3	43.7	56.4	58.2	58.4	53.0	50.7	52.4	22.4	60.0	51.3
Processed other vegetables	62.9	37.7	56.3	51.3	39.1	34.0	34.7	57.4	38.2	42.6	51.8	48.3
Total potatoes	**82.9**	**84.5**	**87.8**	**87.2**	**84.5**	**78.7**	**71.7**	**90.5**	**81.9**	**60.2**	**103.0**	**85.4**
Total other vegetables	**180.4**	**91.5**	**191.3**	**136.7**	**108.7**	**90.3**	**65.9**	**165.6**	**104.0**	**83.4**	**148.8**	**142.4**

Table B7 *continued*

pence per person per week

Number of adults	1		2					3	3 or more		4 or more	All house-holds
Number of children	0	1 or more	0	1	2	3	4 or more	0	1 or 2	3 or more	0	
FRUIT												
Fresh	121.7	51.5	123.2	75.2	77.7	59.1	40.3	96.6	70.3	78.4	91.3	91.3
Other, including fruit products	22.1	5.1	27.1	11.4	10.1	9.2	4.3	17.2	12.3	3.7	8.3	16.0
Fruit juices	29.5	17.2	26.5	23.4	28.4	18.8	9.2	20.5	19.7	28.1	30.0	24.3
Total fruit	**173.3**	**73.8**	**176.8**	**110.0**	**116.1**	**87.1**	**53.8**	**134.3**	**102.4**	**110.2**	**129.6**	**131.5**
CEREALS												
White bread, standard loaves	20.7	15.9	18.0	16.0	13.5	13.5	15.2	21.2	14.1	13.2	16.8	16.7
Softgrain and premium loaves	12.5	10.2	12.7	11.6	12.6	10.1	9.8	12.3	11.2	6.4	15.4	12.0
Brown bread	11.3	3.7	8.6	4.9	3.6	2.5	2.7	6.0	4.2	0.9	4.8	6.0
Wholegrain bread	12.5	2.7	10.1	4.8	3.9	3.3	1.4	7.3	4.4	0.4	5.6	6.6
Rolls	12.0	6.9	13.6	14.1	10.0	9.5	9.6	13.2	9.7	9.0	12.3	11.6
Other breads	24.0	12.5	23.9	20.6	18.7	12.4	8.2	18.8	14.4	11.0	19.4	19.3
Total bread	**92.9**	**51.9**	**86.9**	**71.9**	**62.3**	**51.3**	**46.8**	**78.8**	**57.9**	**40.8**	**74.2**	**72.2**
Flour	2.3	1.5	2.8	1.3	1.4	0.6	0.8	2.0	5.7	7.4	1.1	2.2
Cakes	49.7	27.5	49.3	33.8	32.9	31.1	16.8	44.4	36.6	21.8	36.1	39.3
Biscuits	40.8	36.2	38.5	37.9	38.3	36.7	28.8	32.8	35.7	14.1	37.6	37.1
Oatmeal and oat products	2.5	0.4	2.5	0.6	0.8	1.0	0.6	1.7	0.4	0.2	0.5	1.4
Breakfast cereals	38.5	34.9	34.3	37.4	39.1	40.0	36.4	34.4	35.1	26.9	29.7	36.2
Other cereals	75.0	70.8	79.3	98.6	85.2	66.0	64.7	84.8	77.6	66.4	68.3	79.6
Total cereals	**301.6**	**223.2**	**293.6**	**281.6**	**260.0**	**226.5**	**195.1**	**279.0**	**249.0**	**177.8**	**247.4**	**267.9**
BEVERAGES												
Tea	33.8	9.6	26.2	14.0	11.0	12.4	7.2	22.8	16.5	9.7	21.1	19.2
Coffee	33.6	16.1	37.3	23.6	19.7	13.8	10.5	36.5	16.5	7.1	24.5	26.4
Cocoa and drinking chocolate	2.7	0.7	2.3	1.6	0.9	1.6	1.0	1.9	1.5	...	2.8	1.8
Branded food drinks	2.7	0.4	2.5	1.2	0.7	0.8	0.3	2.0	0.8	...	1.5	1.5
Total beverages	**72.7**	**26.8**	**68.2**	**40.5**	**32.3**	**28.6**	**19.0**	**63.3**	**35.2**	**16.8**	**49.9**	**48.9**
MISCELLANEOUS												
Soups, canned, dehydrated and powdered	20.9	8.5	15.9	10.9	9.2	7.0	3.7	10.5	12.4	0.0	12.4	12.0
Mineral water	6.7	3.4	8.7	3.5	4.7	2.2	1.3	6.1	7.1	0.0	7.1	5.5
Ice-cream and other frozen dairy foods	13.5	15.3	18.1	14.2	14.6	16.6	11.7	15.3	10.4	8.4	10.4	15.1
Other foods	46.1	35.9	55.5	62.8	41.8	35.8	23.6	48.0	36.2	16.1	47.7	46.7
Total miscellaneous	**87.1**	**63.1**	**98.2**	**91.0**	**70.3**	**62.5**	**40.3**	**80.0**	**57.6**	**24.5**	**77.6**	**79.2**
Total food	**£17.43**	**£10.53**	**£18.11**	**£14.68**	**£12.77**	**£10.79**	**£8.57**	**£16.73**	**£12.45**	**£8.62**	**£15.61**	**£14.79**
SOFT DRINKS												
Concentrated	6.3	8.1	6.2	9.0	11.3	12.7	9.1	9.2	8.2	8.2	10.1	8.6
Ready to drink	21.5	28.2	22.9	32.6	25.6	23.5	23.7	29.5	31.6	19.1	35.0	26.1
Low calorie, concentrated	1.8	3.5	2.3	3.7	4.4	4.9	4.7	2.8	3.2	...	1.1	3.1
Low calorie, ready to drink	12.2	12.5	16.0	14.3	14.0	9.9	4.2	17.3	14.3	24.2	18.5	14.2
Total soft drinks	**41.8**	**52.2**	**47.4**	**59.7**	**55.3**	**51.1**	**41.6**	**58.9**	**57.3**	**51.5**	**64.8**	**52.0**
ALCOHOLIC DRINKS												
Lager and beer	35.1	11.4	43.8	42.2	30.8	21.9	16.1	36.4	21.9	6.6	26.8	32.9
Wine	65.1	20.7	101.2	42.7	89.6	37.5	10.5	62.3	41.2	5.6	54.0	67.2
Others	63.7	9.7	59.3	18.0	14.4	11.1	13.1	34.1	10.8	-	27.6	32.8
Total alcoholic drinks	**163.8**	**41.7**	**204.3**	**102.9**	**134.8**	**70.4**	**39.7**	**132.8**	**73.8**	**12.2**	**108.4**	**132.9**
CONFECTIONERY												
Chocolate confectionery	22.7	15.2	25.4	22.9	23.8	22.2	19.0	22.0	19.0	17.8	25.6	22.7
Mints and boiled sweets	8.0	3.8	6.5	4.2	6.3	5.3	5.1	5.8	5.3	0.7	4.1	5.8
Other	1.9	0.9	2.1	1.6	1.2	0.7	0.7	2.3	1.6	1.5	1.0	1.6
Total confectionery	**32.5**	**19.9**	**34.0**	**28.7**	**31.2**	**28.3**	**24.8**	**30.1**	**25.9**	**20.0**	**30.7**	**30.1**
Total food and drink	**£19.82**	**£11.67**	**£20.96**	**£16.60**	**£14.99**	**£12.29**	**£9.63**	**£18.95**	**£14.02**	**£9.46**	**£17.65**	**£16.94**

Table B8 Household food consumption by household composition groups, within income groups: selected food items, 1998

grams per person per week, unless otherwise stated

Income group A
Households with

		Adults only	2 adults and			3 or more adults
			1 child	2 children	3 children	1 or more children
Milk and cream	(ml or eq ml)	1985	2048	2056	2090	1836
Cheese		143	123	108	106	113
Carcase meat		291	189	148	228	251
Other meats and meat products		785	770	625	581	616
Fish		218	128	130	107	112
Eggs	(no)	2.18	1.40	1.45	1.26	0.74
Fats		219	155	124	120	214
Sugar and preserves		113	103	106	102	91
Fresh potatoes		668	490	450	447	826
Fresh green vegetables		390	277	225	171	202
Other fresh vegetables		831	566	487	550	421
Processed vegetables		524	524	453	532	485
Fresh fruit		1150	810	879	733	990
Other fruit and fruit products		573	384	776	702	532
Bread		706	714	584	602	552
Other cereals		837	760	712	921	886
Tea		27	20	23	37	11
Coffee		27	18	8	11	15
Cocoa and drinking chocolate		2	3	2	7	…
Branded food drinks		1	10	3	2	…
FOOD EXPENDITURE		**£23.11**	**£17.91**	**£16.85**	**£16.14**	**£16.42**
Soft drinks, volume as purchased	(ml)	826	1013	875	685	830
Alcoholic drinks	(ml)	1013	296	604	528	447
Confectionery		51	31	68	39	60
FOOD AND DRINK EXPENDITURE		**£29.12**	**£19.91**	**£22.44**	**£18.92**	**£20.20**

(a) Consumption figures are not shown for those households with 1 adult and one child and 2 adults and four or more children because there are fewer than 10 such households in the sample.

grams per person per week, unless otherwise stated

Income group B
Households with

		Adults only	1 Adult	2 adults and				3 or more adults
			1 or more children	1 child	2 children	3 children	4 or more children	1 or more children
Milk and cream	(ml or eq ml)	1966	1433	2043	1852	1837	1911	1878
Cheese		140	81	113	81	86	91	85
Carcase meat		275	60	274	182	152	104	215
Other meats and meat products		807	584	670	559	579	546	643
Fish		192	114	148	104	91	115	110
Eggs	(no)	1.69	0.76	1.50	1.17	1.23	1.47	1.47
Fats		220	109	162	126	125	130	158
Sugar and preserves		141	82	105	84	101	105	129
Fresh potatoes		729	331	643	450	512	426	706
Fresh green vegetables		337	167	214	159	148	90	171
Other fresh vegetables		660	386	508	384	347	260	415
Processed vegetables		634	425	586	459	539	421	528
Fresh fruit		912	621	659	601	490	482	566
Other fruit and fruit products		474	340	432	415	328	186	373
Bread		788	495	693	624	631	548	732
Other cereals		746	230	777	719	709	642	679
Tea		37	10	21	17	20	12	33
Coffee		24	14	12	12	6	5	8
Cocoa and drinking chocolate		4	6	2	…	4	4	3
Branded food drinks		1	…	…	1	2	…	2
FOOD EXPENDITURE		**£18.98**	**£12.06**	**£15.86**	**£12.43**	**£11.07**	**£10.17**	**£12.65**
Soft drinks, volume as purchased	(ml)	900	1264	1029	867	1120	634	1046
Alcoholic drinks	(ml)	669	396	542	371	236	105	264
Confectionery		58	87	50	55	59	60	54
FOOD AND DRINK EXPENDITURE		**£22.14**	**£14.78**	**£18.17**	**£14.27**	**£12.62**	**£11.07**	**£14.15**

Table B8 *continued*

grams per person per week, unless otherwise stated

Income group C
Households with

	Adults only	1 adult	2 adults and				3 or more adults
		1 or more children	1 child	2 children	3 children	4 or more children	1 or more children
Milk and cream (ml or eq ml)	1893	1646	2008	1946	1939	1836	2047
Cheese	118	121	111	94	71	81	79
Carcase meat	315	171	264	198	157	183	180
Other meats and meat products	801	714	748	627	554	476	572
Fish	152	82	111	98	109	68	81
Eggs (no)	1.94	1.37	1.77	1.40	0.94	1.63	1.30
Fats	217	148	193	160	114	103	223
Sugar and preserves	170	103	130	113	94	82	154
Fresh potatoes	798	490	662	645	439	759	477
Fresh green vegetables	290	153	198	143	97	113	169
Other fresh vegetables	560	354	374	314	256	331	284
Processed vegetables	618	634	614	600	533	612	474
Fresh fruit	752	537	493	466	408	316	580
Other fruit and fruit products	339	283	313	298	226	143	257
Bread	813	690	711	740	614	781	585
Other cereals	692	812	698	711	637	585	827
Tea	43	19	26	25	22	14	30
Coffee	22	13	16	12	10	8	6
Cocoa and drinking chocolate	3	2	3	3	6	4	2
Branded food drinks	4	...	3	2	...	1	...
FOOD EXPENDITURE	**£16.04**	**£12.36**	**£13.85**	**£12.09**	**£9.45**	**£8.37**	**£10.51**
Soft drinks, volume as purchased (ml)	917	944	984	1055	1066	655	1084
Alcoholic drinks (ml)	469	133	385	291	223	256	99
Confectionery	55	47	56	65	58	39	46
FOOD AND DRINK EXPENDITURE	**£18.26**	**£13.56**	**£15.64**	**£13.63**	**£10.58**	**£9.40**	**£11.53**

grams per person per week, unless otherwise stated

Income group D and E2
Households with

	Adults only	1 adult	2 adults and				3 or more adults
		1 or more children	1 child	2 children	3 children	4 or more children	1 or more children
Milk and cream (ml or eq ml)	2301	2055	2093	2189	1982	1742	2534
Cheese	102	69	78	77	53	49	82
Carcase meat	291	171	219	182	97	114	215
Other meats and meat products	740	567	809	657	388	397	751
Fish	177	88	107	148	80	40	93
Eggs (no)	2.58	1.35	1.66	1.70	1.20	0.84	2.76
Fats	251	147	167	186	145	90	142
Sugar and preserves	267	130	200	180	167	68	228
Fresh potatoes	966	834	930	598	696	172	911
Fresh green vegetables	308	110	162	142	73	28	161
Other fresh vegetables	535	255	280	309	223	130	360
Processed vegetables	607	581	493	475	514	397	510
Fresh fruit	804	315	364	449	339	216	467
Other fruit and fruit products	338	214	270	268	179	77	181
Bread	896	639	757	685	644	549	800
Other cereals	758	642	607	657	561	402	994
Tea	54	19	33	29	22	9	45
Coffee	17	8	22	15	8	3	19
Cocoa and drinking chocolate	5	1	4	6	...	...	2
Branded food drinks	6	2	2	2	1	...	2
FOOD EXPENDITURE	**£15.01**	**£9.64**	**£11.10**	**£10.44**	**£7.26**	**£5.13**	**£10.98**
Soft drinks, volume as purchased (ml)	666	886	1021	781	877	913	1018
Alcoholic drinks (ml)	344	80	109	100	75	294	29
Confectionery	59	29	53	47	52	6	26
FOOD AND DRINK EXPENDITURE	**£16.60**	**£10.46**	**£12.16**	**£11.31**	**£8.02**	**£5.80**	**£11.56**

Table B9 Nutritional value of household food: national averages 1996 - 1998

		1996	1997	1998 GB	1998 GB[a]	1998 UK	1998 UK[a]
(i) intake per person per day							
Energy	(kcal)	1850	1790	1740	1840	1740	1840
	(MJ)	7.8	7.5	7.3	7.8	7.3	7.7
Total protein	(g)	65.0	64.7	64.3	64.9	64.3	64.8
Animal protein	(g)	39.8	39.5	39.4	39.8	39.3	39.7
Fat	(g)	82	78	75	76	75	76
Fatty acids:							
saturated	(g)	31.6	30.3	29.3	30.1	29.3	30.1
monounsaturated	(g)	29.3	27.5	26.6	27.1	26.5	27.0
polyunsaturated	(g)	14.8	14.0	13.5	13.6	13.5	13.5
Cholesterol	(mg)	233	233	225	226	224	226
Carbohydrate [b]	(g)	228	221	214	232	214	232
Of which:							
total sugars	(g)	92	90	86	103	86	103
non-milk extrinsic sugars	(g)	53	51	48	65	48	65
starch	(g)	136	131	128	128	128	128
Fibre [c]	(g)	12.4	12.4	12.1	12.2	12.1	12.2
Alcohol	(g)	-	-	-	3.8	-	3.7
Calcium	(mg)	820	820	800	820	800	820
Iron	(mg)	10.1	9.9	9.8	10.0	9.8	10.0
Zinc	(mg)	7.8	7.7	7.5	7.6	7.5	7.6
Magnesium	(mg)	229	226	222	232	222	232
Sodium [g]	(g)	2.62	2.58	2.52	2.54	2.52	2.54
Potassium	(g)	2.60	2.60	2.58	2.64	2.57	2.63
Thiamin	(mg)	1.44	1.37	1.36	1.37	1.36	1.37
Riboflavin	(mg)	1.60	1.73	1.68	1.72	1.68	1.72
Niacin equivalent	(mg)	26.5	26.0	26.1	26.7	26.1	26.7
Vitamin B6	(mg)	2.0	1.9	1.9	2.0	1.9	2.0
Vitamin B12	(μg)	4.3	7.2	6.8	6.9	6.8	6.9
Folate	(μg)	248	247	241	245	241	244
Vitamin C	(mg)	55	58	59	64	59	63
Vitamin A:							
retinol	(μg)	580	530	490	500	490	490
β-carotene	(μg)	1680	1740	1710	1760	1700	1750
total (retinol equivalent)	(μg)	860	820	780	790	780	790
Vitamin D [d]	(μg)	3.35	3.40	3.25	3.25	3.25	3.25
Vitamin E	(mg)	10.68	10.15	9.80	9.90	9.79	9.90
(ii) as a percentage of Reference Nutrient Intake [e]							
Energy [f]		89	86	84	89	84	89
Protein		145	145	143	144	143	144
Calcium		120	120	118	120	118	120
Iron		97	96	95	97	95	97
Zinc		98	98	95	96	95	96
Magnesium		88	87	85	89	85	89
Sodium [g]		177	176	171	172	171	172
Potassium		83	83	82	84	82	84
Thiamin		173	165	163	164	163	164
Riboflavin		141	154	149	152	149	152
Niacin equivalent		192	190	189	194	189	194
Vitamin B6		162	161	159	166	160	166
Vitamin B12		317	529	498	504	499	504
Folate		133	133	129	131	129	131
Vitamin C		143	153	155	167	154	166
Vitamin A (retinol equivalent)		139	134	126	128	126	128
(iii) as a percentage of food energy							
Fat		39.7	39.1	38.8	37.3	38.8	37.3
Of which:							
saturated fatty acids		15.4	15.3	15.2	14.7	15.2	14.7
Carbohydrate		46.2	46.4	46.4	47.2	46.4	47.2

a) columns include soft and alcoholic drinks and confectionery
b) available carbohydrate, calculated as monosaccharide
c) as non-starch polysaccharide
d) contributions from pharmaceutical sources of this (or any other) vitamin are not recorded by the Survey
e) Department of Health, *Dietary Reference Values for Food Energy and Nutrients for the United Kingdom*, HMSO, 1991. Before comparison with the weighted Reference Nutrient Intakes, ten percent has first been deducted from each absolute intake given above to allow for wastage, and an allowance has also been made for meals not taken from the domestic food supply
f) as a percentage of Estimated Average Requirement
g) excludes sodium from table salt

Table B10 Nutritional value of household food by region, 1998

		Government Office Regions									England	Wales	Scotland	Northern Ireland
		North East	North West	Yorkshire and the Humber	East Midlands	West Midlands	East	London	South East	South West				
		(i) intake per person per day												
Energy	(kcal)	1780	1650	1700	1750	1770	1640	1740	1740	1850	1730	1870	1700	1680
	(MJ)	7.4	6.9	7.1	7.3	7.4	6.9	7.3	7.3	7.8	7.3	7.9	7.1	7.0
Total protein	(g)	67.2	62.6	63.8	63.9	64.6	62.3	63.5	63.3	67.9	64.1	68.4	63.7	61.4
Animal protein	(g)	41.1	39.6	38.8	38.9	38.9	38.0	38.4	38.4	41.1	39.2	41.9	39.7	37.4
Fat	(g)	76	72	72	76	74	68	75	75	80	74	82	75	72
Fatty acids:														
saturated	(g)	29.9	28.4	28.0	29.8	29.3	27.1	27.6	29.9	31.8	29.1	32.4	29.6	29.2
monounsaturated	(g)	27.3	25.7	25.8	26.7	26.3	24.1	27.0	26.6	28.3	26.4	28.8	26.7	25.3
polyunsaturated	(g)	13.2	12.9	13.0	13.6	13.3	11.9	15.5	13.4	14.2	13.5	14.5	13.1	12.7
Cholesterol	(mg)	238	221	224	221	217	212	220	225	236	223	241	228	213
Carbohydrate	(g)	219	199	212	216	224	208	213	215	228	214	230	205	208
Of which:														
total sugars	(g)	85	80	82	87	89	84	83	90	93	86	94	82	79
non-milk extrinsic sugars	(g)	48	44	45	49	51	46	44	51	52	48	52	47	41
starch	(g)	134	119	130	129	135	123	130	124	135	128	136	123	129
Fibre [a]	(g)	12.3	11.0	11.7	12.2	12.2	12.2	12.5	12.4	13.5	12.2	13.1	11.2	11.6
Calcium	(mg)	800	780	790	840	840	760	770	800	870	800	850	770	800
Iron	(mg)	10.3	9.2	9.9	9.7	9.8	9.6	9.5	9.7	10.6	9.8	10.3	9.6	9.4
Zinc	(mg)	7.8	7.3	7.4	7.5	7.5	7.3	7.4	7.4	8.0	7.5	7.9	7.5	7.3
Magnesium	(mg)	224	209	215	219	224	219	222	226	242	222	239	212	210
Sodium	(g)	2.74	2.43	2.50	2.49	2.58	2.36	2.25	2.53	2.73	2.50	2.67	2.60	2.42
Potassium	(g)	2.62	2.46	2.45	2.57	2.63	2.52	2.62	2.58	2.79	2.58	2.82	2.42	2.45
Thiamin	(mg)	1.42	1.30	1.35	1.36	1.38	1.32	1.33	1.35	1.46	1.36	1.44	1.31	1.33
Riboflavin	(mg)	1.70	1.68	1.68	1.69	1.72	1.61	1.63	1.66	1.79	1.68	1.78	1.63	1.69
Niacin equivalent	(mg)	27.4	25.3	26.0	25.5	26.1	25.5	25.7	25.7	27.6	26.0	27.9	25.9	24.3
Vitamin B6	(mg)	2.0	1.9	1.9	1.9	2.0	1.9	2.0	1.9	2.1	1.9	2.1	1.8	2.0
Vitamin B12	(µg)	7.3	6.8	6.9	6.9	6.8	6.6	6.8	6.7	7.2	6.9	6.9	6.4	6.9
Folate	(µg)	237	225	239	241	246	239	244	241	266	242	258	223	226
Vitamin C	(mg)	57	54	56	57	57	61	67	62	64	60	63	53	44
Vitamin A														
retinol	(µg)	580	440	510	510	470	440	460	520	570	500	500	450	430
β-carotene	(µg)	1710	1590	1650	1740	1610	1780	1720	1690	1960	1710	2000	1490	1440
total (retinol equivalent)	(µg)	870	710	790	800	740	740	750	810	890	780	830	700	670
Vitamin D	(µg)	3.43	3.16	3.47	3.43	3.39	3.13	2.90	3.03	3.56	3.25	3.50	3.14	3.16
Vitamin E	(mg)	9.40	9.22	9.45	10.04	9.84	8.66	11.22	9.60	10.51	9.80	10.77	9.43	9.52

Table B10 *continued*

		\multicolumn{12}{c}{Government Office Regions}			
		North East	North West	Yorkshire and the Humber	East Midlands	West Midlands	East	London	South East	South West	England	Wales	Scotland	Northern Ireland

(ii) as a percentage of Reference Nutrient Intake [b]

	North East	North West	Yorkshire and the Humber	East Midlands	West Midlands	East	London	South East	South West	England	Wales	Scotland	Northern Ireland
Energy [c]	85	80	82	83	84	79	85	84	88	83	90	81	82
Protein	150	140	143	140	144	139	144	142	148	143	150	141	142
Calcium	116	114	116	122	121	112	115	118	124	118	124	113	119
Iron	99	89	97	93	94	93	92	95	102	95	100	93	91
Zinc	99	93	94	93	94	92	96	94	100	95	100	94	94
Magnesium	86	80	83	83	85	84	87	87	91	85	90	81	83
Sodium	187	165	171	167	174	160	155	173	181	170	179	175	169
Potassium	84	79	79	81	84	80	85	83	87	82	88	77	81
Thiamin	170	156	163	161	164	158	163	163	173	163	173	156	163
Riboflavin	150	149	149	148	151	142	147	148	155	149	156	144	154
Niacin equivalent	199	184	190	182	187	185	190	188	197	189	202	187	180
Vitamin B6	165	154	155	156	161	157	165	158	168	160	170	150	170
Vitamin B12	533	502	506	497	497	483	506	491	517	502	500	463	519
Folate	127	121	129	128	131	128	133	131	140	130	137	119	125
Vitamin C	149	141	146	148	148	159	179	164	166	156	164	138	118
Vitamin A (retinol equivalent)	141	116	128	128	120	120	124	132	143	127	134	113	111

(iii) as a percentage of food energy

	North East	North West	Yorkshire and the Humber	East Midlands	West Midlands	East	London	South East	South West	England	Wales	Scotland	Northern Ireland
Fat	38.6	39.4	38.2	39.0	37.8	37.3	39.2	39.0	39.0	38.7	39.2	39.8	38.8
Of which:													
saturated fatty acids	15.2	15.5	14.8	15.3	14.9	14.8	14.3	15.5	15.5	15.1	15.6	15.7	15.6
Carbohydrate	46.3	45.4	46.8	46.4	47.5	47.5	46.2	46.4	46.3	46.5	46.2	45.2	46.6

(iv) contribution to selected nutrients from soft and alcoholic drinks and confectionery

		North East	North West	Yorkshire and the Humber	East Midlands	West Midlands	East	London	South East	South West	England	Wales	Scotland	Northern Ireland
Energy	(kcal)	120	90	100	110	100	120	90	110	110	110	120	130	90
	(MJ)	0.5	0.4	0.4	0.5	0.4	0.5	0.4	0.5	0.5	0.5	0.5	0.5	0.4
Fat	(g)	1	1	1	2	1	2	1	2	2	1	2	2	1
Carbohydrate	(g)	19	15	18	19	18	20	16	17	17	17	17	20	19
Alcohol	(g)	4.3	2.6	3.3	3.6	3.3	3.8	3.2	4.3	3.9	3.6	5.1	4.7	1.5

(a) as non-starch polysaccharides
(b) Department of Health, *Dietary Reference Values for Food Energy and Nutrients for the United Kingdom*, HMSO, 1991
(c) as a percentage of Estimated Average Requirement

Table B11 Nutritional value of household food by income group, 1998

		\multicolumn{6}{c}{Income groups}	
		\multicolumn{6}{c}{Gross weekly income of head of household}	
		\multicolumn{4}{c}{Households with one or more earner}	\multicolumn{2}{c}{Households without an earner}	
		£640 and over	£330 and under £640	£160 and under £330	Under £160	£160 and over	Under £160	OAP
		A	B	C	D	E1	E2	

(i) intake per person per day

		A	B	C	D	E1	E2	OAP
Energy	(kcal)	1720	1640	1690	1610	2100	1800	2020
	(MJ)	7.2	6.9	7.1	6.7	8.8	7.6	8.5
Total protein	(g)	64.5	61.7	63.1	57.7	77.6	65.3	72.9
Animal protein	(g)	39.4	37.5	38.7	34.8	48.0	39.5	46.1
Fat	(g)	74	70	74	68	90	76	88
Fatty acids:								
saturated	(g)	29.6	27.7	28.4	26.9	36.3	29.4	35.6
monounsaturated	(g)	26.1	25.0	26.5	24.0	31.6	27.0	31.1
polyunsaturated	(g)	13.2	12.7	13.7	11.9	15.8	13.7	15.2
Cholesterol	(mg)	225	207	218	204	280	232	291
Carbohydrate,	(g)	211	202	206	203	260	228	249
Of which:								
total sugars	(g)	87	79	79	83	116	91	112
non-milk extrinsic sugars	(g)	45	42	44	49	64	54	66
starch	(g)	124	123	127	121	144	137	137
Fibre [a]	(g)	12.9	11.7	11.5	10.5	15.6	12.3	13.6
Calcium	(mg)	800	770	770	750	980	840	920
Iron	(mg)	10.1	9.4	9.5	8.6	12.1	10.0	10.9
Zinc	(mg)	7.6	7.2	7.4	6.7	9.2	7.7	8.6
Magnesium	(mg)	232	214	212	199	283	224	251
Sodium	(g)	2.44	2.45	2.49	2.31	2.96	2.55	2.73
Potassium	(g)	2.65	2.46	2.47	2.34	3.28	2.59	2.99
Thiamin	(mg)	1.41	1.32	1.30	1.22	1.67	1.39	1.51
Riboflavin	(mg)	1.71	1.59	1.61	1.53	2.08	1.76	2.02
Niacin equivalent	(mg)	26.7	25.2	25.6	23.0	31.9	25.9	29.0
Vitamin B6	(mg)	2.0	1.8	1.9	1.8	2.4	2.0	2.2
Vitamin B12	(µg)	6.7	6.5	6.5	6.2	8.6	6.9	8.5
Folate	(µg)	254	229	228	213	307	246	291
Vitamin C	(mg)	78	60	52	48	81	52	64
Vitamin A:								
retinol	(µg)	490	450	490	370	660	470	720
β-carotene	(µg)	1900	1710	1600	1500	2250	1490	1900
total (retinol equivalent)	(µg)	800	740	750	620	1030	720	1040
Vitamin D	(µg)	3.01	3.13	3.10	2.67	4.22	3.39	4.19
Vitamin E	(mg)	9.55	9.36	9.90	8.50	11.69	9.87	10.82

(ii) as a percentage of Reference Nutrient Intake [b]

Energy [c]	86	81	81	77	94	87	91
Protein	154	144	141	130	150	147	139
Calcium	123	117	113	108	131	122	122
Iron	99	91	90	81	123	96	113
Zinc	101	93	93	85	106	96	101
Magnesium	95	85	81	76	95	86	83
Sodium	177	174	170	156	177	172	159
Potassium	91	83	79	75	90	83	80
Thiamin	176	163	155	147	185	167	167
Riboflavin	160	146	143	135	165	155	160
Niacin equivalent	201	187	185	167	216	189	199
Vitamin B6	170	158	155	145	173	165	163
Vitamin B12	524	497	480	451	547	505	526
Folate	145	128	123	115	146	131	135
Vitamin C	216	164	136	126	192	133	148
Vitamin A (retinol equivalent)	138	124	123	101	151	115	152

(iii) as a percentage of food energy

Fat	38.9	38.7	39.3	38.0	38.7	37.9	39.3
Of which:							
saturated fatty acids	15.5	15.2	15.1	15.1	15.6	14.7	15.8
Carbohydrates	46.1	46.3	45.8	47.6	46.5	47.6	46.2

(iv) contribution to selected nutrients from soft and alcoholic drinks and confectionery

Energy	(kcal)	130	120	110	80	130	90	80
	(MJ)	0.6	0.5	0.5	0.4	0.5	0.4	0.4
Fat	(g)	2	2	2	1	2	1	1
Carbohydrate	(g)	17	19	18	16	17	17	14
Alcohol	(g)	8.0	4.3	2.9	1.6	6.0	1.8	2.8

(a) as non-starch polysaccharides
(b) Department of Health, *Dietary Reference Values for Food Energy and Nutrients for the United Kingdom*, HMSO, 1991
(c) as a percentage of Estimated Average Requirement

Table B12 Nutritional value of household food by household composition, 1998

		\multicolumn{11}{c	}{Households with}
No of adults		\multicolumn{2}{c	}{1}	\multicolumn{5}{c	}{2}	3	\multicolumn{2}{c	}{3 or more}	4 or more
No of children		0	1 or more	0	1	2	3	4 or more	0	1 or 2	3 or more	0
\multicolumn{13}{c	}{*(i) intake per person per day*}
Energy	(kcal)	1950	1460	1980	1700	1520	1460	1330	1860	1680	1240	1840
	(MJ)	8.2	6.1	8.3	7.1	6.4	6.1	5.6	7.8	7.0	5.2	7.7
Total protein	(g)	72.1	52.9	74.5	64.1	55.4	51.5	48.7	71.3	59.8	43.3	68.9
Animal protein	(g)	43.6	31.8	46.1	39.9	33.4	30.4	28.6	45.1	35.5	24.7	43.3
Fat	(g)	82	62	86	74	64	61	55	83	73	45	84
Fatty acids:												
saturated	(g)	32.9	24.5	33.5	28.8	25.7	24.8	22.4	31.9	26.7	18.2	31.8
monounsaturated	(g)	28.5	22.2	30.5	26.4	22.7	21.7	19.5	29.6	26.5	15.5	30.5
polyunsaturated	(g)	14.1	10.9	15.6	13.7	11.2	10.4	9.3	15.1	14.8	7.9	16.1
Cholesterol	(mg)	263	176	266	220	186	170	167	260	196	154	252
Carbohydrate	(g)	245	184	242	206	191	186	170	222	207	177	213
Of which:												
total sugars	(g)	105	69	102	80	74	73	58	88	79	57	83
non-milk extrinsic sugars	(g)	60	39	57	44	40	42	30	49	44	27	46
starch	(g)	139	115	139	125	117	113	112	133	128	119	130
Fibre [a]	(g)	14.4	9.5	14.4	11.5	10.4	10.0	9.0	12.6	11.3	8.1	12.4
Calcium	(mg)	930	700	890	780	730	690	660	830	780	640	810
Iron	(mg)	11.3	8.0	11.2	9.7	8.6	8.4	7.8	10.3	9.2	6.3	9.9
Zinc	(mg)	8.6	6.1	8.7	7.5	6.4	6.0	5.7	8.3	6.9	4.9	7.9
Magnesium	(mg)	264	178	260	214	192	182	163	236	203	148	226
Sodium	(g)	2.86	2.20	2.84	2.54	2.24	2.10	1.93	2.69	2.29	1.44	2.74
Potassium	(g)	2.98	2.08	3.04	2.48	2.22	2.08	1.90	2.78	2.33	1.82	2.71
Thiamin	(mg)	1.56	1.11	1.56	1.34	1.19	1.15	1.05	1.44	1.26	0.92	1.39
Riboflavin	(mg)	1.97	1.43	1.87	1.66	1.50	1.46	1.39	1.76	1.57	1.24	1.66
Niacin equivalent	(mg)	28.8	21.3	30.4	26.3	22.5	20.8	19.6	29.3	23.9	16.6	28.0
Vitamin B6	(mg)	2.1	1.6	2.2	1.9	1.7	1.6	1.6	2.1	1.8	1.4	2.1
Vitamin B12	(µg)	8.1	5.7	7.7	6.5	6.0	5.5	5.2	7.5	6.2	4.8	7.1
Folate	(µg)	285	192	286	230	204	195	184	257	214	163	252
Vitamin C	(mg)	71	42	71	57	54	48	36	61	51	49	61
Vitamin A:												
retinol	(µg)	640	360	600	480	380	340	330	560	400	200	610
β-carotene	(µg)	1940	1240	2150	1600	1410	1250	1170	1970	1440	940	1800
total (retinol equivalent)	(µg)	970	570	960	750	620	550	520	890	640	350	910
Vitamin D	(µg)	3.72	2.51	3.85	3.31	2.65	2.61	2.43	3.81	2.79	1.56	3.57
Vitamin E	(mg)	10.45	8.10	11.26	9.76	8.37	7.82	6.91	10.70	10.35	5.64	11.51
\multicolumn{13}{c	}{*(ii) as a percentage of Reference Nutrient Intake [b]*}
Energy [c]		92	82	89	85	78	74	68	85	80	60	85
Protein		145	153	145	152	143	136	132	143	132	101	141
Calcium		131	112	122	119	114	106	100	117	111	90	117
Iron		116	75	110	92	84	82	76	99	83	56	94
Zinc		107	89	103	99	86	80	75	100	88	61	99
Magnesium		93	83	89	88	83	80	72	83	76	57	81
Sodium		177	178	172	185	170	162	150	169	154	99	176
Potassium		85	83	84	85	83	80	74	80	73	60	80
Thiamin		180	154	175	168	153	146	135	163	151	111	160
Riboflavin		166	149	151	155	144	140	133	147	140	111	142
Niacin equivalent		206	179	206	198	173	159	151	200	171	120	195
Vitamin B6		165	160	167	165	151	144	143	162	147	119	163
Vitamin B12		534	506	501	510	502	471	449	506	453	361	484
Folate		141	122	138	131	123	118	112	129	115	89	129
Vitamin C		176	125	171	153	153	134	103	152	136	129	157
Vitamin A (retinol equivalent)		150	107	143	127	109	96	91	137	104	58	144
\multicolumn{13}{c	}{*(iii) as a percentage of food energy*}
Fat		37.8	38.3	39.1	39.4	38.2	37.8	37.4	39.9	39.3	32.6	41.4
Of which:												
saturated fatty acids		15.2	15.1	15.2	15.3	15.2	15.3	15.1	15.4	14.4	13.2	15.6
Carbohydrate		47.3	47.3	45.9	45.5	47.2	48.0	47.9	44.8	46.4	53.5	43.6
\multicolumn{13}{c	}{*(iv) contribution to selected nutrients from soft and alcoholic drinks and confectionery*}
Energy	(kcal)	110	90	120	110	110	110	100	110	100	50	120
	(MJ)	0.5	0.4	0.5	0.5	0.5	0.5	0.4	0.5	0.4	0.2	0.5
Fat	(g)	1	1	2	2	2	2	1	1	1	1	2
Carbohydrate	(g)	15	18	16	19	19	21	19	18	19	10	20
Alcohol	(g)	4.7	1.4	6.0	3.1	3.2	2.1	1.5	3.9	1.8	0.3	3.3

(a) as non-starch polysaccharides
(b) Department of Health, *Dietary Reference Values for Food Energy and Nutrients for the United Kingdom,* HMSO, 1991
(c) as a percentage of Estimated Average Requirement

Table B13 Contribution made by selected foods to the nutritional value of household food: national averages, 1998

per person per day

	Energy	Fat	Fatty Acids Saturated	Fatty Acids Poly-unsaturated	Total sugars (a)	Starch (b)	Fibre (c)
	kcal	g	g	g	g	g	g
Milk and milk products	179	8.2	5.3	0.3	16.1	0.2	0.1
Of which: whole milk	66	4.0	2.6	0.1	4.4	-	-
skimmed milks	75	2.3	1.6	0.1	7.9	-	-
yoghurt	13	0.3	0.1	...	2.0	0.1	...
Cheese	54	4.5	2.8	0.2	0.1	...	-
Meat and meat products	254	16.7	6.3	2.0	0.8	4.5	0.3
Of which: carcase meat	68	4.7	2.0	0.4	-	-	-
poultry, uncooked	39	2.2	0.6	0.4	-	-	-
bacon and ham	30	2.0	0.7	0.3	...	-	-
offal	...	...	...	...	-	-	-
Fish	27	1.3	0.3	0.4	0.1	0.8	...
Eggs	19	1.4	0.4	0.2	-	-	-
Fats	192	21.1	6.5	5.8	0.3	...	...
Of which: butter	41	4.5	3.0	0.1	-	-	-
margarine	27	2.9	0.8	0.8	...	-	-
low fat and reduced fat spreads	54	5.8	1.3	2.0	0.1	-	-
vegetable and salad oils	57	6.4	0.7	2.7	-	-	-
Sugar and preserves	81	...	...	...	21.5	...	...
Vegetables	187	4.9	1.5	1.3	6.5	25.7	4.6
Of which: fresh potatoes	58	0.1	...	0.1	0.9	12.7	0.9
fresh green vegetables	7	0.2	...	0.1	0.6	0.1	0.5
other fresh vegetables	15	0.2	...	0.1	2.7	0.2	0.9
frozen vegetables	27	0.7	0.2	0.2	0.5	3.9	0.8
canned vegetables	18	0.1	...	0.1	1.3	2.1	0.8
Fruit	79	1.3	0.3	0.4	16.0	0.5	1.4
Of which: fresh fruit	42	0.2	0.1	0.1	9.5	0.4	1.1
fruit juices	17	-	...	...	4.0	-	...
Cereals	610	13.1	5.1	2.2	18.7	94.8	5.4
Of which: white bread (standard loaves)	89	0.6	0.1	0.2	1.1	17.8	0.6
brown and wholemeal	47	0.5	0.1	0.1	0.5	8.7	1.0
cakes, pastries and biscuits	157	6.8	3.3	0.7	10.3	12.8	0.7
breakfast cereals	69	0.5	0.1	0.2	3.5	11.9	1.5
Other foods	54	2.2	0.8	0.6	6.0	1.3	0.3
Total food, (GB)	**1736**	**74.8**	**29.3**	**13.5**	**86.1**	**127.9**	**12.1**
Total food, (UK)	**1735**	**74.7**	**29.3**	**13.5**	**85.9**	**127.9**	**12.1**
Soft drinks	43	-	-	-	11.4	-	-
Alcoholic drinks	30	...	...	-	0.7	-	-
Confectionery	35	1.5	0.8	0.1	5.0	0.3	0.1
Total food and drink, (GB)	**1844**	**76.2**	**30.1**	**13.6**	**103.2**	**128.1**	**12.2**
Total food and drink, (UK)	**1842**	**76.2**	**30.1**	**13.6**	**103.0**	**128.2**	**12.2**

(a) includes sucrose, glucose, fructose, lactose and other simple sugars, as their monosaccharide equivalents
(b) as its monosaccharide equivalent
(c) as non-starch polysaccharides

Table B13 *continued*

per person per day

	Calcium	Iron	Sodium (d)	Vitamin C	Folate	Vitamin A (e)	Vitamin D
	mg	mg	mg	mg	µg	µg	µg
Milk and milk products	361	0.2	136	5.0	19	92	0.2
of which: whole milk	116	0.1	42	1.7	7	32	...
skimmed milks	198	0.1	70	2.8	9	34	...
yoghurt	24	...	11	-	1	2	...
Cheese	91	...	104	-	5	49	...
Meat and meat products	26	1.4	522	1.7	13	162	0.6
of which: carcase meat	2	0.4	21	-	3	1	0.2
poultry, uncooked	1	0.1	15	-	2	4	0.1
bacon and ham	1	0.1	206	0.4	...	-	0.1
offal	...	0.1	...	...	...	98	-
Fish	14	0.2	63	0.1	3	4	0.5
Eggs	7	0.2	18	-	6	24	0.2
Fats	4	...	133	...	...	172	1.1
of which: butter	1	...	41	-	-	49	...
margarine	...	...	28	-	-	30	0.3
low fat and dairy spreads	2	...	63	...	-	92	0.7
vegetable and salad oils	-	-	-	-	-	-	-
Sugar and preserves	4	0.1	4	0.4	...	...	-
Vegetables	50	1.7	240	20.1	78	235	...
of which: fresh potatoes	4	0.3	8	5.3	25	-	-
fresh green vegetables	11	0.2	2	3.3	19	16	-
other fresh vegetables	13	0.3	9	5.4	15	171	-
frozen vegetables	6	0.3	14	3.4	9	25	-
canned vegetables	10	0.3	109	0.8	6	11	-
Fruit	19	0.4	13	29.5	17	8	-
of which: fresh fruit	11	0.2	3	13.4	8	5	-
fruit juices	5	0.1	5	15.5	7	2	-
Cereals	205	5.1	988	1.9	78	22	0.6
of which: white bread (standard loaves)	41	0.6	210	-	8	-	-
brown and wholemeal	16	0.6	119	-	9	-	-
cakes, pastries and biscuits	34	0.7	126	...	5	7	...
breakfast cereals	12	1.7	124	1.6	35	-	0.5
Other foods	22	0.3	299	0.9	22	12	...
Total food, (GB)	**804**	**9.8**	**2520**	**59.3**	**241**	**779**	**3.3**
Total food, (UK)	**804**	**9.8**	**2516**	**58.9**	**241**	**776**	**3.2**
Soft drinks	6	...	14	4.4	2	7	-
Alcoholic drinks	4	0.1	3	-	1	...	-
Confectionery	8	0.1	8	-	1	2	-
Total food, (GB)	**821**	**10.0**	**2545**	**63.7**	**245**	**789**	**3.3**
Total food, (UK)	**821**	**10.0**	**2542**	**63.3**	**244**	**786**	**3.2**

(d) excludes sodium from table salt
(e) retinol equivalent

Appendix C

Supplementary tables for the Eating Out Survey

List of supplementary tables

		page
C1	Consumption of individual foods, 1994 - 1998	150
C2	Consumption of food eaten out by age and gender, 1998	152

Table C1 Consumption of individual foods eaten out, 1994 to 1998 [a]

grams per person per week, unless otherwise stated

	Consumption				
	1994	1995	1996	1997	1998
Ethnic foods	**28**	**26**	**32**	**38**	**41**
of which: Chinese dishes	10	9	13	17	16
Curry	13	12	10	12	16
Indian dishes	3	3	7	7	7
Meat and meat products	**109**	**108**	**99**	**107**	**110**
of which: Bacon, gammon or ham	5	6	6	7	7
Steak	5	5	3	4	4
Hamburger or cheeseburger	16	17	13	15	16
Meat pies (pastry and potato based)	21	19	15	15	16
Roast beef, pork, lamb, and chops	5	4	4	4	4
Meat based dish (e.g. casserole, lasagne, chilli con carne)	19	17	12	15	14
Sausages (including sausage rolls, toad in the hole)	19	19	19	19	21
Chicken or turkey (roasted or fried)	15	16	21	22	23
Fish and fish products	**(b)**	**(b)**	**23**	**23**	**25**
of which: White fish	(b)	(b)	11	12	12
Cheese and egg dishes and pizza	**5**	**26**	**28**	**27**	**27**
of which: Cheese pie or pastry	11	3	5	4	4
Pizza	4	10	12	11	12
Eggs	(b)	5	6	7	7
Potatoes and vegetables	**(b)**	**(b)**	**179**	**192**	**197**
of which: Potato chips	(b)	(b)	69	68	73
Boiled or mashed potatoes	21	18	21	22	23
Roast or sautéed potatoes	12	11	11	13	12
Jacket potatoes	12	9	8	11	11
Other potato dishes	8	7	5	5	4
Peas, sweetcorn or mange tout	12	11	10	11	11
Green vegetables	13	11	11	12	12
Carrots	8	8	7	8	8
Tomatoes	2	3	5	5	6
Beans (not green, e.g. broad beans, baked beans, chick peas)	13	13	14	14	16
Vegetable products (e.g. mushy peas, nut roast, humous)	9	7	8	10	10
Salads	**(b)**	**(b)**	**17**	**22**	**21**
Rice, pasta and noodles	**20**	**18**	**24**	**27**	**27**
of which: Rice	10	9	12	13	15
Pasta or noodles	10	9	12	13	12
Soup (ml)	**18**	**16**	**17**	**16**	**16**
of which: Vegetable based soup (including tomato) (ml)	12	11	10	9	8
Baby food	...	...	...	...	...
Breakfast cereal	**1**	**1**	**1**	**1**	**1**
Fruit (fresh and processed)	**17**	**17**	**18**	**22**	**19**
of which: Apples	5	4	5	5	4
Bananas	3	3	3	4	4
Yoghurt	**6**	**4**	**5**	**6**	**6**
Bread	**13**	**14**	**14**	**14**	**15**
of which: Bread roll, french stick, or baguette	5	5	5	4	4
White bread toasted or untoasted	4	5	5	5	5

Table C1 *continued*

grams per person per week, unless otherwise stated

		Consumption				
		1994	1995	1996	1997	1998
Sandwiches		**36**	**37**	**35**	**50**	**45**
of which:	Meat based sandwich	11	11	11	15	15
	Fish based sandwich	7	7	6	9	9
	Cheese based sandwich	8	8	7	9	9
	Egg based sandwich	3	3	3	4	4
	Poultry based sandwich	4	4	4	6	5
Rolls		**25**	**26**	**24**	**31**	**28**
of which:	Meat based roll	11	11	11	14	11
	Fish based roll	3	3	3	4	4
	Cheese based roll	5	5	5	6	5
Sandwich/roll extras		**9**	**10**	**7**	**8**	**8**
of which:	Salad fillings (e.g. coleslaw, mayonnaise)	7	7	5	5	5
Miscellaneous foods		**16**	**16**	**17**	**18**	**18**
of which:	Butter	4	4	4	4	3
	Savoury sauces (e.g. gravy, tomato ketchup)	8	8	7	8	14
Other additions		**18**	**15**	**15**	**13**	**11**
of which:	Milk based additions (e.g. custard, cream)	14	12	12	10	8
Ice creams, desserts and cakes		**57**	**49**	**51**	**56**	**51**
of which:	Ice creams	8	7	8	7	7
	Cream cakes or buns, and dairy desserts (e.g. cheesecake, trifle)	7	6	7	6	5
	Milk puddings	3	2	3	7	7
	Pies and puddings	17	13	13	15	12
	Buns, scone and other cakes	20	18	19	20	18
Biscuits		**6**	**5**	**12**	**11**	**11**
Crisps, nuts and snacks		**10**	**9**	**12**	**11**	**10**
of which:	Crisps and potato snacks	8	7	9	8	8
Beverages	(ml)	**383**	**389**	**392**	**406**	**392**
of which:	Coffee (ml)	223	212	219	229	215
	Tea (ml)	149	164	161	167	165
Soft drinks including milk	(ml)	**310**	**330**	**336**	**348**	**318**
of which:	Mineral water (ml)	16	24	23	30	28
	Pure fruit juices (ml)	24	26	22	25	21
	Fruit juice drink or squash (ml)	39	38	43	48	41
	Carbonated drink (ml)	197	208	216	214	200
	Milk as a drink (ml)	16	15	19	16	14
	Milk-based drinks (e.g. milkshake) (ml)	10	10	12	12	12
Alcoholic drinks	(ml)	**539**	**535**	**483**	**490**	**435**
of which:	Low alcohol beer or cider (ml)	4	4	7	4	4
	Beers (ml)	295	281	251	238	211
	Lagers and continental beer (ml)	178	183	167	185	161
	Ciders and perry (ml)	20	22	21	16	14
	Wine - full strength (ml)	22	24	24	30	25
	Wine or spirit with mixer, low alcohol wine (ml)	14	15	8	12	13
Confectionery		**21**	**19**	**23**	**19**	**17**
of which:	Chocolate coated bar or sweet	12	11	12	11	9

(a) a change of contractor in 1996 means that comparisons before and after may be less reliable.
(b) comparable data not available in 1994 and 1995.

Table C2 Consumption of food eaten out by age and gender, 1998

grams per person per week, unless otherwise stated

	Infants	Children			Males				Females				
	Infants under 1	1 to 3	4 to 6	7 to 10	11 to 14	15 to 18	19 to 50	51+	11 to 14	15 to 18	19 to 50 not pregnant	19 to 50 pregnant	51+
Number of respondents	72	239	259	360	172	145	1171	930	150	135	1389	40	1103
Ethnic foods	-	5	17	20	26	35	78	18	19	41	64	29	21
Meat products	9	53	126	160	191	211	181	74	145	141	90	149	53
Fish dishes and products	2	8	30	29	22	16	32	23	23	25	26	16	22
Cheese/egg dishes and pizza	1	4	24	40	75	41	38	19	62	64	24	41	11
Potatoes	15	66	196	234	274	204	138	88	219	182	105	143	69
Vegetables (excl. pots)	9	33	105	109	85	51	88	67	58	57	76	61	57
Salads	10	6	10	15	8	5	24	19	12	18	28	24	23
Rice, pasta and noodles	3	15	47	64	34	30	37	10	22	43	32	10	9
Soup (ml)	-	3	6	6	1	1	26	20	14	11	21	-	11
Baby food	5	1	-	-	-	-	-	-	-	-	-	-	...
Breakfast cereal	8	...	-	...	...	-	2	...	1	-	1	1	...
Fruit (fresh and processed)	3	21	24	23	12	8	23	17	22	16	25	3	11
Yoghurt	8	6	11	13	9	2	4	2	6	6	9	-	3
Bread	3	5	5	8	8	12	27	11	18	14	18	19	9
Sandwiches	-	8	19	15	31	43	85	29	39	66	63	56	23
Rolls	-	5	6	7	17	48	59	18	18	36	37	41	8
Sandwich/roll extras	-	2	2	3	4	7	15	4	6	10	13	16	4
Miscellaneous foods	-	5	11	16	20	24	25	15	28	17	22	25	13
Other additions	1	4	20	27	8	2	11	10	14	4	9	13	11
Beverages (ml)	-	-	2	6	11	85	828	371	27	134	544	379	266
Ice creams, desserts and cakes	3	39	119	127	82	22	45	36	75	38	43	43	42
Biscuits	1	19	16	19	16	9	13	4	23	11	14	5	6
Crisps, nuts and snacks	...	4	8	9	16	24	15	3	30	22	12	20	2
Soft/milk drinks (ml)	53	246	342	362	843	847	412	83	759	760	360	633	99
Alcoholic drinks (ml)	-	-	-	-	2	341	1170	789	...	212	293	31	83
Confectionery	1	7	14	21	69	63	20	4	73	69	14	25	2

Glossary

Glossary of terms used in the Survey

Adult   A person of 18 years of age or over, however, solely for purposes of classifying households according to their composition, heads of household and diary-keepers under 18 years of age are regarded as adults.

Average consumption   For the main Survey, the aggregate amount of *household food obtained for consumption* by the households in the sample divided by the total number of persons in the sample. For the eating out extension, the aggregate amount of *eating out consumption* by the people in the extension sample divided by the number of people in the extension sample.

Average expenditure   For the main Survey, the aggregate amount spent by the households in the sample divided by the total number of persons in the sample. For the eating out extension, the aggregate eating out expenditure by the people in the extension sample, divided by the number of people in the extension sample.

Average price   The aggregate expenditure by the households in the sample on an item in the Survey Classification of foods, divided by the aggregate quantity of that item purchased by these households. It is therefore, more strictly an 'average unit value'.

Child   A person under 18 years of age; however, solely for purposes of classifying households according to their composition, heads of household and diary-keepers under 18 years of age are regarded as adults.

Composite meals and snacks   For the eating out extension, these are defined as meals or snacks for which a cost can only be given for a number of foods together. A cost is given for the whole meal, and the individual components are recorded for use in calculating consumption and nutritional values.

Convenience foods   Those processed foods for which the degree of preparation has been carried to an advanced stage by the manufacturer and which may be used as labour-saving alternatives to less highly processed products. The convenience foods distinguished by the Survey are cooked and canned meats, meat products (other than uncooked sausages), cooked and canned fish, fish products, canned vegetables, vegetable products, canned fruit, fruit juices, cakes and pastries, biscuits, breakfast cereals, canned, fresh and dried pasta, instant coffee and coffee essences, baby foods, canned soups, dehydrated soups, ice-cream, and all frozen foods which fulfil the requirements of the previous sentence.

Eating Out consumption   Individual consumption outside the home of all food and drink not obtained from household stocks, regardless of who paid for the food or drink.

Eating Out expenditure   Individual expenditure on all food and drink purchased for *eating out consumption,* whether for consumption by the purchaser or others or both. Expenditure on food and drink for 'business' purposes, i.e. that which is to be reclaimed as business expenses, is not included.

Eating Out extension   An additional section of the National Food Survey which asks half of the main survey households to record their *eating out consumption* and *eating out expenditure.*

Garden and allotment produce, etc   Food which entered the household without payment, and was consumed during the week of participation in the Survey. It includes supplies obtained from a garden, allotment or farm, or from an employer, but not gifts of food from one household in Great Britain to another if such food has been purchased by the donating household. (See also *Value of garden and allotment produced, etc*).

Household   For the Survey purposes, this is defined as a group of persons living in the same dwelling and sharing common catering arrangements.

Household food obtained for consumption   Food purchases from all sources (including purchases in bulk) made by households during their week of participation in the Survey and intended for human consumption during that week or later, plus any *garden or allotment produce, etc* which households actually consumed while participating in the Survey, but excluding sweets, alcohol, soft drinks and meals or snacks purchased for *eating out consumption.* For an individual household, the quantity of food thus obtained for consumption, or estimates of nutrient intake derived from it, may differ from actual consumption because of changes in household stocks during the week and because of wastage. Averaged over a sufficiently large group of households and a sufficiently long period of time, increases in household stocks might reasonably be expected to differ only slightly from depletions.

Income group   Households are grouped into eight income groups (A1, A2, B, C, D, E1, E2 and OAP) according to the ascertained or estimated gross income of the head of the household or of the principal earner in the household (if the weekly income of the head is less than the amount defining the upper limit to income group D). Households without an earner (E1 and E2) are those with no person normally working more than ten hours a week, however of these, *Pensioner Households* and those with at least one person unemployed for less than a year are not counted as households without an earner.

Main Survey   The core part of the National Food Survey, for which the main estimates of *average consumption* and *average expenditure* for *household food obtained for consumption* are derived.

Meals   For the eating out extension, a meal is an eating occasion which cannot be described by a single food item code, but which includes a main dish. In addition a meal must be served and consumed on the premises of one of the following types of outlet: respondent's workplace, school, restaurant, public house, catering facilities on trains, buses or aeroplanes, meals on wheels or other catering facilities such as hospitals, football grounds, etc. A meal is distinct from a meal occasion, which is defined as breakfast, mid-day or evening meal or other eating or drinking occasion and may comprise a meal or drink or snack or any combination of these.

Net balance   The net balance for an individual (a member of the household or a visitor) is a measure of the proportion of the individuals' food needs which are met by meals eaten in the home by that individual during the Survey week. Each meal is given a weight in proportion to its normal importance, the relative weights currently used being breakfast 3, mid-day meal 4, evening meal 7. These weights were changed during 1991; previously, separate weights for tea (2) and supper (5) were used if two evening meals were taken; now a light tea or supper is disregarded in this calculation. The net balance is used when relating nutrient intakes to reference intakes (based on age and sex etc).

Nutrients   In addition to the energy value of food expressed in terms of kilocalories and MegaJoules (4.184 MJ = 1,000 kilocalories), the food is evaluated in terms of the following nutrients:

> Protein (animal and total), fat (including the component saturated, monosaturated and polyunsaturated fatty acids), carbohydrate (including total sugars, non-milk extrinsic sugars and starch), fibre (as non-starch polysaccharides), calcium, iron, zinc, magnesium, sodium, potassium, vitamin A (retinol, B-carotene, retinol equivalent), thiamin, riboflavin, niacin equivalent, folate, vitamins B6, B12, C, D and E, cholesterol, copper, manganese, phosphorus, biotin and pantothenic acid.

Pensioner households (OAP)   Households in which at least three-quarters of total income is derived from state retirement pensions or similar pensions and/or supplementary pensions or allowances paid in supplementation or instead of such pensions. Such households will include at least one person over the state retirement age.

Person   An individual of any age who, during the week of the Survey, spends at least four nights in the household ('at home') and has at least one meal a day from the household food supply on at least four days, except that if he/she is the head of the household, or the diary-keeper, he or she is regarded as a person irrespective of the above conditions.

Price index   A price index of Fisher 'Ideal' type is used; this index is the geometric means of two indices with weights relating to the earlier and later periods respectively or, in the case of non-temporal comparisons (e.g. regional, type of area, income group and household composition), with weights relating to the group under consideration and the national average respectively.

Quantity index   This index is also of the Fisher 'Ideal' type. The price and quantity indices together thus account for the whole of the expenditure difference between the two periods or groups being compared.

Real price   The price of an item in relation to the price of all goods and services. The term is used when referring to changes in the price of an item over a period of time. The real prices quoted in this report are obtained by dividing the *average price* paid at a point in time by the Index of Retail Prices (All Items) at that time.

Regions   Government Office Regions except that Merseyside is combined with the North West because of its relatively small sample size.

Seasonal foods   Those foods which regularly exhibit a marked seasonal variation in price or in consumption; for the purposes of the Survey these are deemed to be eggs, fresh and processed fish, shellfish, potatoes, fresh vegetables and fresh fruit.

Snacks   For the eating out extension, snacks are all eating out occasions other than those classified as meals (but including any eating out occasion referred to as snack by the respondent even if this also fulfils the meal definition). They may be from any outlet and contain any food item or combination of items.

Value of consumption   Expenditure plus *value of garden and allotment produce, etc.*

Value of garden and allotment produce, etc   The value imputed to such supplies received by a group of households is derived from the average prices currently paid by the group for corresponding purchases. This appears to be the only practicable method of valuing these supplies, even though if the households concerned had not had access to them, they would probably not have consumed as much of these foods, and would therefore have spent less on them than the estimated value of their consumption (though they might have spent more on other foods). Free school milk and free welfare milk are valued at the average price paid by the group for full price milk. (See also *Garden and allotment produce, etc.*).

Symbols and conventions used

Symbols The following are used throughout:

   - = nil

   ... = less than half the final digit shown

   na or blank = not available or not applicable

Rounding of figures In tables where figures have been rounded to the nearest final digit, there may be an apparent slight discrepancy between the sum of the constituent items and the total shown.

Additional Information

Analyses of Survey data providing more detail and, in some cases, more-up-to-date information than published in this report are available directly from the Ministry of Agriculture, Fisheries and Food. These analyses are of three main types:

i)   Compendium of supplementary NFS results

ii) Standard analyses

   Quarterly national averages - available approximately 10 weeks after the end of each survey period

   Analyses of components of selected food codes

iii) Ad hoc analyses

   Ad hoc analyses can be undertaken to meet the special requirements of organisations, subject to resources being available

The NFS Annual Report for 1997, the latest quarterly and annual NFS Statistics News Releases, selected annual NFS data and a range of other statistics can be found under the heading "statistics" on the World Wide Web at http://www.maff.gov.uk

Copies of the latest Statistical News Release are also available on "faxback" on 0906 711 0395. Information on forthcoming publications is available, also by "faxback", by dialling 0870 444 0200.

Further details regarding additional Survey information are available from:

National Food Survey Branch
Ministry of Agriculture, Fisheries and Food
Room 513, West Block
Whitehall Place
London SW1A 2HH

Printed in the United Kingdom for The Stationery Office
J89530, C15, 11/99